ANTHROPOLOGICAL PAPERS
MUSEUM OF ANTHROPOLOGY, UNIVERSITY OF MICHIGAN
NO. 15

OASIS AND CASBAH: ALGERIAN CULTURE AND PERSONALITY IN CHANGE

by
HORACE M. MINER
and
GEORGE DE VOS

ANN ARBOR
UNIVERSITY OF MICHIGAN, 1960

© 1960 by the Regents of the University of Michigan
The Museum of Anthropology
All rights reserved

ISBN (print): 978-1-949098-30-3
ISBN (ebook): 978-1-951519-52-0

Browse all of our books at sites.lsa.umich.edu/archaeology-books.

Order our books from the University of Michigan Press at www.press.umich.edu.

For permissions, questions, or manuscript queries, contact Museum publications by email at umma-pubs@umich.edu or visit the Museum website at lsa.umich.edu/ummaa.

ACKNOWLEDGMENTS

Plans for this study were formulated in the spring of 1949, when the senior author applied to the Division of Exchange of Persons, of the U. S. Department of State, for assistance under the Fulbright Act. A research grant was made, involving his informal connection with the Faculty of Letters of the University of Algiers. Despite the fact that this was the first year of the exchange program, the U. S. Educational Commission for France did everything possible to facilitate the practical aspects of the grant during the nine months of 1950 which were spent in Algeria. It was this grant, of course, which made the research possible.

The field period would have been much less satisfactory and productive, however, had it not been for an additional generous research grant made to Miner by the Horace H. Rackham Fund of the University of Michigan. Dr. Paul Fejos of the Wenner-Gren Foundation also kindly loaned a wire recorder and other equipment for use in the field. Once the data were collected, their analysis and the writing of the first part of the report made slow progress until a grant-in-aid from the Division of Behavioral Sciences of the Ford Foundation made it possible for Miner to secure research assistance and to devote two summers to writing.

The callaboration between the authors began in the fall of 1956, when Dr. De Vos scored all of the Rorschach protocols obtained in Algeria and those of American control samples kindly loaned by Dr. Samuel J. Beck. De Vos' interpretation of the Algerian data also reflects the exchange of information and discussion which went on between the authors over a year's period. The first seven chapters were written by Miner, who also collaborated in the last three, written by De Vos.

Grateful acknowledgement is also made of the assistance rendered by Professor Max Hutt, who instructed the senior author in the administration of the Rorschach test and was responsible for the scoring of the Algerian tests and for the hypothesis reported in Chapter VII.

In Algiers, the friendship and assistance the Miners received from Dr. and Mrs. L. Cabot Briggs contributed greatly to their pleasure and to the fulfillment of the research objectives. They were fortunate to have Monsieur André Lebert as the administrator of the oasis area in which they lived. He may so aptly be characterized as "a gentleman and a scholar" that the phrase loses its triteness. A fluent Arabic speaker, he lived up to the admonition of Leon Lehuraux, past Director of the Southern territories, who wrote, "No one will ever be worthy of administering the Moslems who does not know that, before all else, he must love them." If there had been more men like these, things might now be different in Algeria.

It was, of course, the Arabs who were the most helpful. Of the many to whom we owe thanks, particular acknowledgment should go to Khaled and Abdelhafid Meghazi and to Hocine Gharbi. It was primarily through their patronage and efforts that the data were collected.

Professor G.-H. Bousquet extended various kindnesses in Algiers and M. Louis Verriére, of the Service de Statistique Générale de l'Algérie, co-operated by providing data from his office.

Dr. Agnes Miner contributed greatly of her time and talents to the field work here reported and to the preparation of the report itself. Likewise, Mrs. George De Vos was of great assistance to her husband.

Professors Ronald Freedman and Herbert Blalock were generous with their time in helping with various statistical problems. In the statistical analyses, Bernard Berk was Miner's painstaking assistant and Philip Converse also aided both Professors Hutt and Miner in the early stages of the work. De Vos' assistants were Messrs. Hiroshi Wagatsuma, Akira Hoshino, Takao Sofue, and Miss Mayumi Taniguchi.

Some of the content of Chapters VIII and X has previously been published in an article in *Sociometry* (XXI, 1958), "Algerian Culture and Personality in Change"; and in a chapter entitled "Oasis and Casbah—a Study in Acculturative Stress," in M. K. Opler (ed.), *Culture and Mental Health* (1959).

Publication of the complete study was generously assisted by a grant from the publication fund of the Horace H. Rackham School of Graduate Studies of the University of Michigan. We are also indebted to Professor James B. Griffin for opening the pages of the *Anthropological Papers* to us, and to the University Museum of Anthropology for its share in supporting the publication.

TABLE OF CONTENTS

I. A Natural Experiment 1
II. The Course of Time 18
III. The Oasis Setting 30
IV. The Course of Oasis Life 42
V. Contact and Change 66
VI. The Supernatural 93
VII. Culture, Personality, and Prediction 107
VIII. Psychological Characteristics of the Algerians 121
IX. Some Individual Patterns of Adjustment. 147
X. The Cultural Context of Personality 179
Appendixes 190
Bibliography 223
Index 227

CHAPTER I

A NATURAL EXPERIMENT

The Algerian revolt which erupted in 1954 reflects a more fundamental revolution which started a century earlier and will continue for years to come. This more gradual metamorphosis involves the change in native life which followed the French conquest of North Africa. The city of Algiers stands as a symbol of this acculturation. As the modern metropolis emerged from the ancient city of Al Dzeir, the latter declined to the position of a native slum, the Casbah, named after the fortress which dominated the old Barbary pirate port.

While the cities became the principal centers of French settlement and culture, the influence of the French on the predominately rural natives was felt even in the Sahara. The initial impact was biological. Early French records show that until 1872 famine and epidemics of cholera, typhus, and smallpox kept the native population of Algeria down to about two million persons. From then on, there were no more human catastrophies and by 1948 the population had surpassed seven and a half million.

This growth, plus the fact that much of the most productive land was taken over by French *colons*, meant increased human pressure on the land resources. Many nomads were forced to become sedentary agriculturists. Cultivation of the oases was intensified and expanded until the underground water sources were dangerously lowered. Increasingly the children of cultivators were forced to seek employment in the cities, where they became a depressed class of slum dwellers. Between 1886 and 1948 the proportion of the native population living in cities increased from seven to sixteen per cent and reached an absolute figure in excess of a million.[1]

These human conditions provided the setting for the growth of militant nationalism. They also provided the sort of "natural experiment" which social scientists seek to use in the study of human behavior. In the oases, the Algerian Arabs were living much as they had for centuries, with little direct contact with the

---

[1]. Service de Statistique Générale, Gouvernement Général de l'Algérie, *Résultats Statistiques du Dénombrement de la Population Effectué le 31 Octobre 1948* (Algiers: Service de Statistique Générale, 1950), p. xxvii.

French and the industrial civilization they represented. In the cities, Arabs from these same oases were living in close interaction with the whole complex of French urban life. It seemed probable that the comparison of these two groups of people at one moment in time could provide knowledge as to what had happened to the Arab migrant through the years. But our interest was not limited to unraveling and recording the details of change in Algeria. There were more general questions of a theoretical nature which could be explored here. Paramount among these was the problem of clarifying the relationship between personality traits and culture traits, particularly in a situation of change.

The Relationship of Culture to Personality

Of all those who have worked in the area of culture and personality, Dr. Abram Kardiner presents the strongest and most systematic thesis that cultural structure and culture change can only be understood by reference to the personality of the culture bearers. Here we have more than the proposition that the "ethos" or "pattern" of a culture must have its parallel in the personality structure of the people who live in terms of that culture. Dr. Kardiner thus goes beyond the view that a shared norm is both an aspect of personality and a culture trait. Specifically, he believes that culture change can be predicted from a knowledge of personality traits and personality theory.

Kardiner points out that certain aspects of culture, his "primary institutions," affect the developing personality of the child more than other aspects of culture. By the time the individual is an adult, the behavioral predispositions based on these primary institutions will constitute his character and he will create "secondary institutions" as "projective systems" based on this personality structure. "In other words, if we know how the basic personality is established, we can make certain predictions about the institutions this personality is likely to invent." [2] Not only is much of culture change thus determined by personality structure but, Kardiner contends, social structure and integration cannot be considered without reference to personality structure.[3] Religion and folklore are explicitly stated to be projective in origin and, in his analysis of specific societies, Kardiner imputes similar origins to cultural phenomena ranging from the manner of disposal of the afterbirth to warfare. He

---

2. Abram Kardiner, *The Psychological Frontiers of Society* (New York: Columbia University Press, 1945), p. 29.
3. *Ibid.*, p. 25.

feels that, "If we could do no more than predict types of religion and folklore, the usefulness of this procedure would be very limited." [4]

Exploration of the relation of culture to personality in a variety of societies was the means employed to test the validity of Kardiner's "predictive" method. This analysis entailed the co-operative effort of a number of anthropologists, who described in detail the cultures with which they were familiar. From these descriptions and employing psychoanalytic theory, Kardiner delineated the sort of basic personality structure which should be developed by the childhood influences inherent in the primary institutions involved. The rest of the culture was also explored in search of parallels between secondary institutions and the behavioral expectations derived from the particular basic personality structure. There is no suggestion in the reports of this work that any attempt was made to test the theoretical framework by keeping the two types of analysis separate. Insights derived from each were used in developing the other. Conviction as to the validity of the predictive value of personality resulted from the fact that parallels could be found between the cultural and personality systems. As Kardiner says, regarding the analysis of a people, "The more the ethnographer tells us about the traits of these people, the greater the number of institutions that we can place as derivatives of this basic personality type." He does not contend that he could have predicted the form of all the "derivative" culture traits, but he states that this limitation results largely from lack of accurate enough knowledge of early conditioning. By the time fifty, instead of ten, societies have been studied by this method, he believes large-scale prediction may be possible.[5]

Most nonpsychologically oriented anthropologists operate on the basis that one can deal with human phenomena at the cultural level of abstraction alone. Structural and functional relationships among culture traits are frequent objects of analysis. Some anthropologists also express confidence in the ultimate predictive value of such analysis. Unfortunately, the methods employed to demonstrate such value differ little from those of Kardiner. In reviewing the latter's statement of theory, a psychologically inclined anthropologist, Scudder Mekeel, was forced to conclude that the divergent claims for the primacy of culture or of personality must be laid to disciplinary biases.[6] It should be added that even Dr. Ralph Linton, who was the major collaborator with

4. *Ibid.*, p. 29.
5. *Ibid.*, p. 30.
6. Scudder Mekeel, review of Abram Kardiner, *The Individual and His Society*, in *American Anthropologist*, XLII (1940), 526-30.

Kardiner, did not go the whole way with him. Linton saw the fruits of their joint labors primarily as the knowledge gained concerning the interoperation of distinctive personality types and distinctive cultures.[7] He agreed that altered primary institutions could change the personality of a people and that these personality changes could contribute to further culture change, but he never spoke of prediction. Examining the points of agreement and divergence between Linton and Kardiner, it becomes apparent that the fundamental difference between them is on the question of the determinism and prediction.

In historical perspective, this relatively new interdisciplinary field seems to be going through the same sort of argument which once characterized the schools of biological and geographical determinism of cultural phenomena. The problem in all of these is not whether there are extracultural influences on the form of culture traits, but whether such influences can be considered to be the only significant independent variables. In both the earlier and the present discussions of this problem the deterministic position is supported by demonstrable correspondence between the two orders of phenomena. Such demonstrations cannot, of course, prove the claims for prediction, for contradictory evidence is largely ignored. If the historical parallels are truly comparable, it suggests that personality factors limit the range of cultural forms which people may develop, but that the particular forms developed are not determined by personality type and hence not predictable.

In the above theoretical setting, part of the Algerian research is an attempt to test Kardiner's belief that the form of culture traits is predictable from a knowledge of personality characteristics. We wanted to know whether, in this situation of culture change, one could predict which cultural alternatives would be adopted by various individuals, basing such prediction on expectations with regard to the appropriateness of certain cultural forms for the expression of behavioral predispositions already established in the personality.

Considering the degree to which cultural and personality data are intertwined in empirical situations, it is admittedly difficult to test the above hypothesis. The method adopted to secure independent measures of the two sorts of data was suggested by Cora DuBois' work in Alor.[8] While administering a variety of psychological tests to the natives of this East Indian Island, she secured thirty-eight Rorschach protocols. These were analyzed "blind" by Emil Oberholzer. He studied only the responses of the natives

7. Foreword to Kardiner, *op. cit.*
8. Cora DuBois, *The People of Alor*, A Social—Psychological Study of an East Indian Island (Minneapolis: University of Minnesota Press, 1944).

to the "ink-blot" test, without reference to any of Dr. DuBois' personal knowledge of Alorese culture and the individuals involved. On the basis of the protocols, Dr. Oberholzer wrote a description of the personality characteristics which seemed to be present in the whole group, as well as personality sketches of individuals. The correspondence between these characterizations and those which DuBois had made from personal observations in the field, while not perfect, were strikingly accurate. The effect was to give independent support to the field observations. But the experiment did more than this. It indicated that, despite the fact that the Rorschach test had been developed on the basis of European subjects, it could be validly employed to make personality analyses of peoples of quite different cultural background.

The experience of other anthropologists with the use of Rorschach tests was such that Irving Hallowell could state definitely, in 1945, that the basic principles of Rorschach interpretation were applicable to data secured from non-Western, nonliterate people.[9] While other, more recently developed, projective tests share this advantage for cross-cultural study, the Rorschach has the added favorable quality that the stimulus cards are relatively "culture free," since the blots depict nothing specific.

With regard to the Algerian research, the use of Rorschach tests to secure data on personality characteristics had a further advantage. The crucial problem in devising the research design was to avoid contamination between the observations on the culture and on the personality. This was complicated by the fact that both types of observation were to be made by Miner alone. But, as he was trained only in the administration of the Rorschach test and not in its interpretation, there was little danger that the test results would influence his cultural inquiry. Conversely, the Rorschach protocols could subsequently be analyzed "blind" by experts in projective testing, without contaminating knowledge of the culture.

The Rorschach test was not, of course, devised as a technique to secure an appraisal of personality independent of other types of observation. It is essentially a device for securing pertinent additional evidence and it is normally used in conjunction with all available sources of information about the personalities involved. The special utility of the Rorschach which DuBois and Oberholzer discovered in the blind analysis of the test does not make maximal use of protocols for the analysis of personality. It was believed, however, that such blind analysis would provide the best technique for the independent collection of personality data. In fact, the interpretation of the test results without additional data is probably

9. A. Irving Hallowell, "The Rorschach Technique in the Study of Personality and Culture," *American Anthropologist*, XLVII (1945), 204.

only justified by the requirements of a research design which demands such independent observation.

In addition to the special use of the Rorschach protocols just indicated, it would be possible, in the final stage of analysis, to combine Rorschach data with personal knowledge of the people gained in the field in order to describe more adequately some of the personality characteristics of the Algerians.

Shortly after reaching the field situation, it became apparent that the nature of the data being collected would make it possible to test yet another aspect of personality theory. Kardiner's contention that the personality type is fixed by the time the individual has reached late adolescence is a very moderate view. Opinions vary widely. Some scholars see the possibility of postadolescent changes while others consider the personality to be set in infancy and early childhood. The latter position enjoyed an early pre-eminence, but seems to have been giving way to the belief that influences in later childhood are equally important. In view of the wide divergence of opinion on this subject, it was obviously desirable to throw whatever light possible on the problem. As will be demonstrated, it was feasible to investigate the nature and extent of adolescent and postadolescent changes in personality in this situation of culture contact and change.

Culture Traits as Distributions of Behavior

Culture traits are the stock-in-trade of the anthropologist but, aside from polemics on the definition of culture, little attention has been devoted to the elaboration of the "trait" concept. We find in the work of Dr. Ralph Linton, however, a lucid discussion of the relationship between individually varying behaviors and culture traits.[10] He pointed out that when an ethnologist describes a particular form of behavior as a trait of a culture, he usually describes the most frequently occurring behavior in a given situation. Such concentration on the statistically modal behavior neglects the variation which is, of course, also cultural. Linton defined a *real* culture trait as the "limited range of behaviors within which the responses of a society's members to a particular situation will normally fall."

As the Algerian cultural data were collected on an individual basis, it was possible to examine changing culture traits in terms of shifting distributions of behavior. This presented the further possibility of relating various behaviors within the *real* trait to personality variation.

---

10. Ralph Linton, *The Cultural Background of Personality* (New York: D. Appleton-Century Co., 1945), pp. 46-54.

Some of our cultural inquiries dealt with ideals, which were described by informants in response to such a questions as, "What is the best way to punish a child?" Such moral norms show variation which does not necessarily correspond with that of the punishments employed. Verbal response to such a question as "Have you ever used a sorcerer?" may confound ideal and behavior, particularly when the two are in conflict. For that matter, the problem of assigning a particular behavior to an individual presents, in microcosm, the same sort of problem as that of describing a particular behavior as characteristic of a society. But, as our problem did not involve the former kind of variability, it was considered sufficient for the purposes of this research to describe only variation among the verbal responses of the different informants.

There is a price which must be paid for even such a limited description of individual cultural behavior. With the field resources available, only a miniscule segment of the total culture could be so described. The areas of culture selected for such treatment were, of course, some of those which appeared most relevant to the problem—those which seemed likely to be influenced by personality predispositions. But some attempt was also made to round out the cultural picture, particularly in the oasis, through the usual ethnographic description of the culture in terms of modal tendencies.

The Selection of Informants

The basic plan of the study was the comparison of two groups of Algerian Arabs who had a common cultural origin but who varied in the amount of contact they had experienced with French urban society. The comparison, as originally envisaged, was between the Arabs of a relatively isolated oasis in the northern Sahara and the Arabs of the city of Algiers. Had it been necessary to assume a common cultural heritage for the variety of peoples called "Arabs" in Algeria, the design would have been less adequate than that which finally emerged. It was ultimately found possible to compare natives from a particular oasis with others who had been born, and had grown up, in that oasis, but had subsequently moved to the city. Two Arabs were included who had been born in Algiers to parents who came from the oasis.

Because urban movement was sometimes recent or impermanent, the contact variable was handled in terms of the amount of time the Arabs had lived in the city and the proportion of their lives which they had spent there. Most of the urban experience of the individuals who were studied had been in Algiers, but some had also worked in cities of metropolitan France. The amount of

contact varied fairly regularly, from those who had never left
the oasis to the two who were born in Algiers. Although the Arabs
who had lived longest in the city were almost always found in
Algiers, some who had lived for a time in the city were encountered as returnees to the oasis. Although they were interviewed and tested in the oasis, this did not obviate the fact of
their earlier urban experience.

The total group upon which the study is based consists of
sixty-four Arab men. Each of these informants was questioned
concerning the same series of cultural beliefs and practices
and each was given a Rorschach test.[11] Originally it had been
hoped to include both men and women. Three Arab women were
given Rorschachs, but any attempt to secure more such subjects
was abandoned as a result of the practical difficulties encountered
in finding an adequate female interpreter. Both cultural and
Rorschach data were also secured from one young man of French
extraction, who had been reared in the Casbah and who was in the
process of officially becoming a Moslem, preliminary to marrying
an Arab girl. This case was collected for comparative purposes
and, as with women, was excluded from the major analysis.

With regard to the age of the informants, it was thought desirable to select Arabs who were postadolescent, but presenescent.
The final age distribution ranged from seventeen to seventy-three
years, but there was only one case under twenty years and but four
over sixty-two. In connection with the question of selection of informants, it seems useful to describe the attempt made to draw a
random sample of the oasis population.

Anthropologists are not given to selecting their informants
by random methods, whereas their confreres working in modern
society are using such methods to an increasing extent. While
both pursue their ways with good reason, there is considerable
misunderstanding between them. As a combination of these
approaches seems to be an inevitable future development, it is
important to recognize the special qualities inherent in the two
techniques. Workers using each of the methods desire both
intensive inquiry and representative coverage. Each succeeds
in one dimension better than the other.

The anthropologist, through observation and the intensive
interrogation of a few selected informants, tries to trace all of
the ramifying interrelationships between the various facets of
the culture. He selects *informed* informants—those who are
particularly aware and communicative concerning their own

---

11. For the original protocols, see Horace M. Miner, "Rorschachs of Arabs from Algiers and from an Oasis," in Bert Kaplan (ed.), *Primary Records in Culture and Personality*, Vol. 3 (Madison: Microcard Foundation, 1960).

culture. He is concerned about the typicality of his information for the society as a whole and has developed techniques for controlling fabrication, misrepresentation, and idealization on the part of informants. While there is variation in cultural behavior among the members of any society, the relative homogeneity of the simpler societies minimizes the importance of recording individual variation.

The anthropologist's approach to informants is also distinctive. The field worker uses the methods of establishing social contact which prevail in the society he is studying. He expands his circle of social relations through chains of friendship and kinship. He is introduced, and vouched for, in each new contact. Through long association he comes to have an intimate knowledge of his informants and the social forces playing upon them. In brief, he has optimum rapport and excellent information upon which to judge the motives of his informants.

In modern society, the survey questionnaire can be used to greatest advantage because its designers already have a considerable knowledge of the culture and because the technique is well adapted to the portrayal of heterogeneity. Used with a random sample, the survey is admirably suited to the rigorous testing of hypotheses concerning interrelationships among variables. But no matter how "open ended" the questionnaire, the survey cannot generate hypotheses concerning these interrelationships as well as can more intensive analysis. The former is a relatively weak exploratory method and of limited assistance in conceptualizing social structure. Informants are selected not for what they know, but because of the requirements of random choice. This fact is the basis of both the strength and the weakness of the method. Finally, the direct approach to the informants provides minimum rapport and knowledge about their motivations in the interrogation situation.

Recognizing the above advantages and limitations of the two methods, there were several factors in the Algerian research which argued for the use of sample survey. The interest in culture traits as distributions of behavior within the group made it necessary to question numerous informants about the same areas of culture. The design called for the testing of hypotheses. The question of the representativeness of the sample was important, at least at the stage when the comparison was envisaged as being between an isolated oasis population and an urban group and before the amount of urban contact was handled as a measurable variable. For these reasons, a random sample of the oasis population was drawn early in the investigation.

The group to be sampled consisted of the inhabitants of the oasis who had been listed in the registration of the population eighteen years previously and who had not been subsequently reported as deceased or departed. From this alphabetical listing of some four thousand names, a random group of forty-two men was drawn, ranging in age from twenty to fifty years at the time of the field work. When these forty-two names were checked with the caïd or village headman, it was discovered that all but fifteen of them had actually left the oasis: thirteen for France, seven for Algiers, four to other North African cities, and three to points unknown. It was further reported that six of the fifteen locally available men had worked in Algiers or France and returned to the oasis.

While the French administration was aware that active males were moving to urban centers for work, the sample produced our best evidence of the magnitude of this movement. In this instance, sampling was a good exploratory procedure but it will be useful to recount our experience in the attempt to contact the fifteen remaining members of the sample.

Rapport with the natives of a society dominated by Europeans is inescapably influenced by the natives' perception of the anthropologist's relationship to the administrative officials. Ten years earlier, while working in French West Africa, Miner had found it necessary to become almost completely isolated from the French administrative and military personnel in order to gain the confidence of the native population. Practically, however, entrée to any community must be initiated through its power figures if the work is to proceed smoothly. Much is also to be gained from their special knowledge. Therefore, upon arrival in the desert area of Algeria which had been chosen as a potential research location, Miner contacted the local French administrator in Ouled Djellal. After hearing what the research requirements were, this official took the anthropologist to survey the possibilities of the oasis of Sidi Khaled and put him in touch with the head of the local *djema'a* or village council. The oasis proved to be excellent for the research purposes and the head of the council became the principal contact and translator during Miner's initial, three-month stay.

As the study progressed, the random sample was drawn and the assistant began trying to secure the co-operation of the men in the sample. Because access to the home of an Arab is normally permitted only for close kinsmen, it was necessary to bring informants to the anthropologist's home for interview and testing. A number of his assistant's friends had already been through this process and the results had been entirely satisfactory. But, when the council headman began searching out the men whose names had been randomly selected, he encountered marked resistance. Despite his own local status and his explanation of how the names had been secured, only five could be induced to co-operate. Finally, he suggested that each inquiry be conducted in the garden where the man worked. This was undertaken but, as the anthropologist's jeep approached the field where the informant was working, the latter departed hastily over the garden wall. Investigation finally revealed that on all previous occasions when the headman had ridden out in a jeep with a "European," searching for a particular Arab, the purpose of the trip had been to arrest the man!

More careful preparation ultimately made possible six interviews in the gardens, but the four remaining men in the sample still refused to co-operate. Months later, when Miner returned to the oasis from Algiers, two of them did agree to be interviewed. They were frank in admitting that their final decision to assist was based on the fact that nothing untoward had happened, in the interim, to those who had worked with him earlier. Of the two complete recalcitrants, it was said that one was such a deviant that he would not even talk with the other members of the community.

While the expansion of the migration-reduced sample had been contemplated, the time and effort consumed in the direct approach to informants made the method obviously impracticable. There were no complications in securing informants in Algiers or Sidi Khaled as long as they were the friends and relatives of others whose assistance had already been secured. Initial contact with non-French-speaking Arabs was established through interpreters, the selection of informants being guided only by a desire to secure the desired age range, to get a distribution of occupational positions, and to find as many men as possible in the oasis who had never been to the city. Direct initial contact with those Arabs who spoke adequate French was, of course, possible. However, only six of the thirty-one men interviewed in the oasis were bilingual, this constituting almost all of the local French-speaking natives. In contrast, twelve of the thirty-three Arabs selected in the city were bilingual and a knowledge of French was no rarity.

Migrants from Sidi Khaled to Algiers do not live in any particular part of the city. The difficulty of finding housing forces dispersion; but here, even as in Paris or Lyons, the migrants from one village have a focal point of assembly where men spend their leisure time. As in the oasis, men only go home to eat and sleep. The center of social life of the men from Sidi Khaled is a section of the Casbah where, within a fifty-yard radius, are located two coffee shops, a cheap jewelry store and plating establishment, and a barber shop—all operated by natives of the oasis. The feeling of solidarity among the Sidi Khaled migrants is striking. A number of destitute, young men of the group, who were seeking employment and doing odd jobs, were even permitted to sleep on the tables of one coffee shop after it closed at night.

This concentration of men from the oasis made the problem of securing urban informants relatively simple. Beginning with the relatives of friends in the oasis, who had informed their kinsmen that "the American" was coming, the range of contacts was expanded through their acquaintances. Special attention had to be given to finding a good representation of regularly employed men, for they were less easily available than the unemployed.

While the study makes no claim as to the typicality of the informants from the oasis and the city, it is essential to know in what ways, if any, the Arabs in our sample of urban migrants differed from those in the nonmigrant sample before the former left the oasis. Selective migration or fortuitous sampling bias could vitiate all conclusions stemming from the comparison of the two groups. Careful examination of the personal backgrounds of the oasis and urban groups reveals a few significant differences. These are controlled in all of the subsequent analyses of change in culture and personality.

The Interview and Test Situation

The use of interpreters is only justifiable as a practical necessity. As there was more to be gained by their use, even with the introduction of French as an intervening language, than there was in trying to secure detailed information through an inadequate knowledge of Arabic, the former course was adopted. The dangers which this decision involved were continually kept in mind. Only Arabs with a real command of French were employed as interpreters and it was found preferable to work through them even with Arabs who knew a little French. One linguistically qualified, potential interpreter was rejected because of his obvious disdain for many of his people's beliefs. The use of four different interpreters permitted subsequent search for interpreter bias in the Rorschach data secured through them.

The first meeting with each interpreter was devoted to covering the standard cultural inquiry and administering the Rorschach test to him. This not only familiarized him with the procedure in which he was to be involved, but it also provided a picture of his particular beliefs and attributes. Such knowledge, plus the intimate association which developed, provided an excellent basis upon which to evaluate his performance and direct his functions. The cultural inquiry did not deal with material which was particularly delicate or otherwise difficult to obtain. It is probably with regard to the Rorschach testing that the greatest question arises concerning the use of interpreters.

Before going into the field, Miner revisited the site of an earlier study in Quebec and gave the test to several French-speaking friends. Professor Hutt's subsequent analysis of Miner's translation of these protocols indicated that his procedures were quite acceptable. It was recognized, however, that the problem of translating from French was a much simpler one than that of translating from Arabic through French.

The technique employed to overcome this problem was to make a wire recording of the Rorschach inquiry, so that both the informant's responses in Arabic and the French translations could be played back. By playing this material back for another interpreter, any significant differences in interpretation could be noted. In point of fact, few such differences did appear, except in the case of a woman interpreter whose services were discontinued. The recording of the most lengthy part of the Rorschach procedure had the added advantage of obviating note-taking and of shortening the time required for the test. As it was, the total time spent in interviewing and testing each informant ran from an hour and a half to four hours, with most sessions taking from two to three hours. Only in the cases of three voluble informants was the time divided into two sessions. The interview and the test each took about the same amount of time. It was found preferable to begin the session with the Rorschach test and to follow it with the less fatiguing discussion of familiar customs and family data.

Sessions with the informants, even in the gardens, were almost always in private except for the interpreter who was sometimes present. Ten of the informants showed notable anxiety during the session, five of these being from the random sample. With the nonacculturated group, particularly when the informant was an intimate of the interpreter, the presence of the latter in the situation was a positive advantage. There is no denying that, despite attempts to make the sessions as nonthreatening as possible, they were an extremely unfamiliar situation for even the urban Arabs. The active presence of the interpreter, with whom all but the random sample were closely acquainted, did more than anything else to put informants at their ease. One very eccentric man did bring his small and very spoiled daughter with him. She was a distraction, but even she may well have made this anxious man feel more "at home." In testing the three Arab women in their own homes, Dr. Agnes Miner felt that the presence of their children, albeit better disciplined, was a distinct asset in putting the mothers at ease.

In the oasis, most of the interview and testing was conducted in the familiar setting of a bare room of a native house in the village. All participants in the sessions sat on mats, following native custom. Mint tea or a nonalcoholic, synthetic fruit *syrop* was usually served during a break after the testing. The only unfamiliar things in the setting, aside from the investigator, were the test materials and the battery-operated recording equipment. The recorder itself was kept to one side where it could be reached unobtrusively. A sensitive, multidirectional microphone was already placed on the floor when the informant entered and he was seated so as to keep it between himself and the investigator. This arrangement, with the "host" facing his guest, also conformed to Arab etiquette.

While few had seen the recorder, its existence was general knowledge. A day or two after arrival in the oasis, a public recording was made of some music which was part of the celebration of the whitewashing of a mosque. The participants had been pleasantly fascinated by the playback of the music. Some of the children present remarked that there must be genii in the recorder box, but their elders ridiculed the idea. The French had given a public showing of one talking movie in Sidi Khaled, so recorded sound was not entirely unfamiliar. There was also a telephone in the oasis and a few radios, which had once been operative. Anyway, "Europeans" could not control genii.

Initially in the test situation, the function of the recorder was explained to the subjects before it was put in operation. It was soon noted that the explanation tended to focus attention on the instrument. The interpreter suggested that the machine was sufficiently unfamiliar and its operation so little noticeable that most informants would ignore it in their concentration on the equally peculiar ink blots. Subsequently, no mention was made of the recorder until after the completion of the test, unless the informant asked about the equipment. In either case, the use of the instrument was described and the subject promised that he could hear as much of the recording as he desired.

In the lower Casbah, where migrants from Sidi Khaled congregate, is a hotel with perhaps a dozen rooms. The manager of this establishment, which might more accurately be described as a "flophouse," slept in his tiny office just inside the entry. As the residents were largely permanent and kept their own keys, his days were spent in the coffeehouse sixty feet away. The daytime use of this office was secured for research work in the city. It was furnished, in addition to the bed, with a table and chairs, these being part of the life-setting of the Arabs in the city. Work was conducted in the office following the same routine as in the oasis. Cigarettes, which were virtually unused in the oasis, were available to those informants who smoked and tea could be brought in from the "coffeehouse." The presence of electricity made it possible to dispense with the battery in the operation of the recorder.

As those familiar with the Rorschach test are aware, its administration requires that one go through the standard series of ten cards twice. On the first run-through, the subject simply describes what he sees in the blots. These reactions were noted on paper, the recorder being inoperative at this juncture, for it is necessary to refer to the responses in the second part of the procedure. A common query concerning the use of the Rorschach with Arabs is whether they experience any difficulty in seeing anything in the blots. The old Islamic tradition against the portrayal of life forms could, conceivably, have such an effect. Actually, no such difficulty was encountered. All of the local Arabs have seen pictures and there is even some reproduction of human forms in the blankets woven by the women. In Western society, the most common parallel to the type of perception required in the test is "seeing figures in the clouds." The Arab parallel was seeing figures in their urine on the ground.

The second part of the test, or inquiry, involves the determination of where on the blot the respondent saw something and what it was in the blot — form, color, shading, etc. — which led him to see it. The nature of this inquiry and the necessity of avoiding leading questions made accurate translation particularly important at this point. It was here that the recorder was used, it still being necessary, of course, to record manually the areas of the blot used in the responses. The latter task was explained to the subjects and they were very co-operative in assisting with it.

With regard to the translation situation, there were so many subjects and the procedure was so repetitive, even to many of the responses, that the anthropologist acquired a good knowledge of what might be called "Rorschach Arabic." As a result, a considerable amount of direct control of the translation was possible. Similarly, a relevant vocabulary was developed in the areas covered by the cultural inquiry.

The interview concerning the informant's cultural beliefs followed a set list of topics, each of which was introduced with a direct question but was subsequently pursued as the situation seemed to merit. The validity of the Rorschach, as an objective measure of individual differences in patterns of communication, was soon evident. Those subjects who gave few test responses and who were indefinite and inconsistent in their responses made poor informants during the ensuing interview. Subjects with other qualities were equally consistent. In addition to keeping a record of the interview, the investigator also noted the degree of French known by the subject, what items of European clothing he wore, and whether he smoked, as well as making a subjective rating of his degree of cleanliness. Following the interview, further record was made of his behavioral characteristics, such as his degree of confidence and any nervous habits he exhibited.

Analytic and Descriptive Scheme

It has been wisely said that the best collaboration takes place under a single hat. In practice, however, individual limitations may necessitate the co-operation of people with different skills. That part of this study which involved independent measures of culture and personality made collaboration essential. Further, it seemed desirable to focus the anthropological and psychological points of view on the panorama of behavior of the Algerians and to see their commonalities and differences in the context both of culture and personality. This study attempts to provide such a double view. The individuality of the collaborators is evident in their styles and terminology as well as their outlook, but the utility of the collaboration is demonstrated by the insights which each provides the other.

Thus, there is nothing new in the observation that the oasis Arabs seclude their women until they are old. Nor is it surprising to anyone who knows the Arabs that Rorschach tests show the Algerians to be rigid and unadaptable. We note further that migration to the city makes no significant difference in the age at which seclusion ends. We also find that urban Arabs are no less rigid than oasis Arabs. The dual view comes into real focus, however, when we find that, among the Arabs, those who are the most rigid are the ones who seclude their women the longest.

The organization of this volume reflects the two viewpoints. The early chapters deal with the culture of the Arabs; the later sections are devoted to Arab personality and its relation to the culture. Throughout the presentation, however, particular attention is devoted to change, the nature of which is derived from the comparison of oasis Arabs, who have virtually never left Sidi Khaled, with others who have spent much of their lives in the city.

The cultural section opens with a sketch of the history of Algeria, particularly as it has affected the oasis of Sidi Khaled. With this introduction, the nature of the community and its culture is treated in some detail. This material does not purport to be a complete ethnography, but it is included to portray the degree to which the oasis is isolated from French influences and to study the local factors leading to emigration to the cities. The sketch also provides a basis for understanding how the oasis culture affects the development of Arab personality and provides expression for it.

Undeniably, it would be ideal to be able to provide a description of the Franco-Arab culture of Algiers and particularly of the structural factors conducive to change. The research design did not, however, require a study of the dynamics of urban acculturation and the magnitude of such a project precluded its fulfilment as part of this investigation. We simply assume that a general

A NATURAL EXPERIMENT

knowledge of Western culture suffices for understanding the general form of the French traits which the Arabs come to know in Algiers.

Comparison of the oasis and urban groups is made in terms of the culture traits about which data were secured from all of the informants. We would expect some distinctively Arab traits to disappear under the impact of French contact. But, knowing that urban Arabs do not become French in all things, we shall be exploring and seeking to explain the different rates of change among traits.

Turning to the psychological data produced by blind analysis of the Rorschachs, we are able to test the proposition that culture can be predicted from personality. There follows a more rounded description of the nature of Arab character, based on both Rorschach evidence and field observations. In conclusion, the anthropological and psychological evidence is combined in an analysis of the covariation of specific cultural beliefs and personality traits.

In the following pages, the reader will note that the period of the field work is often treated as though it were the present. It is hoped that some of the dynamic immediacy of the field situation may thus be transmitted along with the data. It should be clear, however, that the revolution and French reform measures have brought about radical changes since 1950.

CHAPTER II

THE COURSE OF TIME

The Atlas Mountains, stretching from Morocco to Tunisia, separate the Sahara from the Mediterranean. One hundred and seventy miles south of the port of Algiers, the Saharan Atlas drops dramatically two thousand feet to the desert plains below. Here is the Zibane — a narrow, east-west strip of land through which runs the Oued Djedi. This "river" is a dry bed except for intervals each year. But the proximity of water to the surface along its course made it an old route of travel and occasional settlement. Here, on the north bank of the Oued and thirty miles south of the Atlas, lies the oasis of Sidi Khaled. The relationship of this village to the region may be seen on the accompanying figure.

The Early Christian Years

The area has been inhabited for millenia. In the vicinity are sites attesting to the presence of paleolithic men who were the precursors of the Berbers. Of the latter, little is known until the time of the Roman occupation. The Romans actively propagated Christianity among them and established the seat of a bishopric at Vescera, known today as Gafsa. This oasis, fifty miles from Sidi Khaled, was the center of the southernmost part of the Roman colonial territory. A series of frontier posts, extending at some points to the Oued Djedi, protected the colony from the desert tribes. Sidi Khaled was established much later just outside this old defense perimeter. The closest Roman sites are at the oasis of Doucen, fifteen miles to the north and around the oasis of Ouled Djellal, five miles east on the Oued Djedi.

The Roman period ended with the fifth century conquest of North Africa by small Vandal forces whose impact on the natives was slight. The church organization, however, was disrupted and the Bishop of Vescera sent into exile.

The next century saw the return of Christian influence but the conquering Byzantines never occupied the southern territory. In the latter part of the century, there came from the Arabian Hejaz a holy man named Sidi Khaled ben Sinan. He preached Christianity among the Berbers and some say that he prophesied

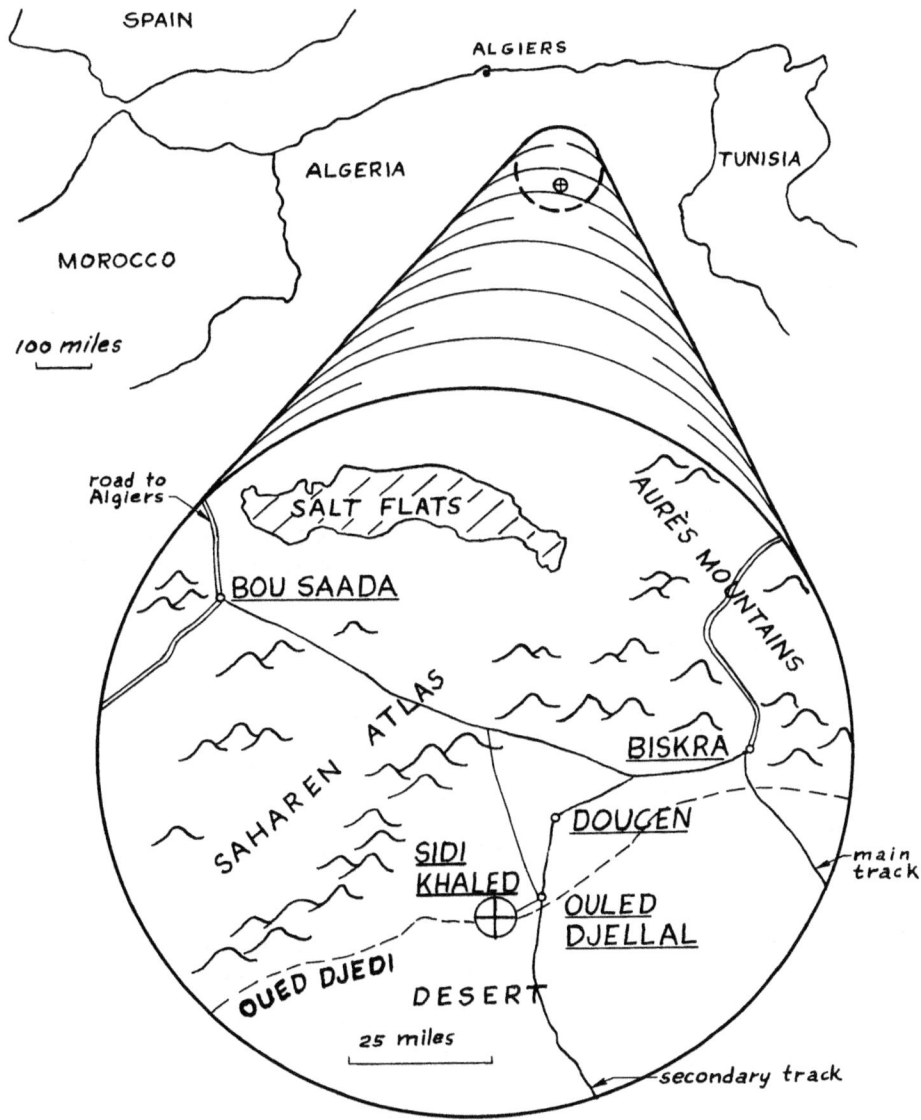

Figure 1. North Africa and the Zibane.

the coming of the Prophet Mohammed. Today, Khaled is recognized by the Moslems as a saint and even as a minor prophet. He is best remembered, though, for miraculously extinguishing a forest fire in the cedar-covered Aurès Mountains near Gafsa. The following account of this miracle was written by a modern Moslem "saint" from the oasis of Sidi Khaled:

> A fire attacked the atheists and non-followers of the true religion. At nightfall the fire appeared and flamed, and by day became smoke. This fire burned all who encountered it and was visible for a distance of three days journey. It looked like a glowing mountain. When Sidi Khaled reached the people, he approached the fire and beat it with a stick, saying some of the sacred names of Allah. This "brazier" was extinguished immediately, before the eyes of all.

Upon his death Sidi Khaled was buried on the south bank of the Oued Djedi, across from the present location of the oasis which took his name. There is, however, no indication that the locality was settled at the time.

The Years of Islamic Dominance

The appearance of the Prophet Mohammed and the militant spread of his religion out of the Hejaz led to the seventh century advance of Arab forces, under Sidi Uqba, into North Africa. Against powerful Byzantine and Berber resistance, he established his followers in what is now Tunisia. Ultimately he met his death in a skirmish with the Berbers outside Gafsa. The Arabs were momentarily forced out of the new territory, but by 700 A. D. they returned and subdued organized resistance. A new policy was adopted of enlisting Berbers into the Moslem army.[1] This scheme was so successful that it was a Berber army which crossed the straits of Gibraltar in 711 A.D. and opened the way to Spain.

The religious conversion of the Berbers was relatively rapid but superficial and a series of local schismatic movements developed. The real period of Arabization of the Berbers followed the seventh century Hilalian invasion by Arabs from Egypt. These nomads, moving as tribes not armies, pillaged what is now Tunisia and eastern Algeria. Not so readily assimilated as the armies which preceded them,[2] they drove out many of the inhabitants and contributed a solidly Arab element to the population. Their invasion penetrated the south and one of the early

---

1. Philip K. Hitti, *History of the Arabs from the Earliest Times to the Present* (5th ed.; New York: The Macmillan Co., 1951), p. 361.

2. Galbraith Welch, *North African Prelude, The First Seven Thousand Years* (New York: William Morrow and Co., 1949), pp. 278-81.

chiefs of Ouled Djellal was a Hilali. Later, whole groups of invaders became sedentarized in the Zibane, into which they were forced by the power of the Almohade Moors. Arab influences came to dominate the culture of the area, both in the oases and the desert. Only in the Aurès Mountains did the Berber tongue continue to be spoken but even these natives were Moslem. The region around Ouled Djellal was also sufficiently removed from the caravan routes to the south that Negro influences from the Sudan tended to pass it by. But "Arabs" from all over North Africa later joined with the population and no one, except perhaps a native, would claim the stock was of purely Arabian origin. It is, however, much closer to it than in many other parts of Algeria.

The Arab tribal history of the area is the story of warring sedentary and nomadic populations. Not only did the nomads prey upon the oasis farmers, growing dates introduced from the East, but nomad tribes and oasis communities fought among themselves. But there was a kind of uneasy symbiosis between the nomads and oasis dwellers. By giving dates to a particular tribe of nomads, the farmers received protection against other nomads, both at home and during the necessary trips to the Atlas to sell dates and to purchase grain. The only real power of the oases was religious. The supernatural power of saints, both living and dead, tended to be localized in the sedentary groups.

During the sixteenth century, when Ottoman rule was reaching North Africa, two men of historic importance moved their families to the region of Ouled Djellal. One settled in that oasis and became the marabout of a new religious fraternity or *zaouia*. which eclipsed those of two earlier local saints. Such fraternities developed all over North Africa around the persons of charismatic holy men. Some of the sacred power or *baraka* of these men could be secured by the faithful through practicing the simple rules and saying special prayers revealed by the saint. There were also financial obligations for the support of the order. Leadership of the brotherhood and its subgroups also depended upon *baraka*. The saint's power passed patrilineally in his family. It could also be transmitted to unrelated holy men who continued the old line or expanded into new localities.

The fortunes of these *zaouias* [3] varied. Many became rich in land and palm groves and exerted a marked stabilizing influence in the country. Their power and beneficence was recognized by

---

3. The plurals of Arabic words are not rendered in their Arabic form as it often differs markedly from that of the singular. The orthography follows the French spelling of the only dictionaries of Algerian Arabic. See Aug. Cherbonneau, *Dictionnaire Français-Arabe pour la Conversation en Algérie* (Paris: Librairie Hachette et Cie., 1884) and Th. Roland de Bussy, *Petit Dictionnaire Francais-Arabe et Arabe-Francais de la Langue Parlée en Algérie* (Algiers: A. Jourdan, 1874).

the Ottoman rulers. In 1797 the brotherhood just mentioned as having been established in Ouled Djellal was granted exemption from all taxation by the Ottoman Bey of Constantine. Each local *zaouia* provided religious leadership, education, alms, and shelter to the faithful. It also offered sanctuary in troubled times.

The other sixteenth century settler of importance was Sidi Abderrahman ben Khalifa, who is the first man known to have established his family near the tomb of Sidi Khaled. As the tomb is even today a place of annual pilgrimage, it seems likely that the sanctity of the spot was what drew Sidi Abderrahman to it. His tribe, the Ouled Ben Khalifa, represents another pattern of the religious influence of sedentary people. The Ben Khalifa were, and continue to be, revered by the powerful nomadic tribe of Ouled Naïl The latter give annual contributions to the venerated Ben Khalifa, who makes regular trips to the mountains to receive these gifts.

The Ouled Naïl did not control this part of the Zibane at an early date. Domination by a desert tribe from the west was broken when the oases established a protective arrangement with the Gueraba Arabs. These nomads came under increasing pressure from one of the Naïl subtribes, the Ouled Zekri, who managed to push south to the Oued Djedi by the time of the French conquest.

Despite the nomads, the settlement at Sidi Khaled prospered and, in the seventeenth century, was moved across the Oued Djedi to its present location. The old site is now a cemetery where new graves still cut into the old village remains. While some attribute the move to respect for the tomb of the Prophet, there was a more fundamental cause. Water was more abundant in the wells along the north bank of the Oued and the gardens prospered there. When, for a few days each year, there was water in the Oued the gardens were isolated and difficult to protect. Sacrilege to the tomb may have been the immediate cause of the relocation, but it was a practical move.

The town was rebuilt so that it presented, to the exterior, the continuous outer walls of houses and courtyards, broken only by a few gates. These portals, except when closed at night, gave access to the narrow, sandy streets onto which opened the doors of the courts of the individual families. As other families joined the community and extended its perimeter, it still retained its defensive character. One of the gates of the old Ben Khalifa settlement came to separate this quarter from the newer ones. Distrust of unrelated neighbors was evident in the fact that the gate continued to be secured nightly. The defensive character of the town's construction was intended primarily to keep out the nomads, but it also served against other local lineages and particularly against the population of the nearby oasis of Ouled Djellal.

Ouled Djellal came to dominate the two other oases of the region by force of arms. Following the murder of a local man by a native of Doucen, forces from Ouled Djellal virtually depopulated Doucen in a two-day battle. The struggle with Sidi Khaled began when a widely venerated shereef of that oasis died and was buried near the Prophet's tomb. His body was stolen by men from Ouled Djellal, who sought to bring his *baraka* to their oasis. The outraged inhabitants of Sidi Khaled attacked Ouled Djellal and were successful in recovering the body. These events initiated a feud between the oases. A Djellal man, caught wandering near Sidi Khaled in search of firewood, was killed and his body desecrated by butchering it and displaying it with mutton in the market. Thus insulted, Ouled Djellal took revenge by killing inhabitants of Sidi Khaled, cutting palm trees and setting fire to houses in the village. The villagers were forced to maintain a constant state of alert, with a watchman in the minaret of the principal mosque. On several occasions, the booming of the warning drum summoned the men to protect their homes and gardens. All of these skirmishes were lost and finally Ouled Djellal accepted a payment of blood money and peace was restored. But the bitterness remained.

In 1843 a descendant of the first Ben Khalifa settler was invested with maraboutic powers by the head of the Rahmania, a brotherhood devoted to a fifteenth century saint. The marabout was a native of Sidi Khaled but moved to Ouled Djellal, where his *zaouia* soon eclipsed the older ones, both among the farmers and the newly-arrived Ouled Zekri. Another marabout, the grandfather of the present local saint of the Rahmania, was recognized in Sidi Khaled and by the Gueraba nomads.

The French Years

At this period, however, the French military penetration of Algeria was the principal concern of the population. Following the capture of Algiers in 1830, the conquest of the country was long and painful. French forces did not reach Ouled Djellal until 1847, when they sustained seventy-five casualties in its capture. Having demonstrated their power, the French withdrew, leaving no garrison. But two years later the Zibane was in revolt. The uprising was quickly crushed and, in reprisal, a village and oasis north of Doucen were razed and many of the insurgents were exiled to the mountains. The natural disasters which occurred after the revolt stand in the folk memory as "The Year of the Cholera" (1867), followed immediately by "The Year of the American Grain," a time of famine mitigated only by relief shipments from the United States.

A generation of French domination brought little change to Sidi Khaled, except in its relation to the nomads. There was no direct contact with the French but important shifts occurred in the nomadic populations. The Gueraba withdrew further into the Sahara, leaving a few sedentarized families in the oasis, and the Ouled Zekri expanded into their territory.

The beginning of real French influence dates from the completion of the fort at Ouled Djellal, in 1887, and the establishment there of a garrison and a military administrator. The conquerors brought to a definite end the pillage and internecine strife which had so long characterized the area. Arabs from rich and powerful families were given titled positions with territorial and tribal responsibilities. Such native leaders were paid by the French and backed by the administrator's French-trained native troops, drawn from other areas of North Africa. The titles of *sheikh* and *caïd* had once designated chiefs who held office by popular consent. Now, at the pleasure of the French, these titles and new prerogatives could be given and withdrawn. It is small wonder that those Arabs who were lured into active support of the administration became known as the *Beni Oui Oui* or "Tribe of Yes Men." No native leadership responsible to the people was permitted. Morocco had its Sultan and Tunisia its Bey, but northern Algeria became part of France and the Algerian Arabs became second-class citizens. Even religious leadership was stifled. The revenue-producing properties belonging to the mosques were confiscated and the religious officials were paid salaries by the French. The system was realistic, in a shortsighted way, and ultimately it was an almost leaderless, pervasive nationalism which brought the whirlwind of revolution.

The government organization, which the French imposed, involved setting a caïd over both Ouled Djellal and Sidi Khaled. He was primarily an intermediary for the administrator, passing orders to the people, assisting in the collection of taxes, and keeping the French informed of any disorders. In this task, the caïd was assisted by a sheikh in Sidi Khaled. In the early 1920's the caïd was drawn from a Gafsa family which had been favored by the French ever since it gained the ascendancy by supporting their conquest. This caïd was later promoted to the position of *bache agha*, a title derived from the Ottoman regime and attached to a largely ceremonial office. The caïdship was passed to a close friend of the agha and relative of a new marabout of growing popularity. Later the position was given to the retiring caïd's cousin, who had been reared in the chief's household.

The fortunes of the position in Sidi Khaled illustrate another aspect of the French occupation and another method of producing native officials. Shortly after 1910 the administration opened a school in Sidi Khaled with the primary objective of teaching French to the natives and, through French, the three "R's." Education was nothing new to the population, two-thirds of whom sent their sons to native *talebs* who taught the Koran and the reading and writing of Arabic. There was, however, bitter opposition to the French school. To secure students, administrative pressure had to be used to force a few parents to send their children to it.

Up to six years' training was provided by the lone instructor, teaching the single class entirely in French. Few of the students completed the six years, but those who became literate in French began to find positions with the administration. A member of the first class became an assistant to the doctor at the infirmary at Ouled Djellal. As such utility of the additional language became apparent, popular attitude toward the school altered but only a few of the boys had any exposure to such instruction and the girls had none.

One of the students in the early years was the son of a Zekri nomad who was a man of importance. He had three wives, a half dozen Negro slaves, fourteen horses, fifteen herds of sheep, and two herds of camels. His wealth was in the desert but he had found sedentary life agreeable. Retiring from the position of caïd in an eastern oasis, he moved to Sidi Khaled before the turn of the century. For his sons born in this oasis he provided years of Koranic schooling and two of the boys subsequently became *talebs* themselves. One of these had also been sent to the French school for six years, for the retired caïd was susceptible to administrative pressure. Subsequently, when the administrator was seeking a secretary for the sheikh of Sidi Khaled, this French-schooled caïd's son was a natural choice. After serving five years as secretary he replaced the sheikh, who had displeased the administrator and had been removed. When the administrative status of Sidi Khaled was later changed, the sheikh became the present caïd.

The outstanding problem facing the population and the administration was a shortage of water. Man's dependence upon water is a stark reality in the desert. Rain is scarce and sparse, the average rainfall being but seven inches. The oasis exists only so long as ground water is tapped by wells and hauled up to irrigate the gardens and palm groves. While the amount of such water has remained relatively constant, population growth has made this amount increasingly inadequate.

At the time of the conquest Sidi Khaled seems to have had between two and three thousand inhabitants. Judging from the extent of the village inclosed by the old gates, it was less than a quarter of a mile square. By the time the Army mapped the town in 1909, it was half again larger. A whole new section had been added to the village by Ouled Zekri who had taken up sedentary life. The 1932 registration of the population revealed that the community had grown to 4,200 persons. This registration was also noteworthy in that it established surnames for the Arabs, who had managed without them for centuries. The new names were required for all official dealings and, presumably because such formalities necessitated the writing of the surname before the given name, the tradition arose of stating names in that order. The new names carried with them a new duty — that of registering births and deaths. The vital statistics from the time of registration to 1950 show a further population increase of 1,300 by natural increase alone. The village now covers more than twice the area it did before the arrival of the French, as will be seen in Figure 2.

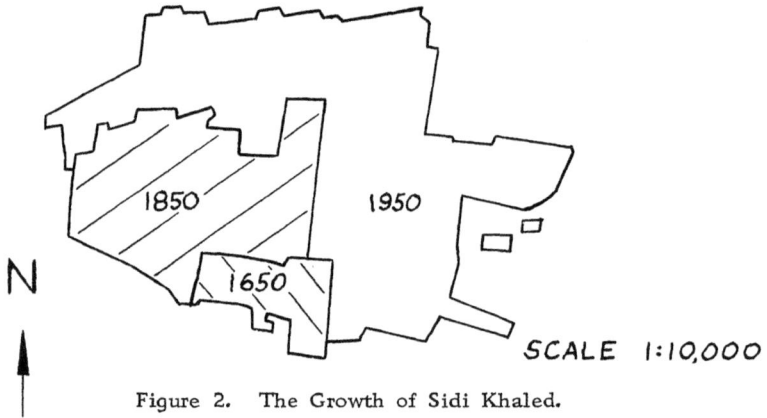

Figure 2. The Growth of Sidi Khaled.

While the community grew, new gardens and palm groves were planted and watered from new wells. But, as more and more water was used, its subterranean level sank lower and lower. The wells were dug deeper, down to twenty feet or more, and then a new problem arose. The old *shaduf*, or bucket suspended from a counterweighted lever, became increasingly impractical as a means of bringing water to the surface. The alternative "Tunisian" system of hauling up the bucket by animal power was both slow and expensive. To keep the water level from sinking even lower, the administration virtually stopped the digging of new wells. To the Arab farmer, who knew that water was a gift of Allah and accorded in quantities which He saw fit, the French prohibition on digging wells on one's own land seemed oppressively cruel.

Other oases faced the same problem. A proposal was advanced by the administrator to build a small dam across the Oued, between Ouled Djellal and Sidi Khaled, in order to collect the water which rose in the river bed in the late spring. It was to be a joint project between the oases. Ouled Djellal was to have the use of the surface water, which could be drained down to it, and Sidi Khaled was to benefit by a higher water level in its wells. Sidi Khaled, distrustful of both the French and its neighboring oasis and knowing nothing of hydrology, refused to help construct a dam to hold water for the gardens of Ouled Djellal. The administration was later successful in drilling an artesian well in Ouled Djellal, which did much to mitigate the difficulty there. An attempt to reach artesian sources at Sidi Khaled failed and the effort was abandoned.

Following World War I the natives found a partial solution to the economic stricture produced by growing population and limited water resources. Arabs who had been in the Army and others who had gone to the cities in France [4] and Algeria to do war work returned and described the good wages and standard of living they had experienced. Young men for whom there was no economic opportunity in the oases went to work in the cities. Those who were married left their families in the desert, for most of the migrants intended to return and settle down with the money they would save. In the first half of the 1920's, 200,000 Algerians crossed the Mediterranean to work in France and seventy-five per cent of them returned in that period. During the depression years returnees outnumbered the departures for the continent. Then, from 1935 to 1948, a third of a million Arabs left for France where almost half of them remained. The movement to the more available Algerian cities was even more marked during these years. In the metropolitan area of Algiers (Arrondissement d'Alger) the Moslem population increased by 100,000 through urban migration alone.

Evidence from Sidi Khaled indicates that those who lived in the cities as much as five years, even discontinuously, ultimately settled there. If already married, their families joined them. If not, their brides were often sought in the oasis. Some men married city women, though, and a few "fell so low" as to marry French women.

Those who did come back to live in the oasis brought in new ideas. Most had worked as unskilled laborers in the city but a few had acquired new skills, particularly of a mechanical sort. It was these men who solved the old problem of raising the water from the deep wells. With the money and knowledge acquired in the cities, gasoline pumps were introduced in the thirties and soon became general. At this time also, the first automobile was brought to the oasis, even though few of the streets were wide enough to permit its passage. A road now connected Sidi Khaled with Ouled Djellal and a bus line linked that oasis to Algiers and

---

4. What the French would call "Metropolitan France," as northern Algeria is divided into three departments which are integral political parts of France.

the world beyond. Briefly, the line extended to Sidi Khaled but the amount of movement was insufficient to maintain it. Yet for all but the nomads, the Oued Djedi was no longer a route of movement and the camel was replaced by the truck.

World War II brought an increase in urban opportunities but it is remembered primarily for the successive years of drought which accompanied it. Palm trees died and grain prices soared. Horses could be bought for the price of a day's feed. Much of the livestock had to be turned loose to forage and die in the desert. Many of the nomads lost their herds and were drawn to the village. Again, it was American shipments of grain which helped avert famine.

The war also closed the French school, which was just resuming operation after a number of years during which there had been no teacher. But education was not forgotten by the administration. The construction of a school building and residence for teachers was undertaken with German prisoner-of-war labor. Located a hundred yards east of the village, it brought the first French residents to the oasis. This time, when the school opened in 1946, it was besieged by parents trying to secure the admission of their children. Despite expanded facilities, many boys were turned away. But only a few parents of girls could be induced to let their daughters attend the class in French and sewing taught by the wife of the school director. The class included two daughters from the family of a pensioned native soldier and two French girls whose Arab stepfather had married their naturalized Polish mother in France. Two other men had brought back childless French women to a life of isolation from both the French and Arabs.

The end of the war saw the reopening of the post office. One of the principal functions of the office was to handle the postal money orders sent by urban workers to their families. The *poste* was first opened in the midtwenties and was operated by a native of Ouled Djellal. Two years later he absconded with the funds of a private concern and the Sidi Khaled office was closed, for it had been little used. It was re-established under the direction of a graduate of one of the early French classes who had subsequently gone to work in France, returned and installed a gasoline pump, and introduced the first auto and radio.

The history of French influence on Sidi Khaled is inescapably an account of individuals, for it was only a few whose lives were much altered from the traditional pattern. Those few stood as intermediaries between the Arabs and the French, in commerce and in government. They were also the innovators, but the innovations which became widely accepted were principally in material culture. In 1950 there were some eighty pumps in the gardens; otherwise, agriculture went on as before. The number of radios had increased to six, but none was operative. There were three old cars, three trucks, and perhaps ten men who could repair them and the pumps. But the age of mechanical transportation could hardly be said to have arrived, except as a means of helping the urban migrants leave the oasis. The bus to Ouled Djellal no longer operated. A ride in an automobile was an exciting and even terrifying experience. Practically everyone walked or rode an ass, and many had never been outside the oasis. A quarter of the men had attended the French school for a year or so, but the teachers spoke no Arabic and had never been in a local Arab home. Not more than a half dozen Arabs had learned to speak more than a few phrases of French.

Like the school teachers, little that was French had penetrated the home. The women, living out their lives behind courtyard walls, had only heard of most of the new things. They had seen only the matches, soap, carbide lamps, utensils, and gay-colored textiles which the men brought into the houses. But for men and women alike, French authority was omnipresent — exacting taxes, controlling the water, and failing to provide the economic expansion required to employ the mass of young men being forced to migrate to the cities.

CHAPTER III

THE OASIS SETTING

The most striking feature of life in Sidi Khaled is its sharp cleavage into a world of women behind closed doors and the external world of men. These two worlds are quite literally separated by a solid wall. Each home is not a house, in the Western sense, but a courtyard inclosed by a mud-brick wall, fifteen to twenty feet high, and topped with dry briars or broken glass. There are no windows in the wall, only a solid wooden door which is always kept locked. Around the inside of the court are one or more rooms, also of mud brick, and each having its own door giving onto the court.

The rooms are used mostly for sleeping and to secure protection from the climate. One might expect the desert to be continuously hot, but the Sahara has been aptly described as "a cold country with a hot sun." The average temperature of the Zibane in January is 51°F. and it has been known to fall to 9°. Like all precipitation here, snow flurries are rare. A snowfall heavy enough to cover the sands is sufficiently unusual to be remembered as "The Year of the Snow." Diurnal variation in temperature is great and near-freezing nights are not unusual in winter. The Arabs sleep in their robes and, if possible, under blankets. Usually no attempt is made to heat the rooms, although some families may afford the luxury of huddling over a charcoal brazier.

Summer, of course, is a different story. Then the temperature may reach 127°F. and not fall below 90° at night. The cavelike rooms are cooler than the courtyard at midday. During the early and late hours, however, life in the yard, as in the streets, follows the shadows cast by the high walls. Little movement of air can reach the court, but sleeping is better there than under the roof. While the most airy spot is on top of the roof, practically no use is made of it. In fact, it is greatly resented if a person lingers on his roof. There being no space between the houses, a rooftop usually overlooks the sanctum of the neighboring courtyard.

Only close male relatives have access to a man's home, [1] where his womenfolk can be seen. If a man is to entertain his

---

[1]. These include what G.P. Murdock calls his "primary" and "secondary" patrilineal kinsmen. See his *Social Structure* (New York: Macmillan Co., 1949).

friends there, he must have at least one room near the entry to the court, into which his guests can be ushered while the women withdraw to another. Some courts are divided by a wall which, on such occasions, separates the women from the men. It is always the host who serves his guests the tea or food prepared by the wife.

Women leave their homes rarely and under unusual circumstances. Being confined to their courtyards from adolescence and knowing that the outside world is for men only, they are content. When the men are away, a knock at the outside gate may bring a woman to the door, but not to open it unless she hears the reassuring voice of some relative who may be admitted. In some instances, she may not even be able to open the door, for her husband has carefully locked her in.

In 1950, the everyday life of the people on either side of the walls revolved around the activities of some fifty-three hundred people. This figure includes a relatively small proportion of economically active males, two-thirds of the men between the ages of twenty and fifty having gone to the cities. A large number of the 965 elementary families represented in the oasis were supported by these emigrants who received, in addition to wages, the "family allotments" paid by the government.[2] Only 500 operators of agricultural enterprises were listed by the government statistical office, despite the fact that farming is the major pursuit of the population.[3] More families actually live by agriculture than this figure indicates, for half of the operators had more than one garden and many married sons worked in, and lived from, their fathers' gardens.

The size of an oasis often is stated in terms of the number of palm trees, rather than of its inhabitants. In these terms, Sidi Khaled is an oasis of more 28,000 palms. Its groves stretch for almost two miles to the west of the village, along the north bank of the Oued Djedi. The nature of date cultivation does much to contribute solidarity and continuity to the families who live from the products of the palms. The plant itself is slow to mature and minor variations in soil and drainage affect its rate of growth. Some have been known to take thirty years to give fruit, but this is exceptional. Once a palm begins to bear, however, it will continue to do so for generations under proper care. A superior

2. In 1950, $5.50 per month for every child under 15 years of age. These payments, designed to increase the French birth rate, had to be made to "Moslem citizens," whose increase was certainly not desired. For discriminatory practice in this and other welfare laws, see David S. McLellen, "The North African in France, a French Racial Problem," *Yale Review*, XLIV (1955), 421-38.

3. See Appendix A for detailed demographic data.

palm produces eighty to a hundred pounds of dates annually, but the average plant yields forty to fifty pounds. Some of the best palms in the oasis were planted by the grandfathers of those who now reap the harvest. Thus, men live from the efforts of their progenitors and plant for the benefit of their descendants.

The palms are planted irregularly, but the average distance between them is about seven yards. Around the base of each is a shallow earth-basin, three to four yards in diameter. These basins are all connected by an intricate system of irrigation channels, through which water from the wells can be directed. This life-giving flow is sent coursing through the gardens six times a month in summer and four times a month in winter. Water is diverted from one channel to another by the simple expedient of digging through the side of the trough at one point and filling in at another. None of the water is wasted. The saturated sides of the irrigation channel have maize, squash, and melons planted along them; nor is the land between the palms left idle. Here are planted peaches, apricots, pomegranates, and figs. To these are added roses, bougainvillea, jasmine, and hibiscus, just for their beauty and fragrance. An irrigated grove in midsummer, cooled by the shade, the streams of water, and the scented breeze, and offering lush fruits for the picking, seems like a different world from the brown desert with its glaring sun and stifling heat.

All of the gardens once had their own wells, but now the number of deep wells and gasoline pumps is more limited. A few cultivators still draw water from the depths by the "Tunisian" method.[4] Most of those who have no pumps, however, pay for water secured from neighboring gardens where the wells are so equipped. In 1950, the water from a "three-inch" pump cost thirty-five cents an hour which amounted to about five dollars for one irrigation of a good-sized garden. The income from such service paid the pump owner for the gasoline and an annual overhaul of his pump.

The cultivation of dates involves more than the planting of the palms and their irrigation. The blossoms must be artificially pollinated to produce fruit. As only the female palms are productive, small gardens do not even have a male plant. The palms blossom in April and the stamens of the males are cut and

4. This technique was introduced from Tunisia but did not originate there. It involves the use of a draft animal, usually a mule, attached to the well rope. The animal is driven down a specially excavated decline running out from the well mouth. As the mule moves down the slope, it pulls the well rope, raising a leather bucket from the bottom of the well. When the bucket reaches the surface, a trip device dumps the water into an irrigation ditch. The animal is led back to the well mouth, letting the bucket descend into the well, and the process is repeated.

Figure 3. Cultivating at the Foot of a Palm.

collected at that time. The male palms are so prolific that excess stamens are given away to garden owners who have none. Then, men climb to the top of every female palm, dust the pollen from a stamen on each of the blossoms, and tie them shut so as to assure fertilization. Care is required as this is also the time of year when some rain falls. There is rarely enough to disturb the pollen, but the sandstorms during this period may be so intense that the trees must be repollinated. When this happens, the stamens are in short supply and are brought in from more fortunate oases and sold in the market. After successful pollination, all of the palms must be climbed again to untie the blossoms, and then again in the fall to bring down the great clusters of ripe fruit.

While dates are the principal product and cash crop, some other produce is raised for local consumption. To the squash and watermelons already mentioned may be added kidney beans, tomatoes, carrots, turnips, and pimentos. Most of these are used in soups or in sauces for the staple food, couscous. This dish is made from wheat flour, which must be purchased. The hoe-cultivated vegetable gardens are separate from the palm groves but must also, of course, be irrigated.

All gardens, like house sites, are privately owned. Unimproved land belongs to no one and ownership is established by planting it or building on it. In the old days, the making of a garden created continuing ownership of the land, even if it was subsequently uncultivated. The French would not support such a claim, it is believed, although no such cases have arisen. One clear exception to the rule of creating ownership through the use of land is the instance of cultivation without irrigation. Occasionally, in a year when the rainfall is heavier than usual, some optimistic farmers may plow shallow furrows in a small stretch of the desert lands which surround the village. Seeded in grain, these fields will produce a meager crop if a few more rains fall. No one can make a living, however, by wagering good grain that it will rain in the desert. On the other hand, irrigation of wheat and barley fields had become so expensive by 1950 that these crops had dwindled to half their prewar position. Only enough grain was being grown to supply the requirements of the community for about two weeks.

Nature does not provide all of the hazards which face the gardener. Even if the crops are brought to maturity, they will be stolen if left unguarded. Nomad raids have ceased but thievery has supplanted them. Out of the old pattern of paying tribute to a nomad tribe for protection against other tribes, there has evolved a similar arrangement between individual farmers and individual nomads. The garden owner induces a nomad to camp in his garden and guard the crop. The inducement to the nomad varies greatly. One farmer paid the equivalent of sixteen dollars a month, plus six hundred pounds of dates and one-twelfth of the vegetable crop. Other farmers gave an eighth or a tenth of the the total crop. Still another gave the nomad all of the produce of a small palm garden where his tent was pitched and from which he patroled the walls of the main grove. The gate to the latter was kept locked to protect it from the guard! The usual pattern of theft, however, is for the guards to steal from unprotected gardens. Sometimes it has been difficult to find nomads who would give up their mobile life of herding, but the decimation of flocks by the drought of the war years made them more available.

It was noted earlier that the same drought also eliminated most of the larger domestic animals of the oasis. It is claimed that before the dry years there were some fifty horses and two hundred mules in the oasis and "almost every family" had a donkey. In 1950 there were but seven horses, eleven mules, and sixty-nine donkeys. Many families keep a few goats for their milk. A few of the sedentarized nomads retain small flocks of goats and sheep, and even some camels.[5] When not grazing or

---

5. Totals for the oasis: 254 goats, 38 sheep, 5 camels.

working, domestic animals are all kept behind walls, close to the house. The donkeys and goats simply live in the family courtyard.

Every household has its gaunt cur which serves as a watchdog, not as a pet. There are no cats, for they would kill the rabbits which are raised quite generally. A few wild animals, such as gazelles and foxes, are half-domesticated. Nearly all households raise chickens. The hens not only produce eggs but are considered useful in keeping down insects, particularly scorpions. The latter are prevalent in the walls of older houses, being especially active in midsummer. Small boys delight in hunting and killing the scorpions when they emerge at night. Everyone treads cautiously for more than one barefooted Arab has died from stepping on a scorpion, although usually the sting is not fatal.

The principal threats to health are pulmonary diseases, especially in winter, and intestinal ones in summer. Chronic bronchitis, pneumonia, dysentery, and typhoid are prevalent, but tuberculosis is the greatest problem. During the field period a team of clinicians from the United Nations tested the entire regional population for tuberculosis and found seventy to eighty per cent to be infected. The French doctor in Ouled Djellal claimed that syphilis was the next most common disease but admitted that he had never seen a case from Sidi Khaled. While there are no prostitutes in this oasis, its men sometimes frequent some of the fifty-two prostitutes in Ouled Djellal. The medical examination of these girls, however, showed only four with positive Wassermans.

It might be added that the medical service provided the population by the government was most limited. In the first place, only marginal professional men were drawn to such a post. In addition, the budget for medical care amounted to only a few cents per capita. The Arabs were supposed to come to the dispensary in Ouled Djellal for all treatment. The doctor carried on a private practice as well as his work as a civil servant, but only my intervention ever induced him to visit cases in Sidi Khaled who were too seriously ill to make the trip to the dispensary.

In case of sickness, the Arabs place great faith in charms written by a *taleb*. Such men of learning are also the native teachers and the tailors of the community. It is difficult to say how many there were with such training, for not all made professional use of their Koranic knowledge. At least one had a small class of boys but did no sewing and was generally regarded as more likely a source of the evil eye than a producer of charms against it. Four other active Koranic teachers were tailors also. Two of these had sewing machines installed in shops which sold cloth. This symbiotic relationship with the merchant made it possible for a purchaser to arrange the making of clothes for himself, or his family, at the same time that he bought the cloth. The tailor not only brought business to the tradesman but the latter had the added satisfaction of sponsoring and helping support a scholar who could also give his children a basic education in Arabic. The two nonmechanized tailors continued the ancient tradition of the savants. They specialized in making embroidered robes, on which they worked while their pupils chanted verses of the Koran. One of these tailor-teachers was also the imam, or prayer leader, of the village mosque, for which duties he received a stipend from the government.

Each of some half dozen, hole-in-the-wall stores served a faithful clientele. The merchandise was general in character, ranging from cloth to staples, like tea and sugar, and including such a local luxury as cheap perfume, much desired by men and women alike. Wealthy storeowners also owned palm gardens but their shops did not deal in agricultural produce. Aside from the date crop, most of which was sold wholesale, garden products were retailed in the open market place by the producers themselves. Here men bought and sold small quantities of vegetables, fruits, and occasionally firewood. Vegetables were usually offered for sale as they were harvested and then, if unsold, taken home for family consumption. Everyone who did not raise dates bought them in quantity, if possible, and almost all families bought imported wheat. The trade in grain was conducted by men who owned or had access to the three trucks in the village.

The butcher, who daily slaughtered a single goat or possibly a sheep, was also in the market place. The addition of meat to the diet of most families occurred only on feast days. Unlike markets in the more commercially oriented towns, that in Sidi Khaled was frequently emptied of vendors before midday. The social life of idle men, however, continued in the vicinity. A few were always in front of the office of the caïd, but more frequented the two teahouses. In the dark interiors of these establishments they squatted around low tables, sipping mint tea, playing dominoes, and talking away the hours until the 10:00 p.m. closing time imposed by the French.

A few crafts and special occupations completed the economic fabric of the community. There were families of carpenters, slipper-makers, masons, and jewelers. Others made charcoal or dug a type of fuller's earth to make a poor living. Mention has already been made of the young men who repaired the pumps and ancient motor vehicles and who acted as drivers. The pilgrimage mosque of Sidi Khaled and the village mosque each had its caretaker and muezzin. There was also a town crier. To this enumeration should be added the day laborers who found most of their employment in the gardens, but who would undertake any work when they were unemployed.

Village Organization

Kinship is the cement of Arab social organization. Everyone belongs to a kin unit called an 'arch, which is usually translated as "tribe" but which is, strictly speaking, a "sib."[6] Membership in the sib is normally patrilineal and all sib members are believed to be related to one another, which they usually are. Sometimes, however, unrelated individuals or groups become attached to a sib and, in time, their descendents acquire fictional kinship. Sibs are divided into subsibs and these may be further subdivided until the unit constitutes a lineage, within which geneological relationship can actually be traced. The presumed kinship of members of a sib, or its subdivisions, is evident in the names which identify the specific groups. These names usually consist of two words: the first is *Ouled* ("Children of") or *Beni* ("Sons of"); and the second is the distinctive group name, which is commonly that of the presumed original ancestor. Thus, most of the sedentarized nomads in Sidi Khaled are Ouled Harket, a subdivision of the Ouled Zekri, who constitute one branch of the Ouled Naïl.

The tie to kinsmen is the only social relationship which endures and upon which one can count. A mutual obligation for defense, blood revenge, and the payment of blood money rests in the sib. Serious quarrels between sib members are greatly decried and every effort is made to avoid or resolve them. Sib units are also the basis of the political organization. This is particularly marked among the nomads, whose territory-holding tribes and daily co-operating bands are composed of such kin and their wives. Even the ideal marriage is one which unites the children of tribal "brothers" or, better still, those of actual brothers, thus holding together the authority and patrimony of the lineage.

It seems probable that sedentary villages whose populations consisted of single sibs once possessed very similar characteristics. The names of many villages suggest such original homogeneity. But, while the oasis of Ouled Djellal bears such a name, its population now consists of three different sibs and the original Ouled Djellal have entirely disappeared. At one time the Ouled Ben Khalifa composed the total population of Sidi Khaled. They appear to have been joined first by the Ouled Hasine and later the Ouled Abed, each of which added a new section to the village. The settlement of new groups continued, culminating with the sedentarization of families from two subgroups of the Ouled Zekri in the last century. There are now eight unrelated sibs in Sidi Khaled, plus scattered families from still other groups.

6. Following the usage of Murdock, *op. cit.*, p. 47.

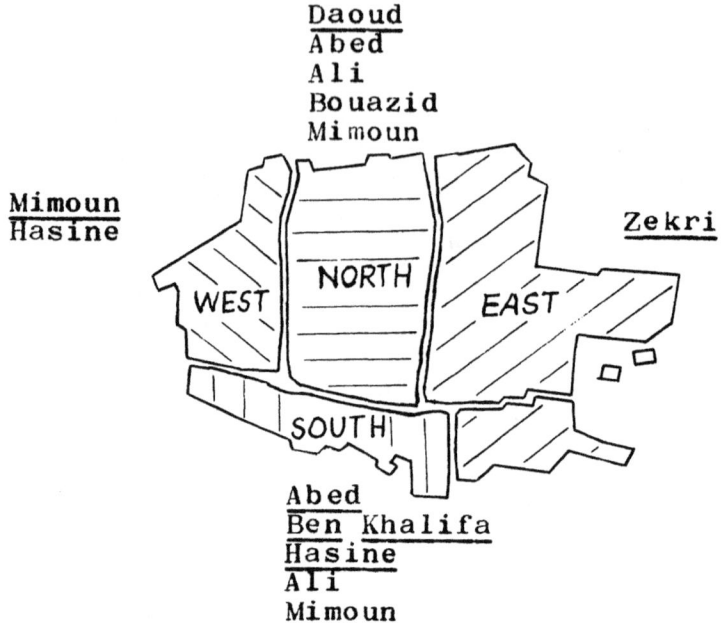

Figure 4. Sidi Khaled — Quarters and Sibs 1950. (Original settlers in each quarter are underlined.)

While these various sibs never trusted one another, suspicion of the sedentarized nomads is particularly marked. The settled Zekri continue to be called "bedouins" by the rest of the population. In recent years, an attempt on the part of the Zekri to expand out of their quarter was met with such violent resistance by the older sibs that the project had to be abandoned. Antagonism to the plan was clearly based on the sentiment that it was bad enough to have these "thieving nomads" in the village without having them for close neighbors. Except in matters affecting the whole village, centuries of residential propinquity have been required to create even limited intersib bonds.

Sibs which settled close together ultimately came to be regarded as a unit for some purposes. The village is now divided into four quarters, named after the cardinal directions, with each containing several sibs, as indicated in Figure 4. In the early days, all of the families of men from one sib lived in one quarter. The leading man of each sib was known as the *kebir* ("Big One"). His prime function was to settle differences within the kin group and to deal with other sib heads. He also officiated, along with a *taleb*, at those marriages which were not formalized by the cadi or native judge, who lived in Ouled Djellal.

Through time, the relation of the sibs to the quarters became confused. Four of the sibs, through growth, intermarriage, and inheritance, came to be represented in more than one quarter. As the sibs remained the really effective units of social control, it seems probable that this scattering resulted in a decline in the functions of the quarters. A *kebir* in one quarter was no longer in as good a position to mediate quarrels between his sib and families belonging to other sibs whose leaders might live in a different quarter of the town. Such quarrels were doubtless referred to the *djema'a*, which was an assembly of village elders. This informal council of sib chiefs and other men of importance was the closest approximation to a village government. Its principal weakness lay in the fact that it lacked the most important element of its prototype, the tribal council. In the village, the elders belonged to different sibs and the feeling of co-operative unity found in a homogeneous tribe did not exist.

The French formalized the *djema'a*, limiting it to sib representatives designated by the administrator. Later, when Sidi Khaled became part of a *commune mixte*, election of a twelve-man council was instituted. As so often happens with the introduction of the vote, it was used to perpetuate the indigenous system. There was an agreement to allocate the twelve positions on the *djema'a* to the various sibs in accordance with their size. Each sib nominated its own leader, or leaders, and the entire slate was voted in by the population. There have been opposition candidates only twice. Some of the young men who had returned from the city decided that the traditional members of the council were only looking after their own interests, rather than those of the community. The youths proposed their own candidates from the sibs, but their slates were defeated in both instances. It was among such young men as these that the spirit of nationalism burned brightest. The French system of control through quasi-traditional channels could not encompass *les déracinés*.

Religion constituted the single focus around which the disparate kin groups of the village could really be organized. Two of the six mosques are maintained by and serve the entire community. Across the Oued is the Mosque of the Prophet (Sidi Khaled). The periodic whitewashing of this structure, with its towering minaret, is practically the only activity which still reflects the old organization of the village into quarters. Each quarter is responsible for calcimining one side of the mosque.

The only other place of worship dignified by a minaret is located on the market place and is known simply as the "Mosque." Here the Friday prayers of the community are conducted. Each of the four other mosques is located in a separate quarter, but they do not serve the quarters. Two mosques belong to individual sibs which are the oldest and the newest in the community, thus representing the exclusiveness of long tradition and the solidarity born of rejection. The remaining mosques were erected in veneration of holy men, including the original local saint of the Rahmania brotherhood.

Figure 5. Competitive Gunplay.

Figure 6. Idle Hours in the Early Sun.

The organization of maintenance work on the Mosque of the Prophet is sufficiently distinctive to deserve further mention. The imam of the village mosque decides whether or not the Prophet's sanctuary needs whitewashing. He has the public crier announce the date on which work is to begin. The *kebirs* of each quarter send men out to lime-bearing deposits, several miles away, where they dig out donkey-loads of the material for transport to the village. The raw material is distributed among the families of the quarter, who burn it into powder and deliver the sacked lime to the *kebir*. Everyone does his share, either out of religious devotion or fear of the ill luck which would ensue if he refused.

On the day set by the imam, the South Quarter streams in ragged procession across the river bed to the Prophet's tomb. The crowd of men, children, and even a few old women is preceded by flag-bearers, drummers, and an armed escort. The day is spent applying the gleaming whitewash to the walls and cupolas on the south side of the mosque. A meal of couscous and meat is provided for the workers by the more wealthy families of the quarter. The work finished by late afternoon, the group troops home, as it came, singing and laughing. On the following day, the next oldest quarter decorates its corresponding western side of the mosque. The other quarters follow, in order of settlement, until all of the surfaces of the building have been whitewashed. That evening there is a general gathering in the market place to watch the gunplay. As seen in the illustration, members of the ceremonial guard discharge their weapons in friendly competition to determine who can make the loudest noise.

Marriages provide another occasion when the even pace of life literally explodes into gunplay for the men, dancing for the women, and feasting for all of the kin. In the next section we turn to the life crises of marriage, birth, and death, all of which occur more frequently in the Arab family than in ours. But while the glamor of a fourth marriage may be somewhat dulled and the sadness of the loss of yet another child be somewhat assuaged, the contrast of these events with the monotony of day-to-day living makes them momentous.

CHAPTER IV

THE COURSE OF OASIS LIFE

The Beginning

While the life of men proceeds in the mosques, gardens, and streets, the activity of the women centers on the home, preparing food, and caring for children. Failure to bear children means loneliness and ultimate divorce, for a man's sons are his pride and his security. A pregnant woman experiences preferential treatment which is not usually her lot. Her husband is less apt to berate her, for she should not be upset. He should provide her with milk and other mild and nourishing foods. If she does not eat well, the baby will be birthmarked. If she is still nursing a previous child, after the third month of pregnancy it must be weaned or given to a wet nurse. The expectant mother must be careful to avoid indigestion and must not take "French medicine" (castor oil) in her later months. Heavy work must be avoided after the sixth month and intercourse is forbidden after the seventh.

Babies are normally born in their fathers' homes if there are women or older children to do the cooking and washing during the mother's confinement. If such assistance is not available, parturition takes place in the home of the mother's parents. Neither grandmother assists at the birth. A midwife is called in and is the only one present during labor. Although husbands must absent themselves during the accouchement, they are informed as to its details for they question the midwife to learn what happens.

Even before the event, the husband ties a rope to a rafter in the center of the sleeping room. He knows that his wife holds onto this rope as she squats to give birth to the child. When the mother has been delivered of the baby and the placenta, the midwife cuts the umbilical cord with a knife. She shapes the infant's head, straightens its limbs, and examines the anus and genitals to be sure there is no obstruction. As washing the baby at birth is believed to subject it to attack by genii, its skin is only rubbed with olive or peanut oil. After the midwife attends to the mother and child, she buries the placenta in the cemetery. Implicit in this act is the idea that if the placenta is committed to the graveyard, the baby will not also have to be buried. Later, when the umbilical cord dries and falls off, it too is interred.

The mother is not bathed after the delivery, but the midwife binds her abdomen with soft cloth and she remains in bed for ten days. She keeps the baby with her and, as it is particularly susceptible to the evil eye and to genii at this time, a *kitab* or written charm is secured from a *taleb* and tied to the infant's head. Grandparents may visit the mother and child as soon as they wish. They bring gifts of meat, sugar, or cloth and are free to compliment the newborn. The baby is, however, isolated from the contact and comments of others. Even the baby's siblings who are less than three years old may not approach it for a month. Otherwise, it is believed that their jealousy and envy would harm the baby. This is the basic mechanism of the evil eye.

On the fourth day the infant is bathed and begins to nurse. Thereafter, whenever it cries, it is given the breast. If the mother has insufficient milk, a wet nurse is sought. A sister of either parent or even a neighbor may assume this function. The baby is taken into the home of the wet nurse, where it lives until weaned. Weaning usually takes place around the end of the second year,[1] but before that time the infant is taken to the home of its actual parents fairly frequently. Its real attachment, of course, is to the woman who nurses it and to brothers and sisters "of the same milk." These bonds are formally recognized in the fictitious kinship which nursing establishes and which constitutes a block to marriage.

An extreme example of this involves a woman, with a baby boy of her own, who was briefly caring for the baby girl of her brother-in-law. She lay down on a bed with the infants beside her, as is the usual practice, and drifted off to sleep. She awoke to find both babies nursing. When she told her husband what had happened, he was furious because the incident had made siblings of the infants. They were actually the offspring of brothers and constituted an ideal marriage match, an arrangement which the brothers had already agreed upon and which had now become impossible. If the mother was really opposed to the match, this "accident" was a typical Arab solution to her problem.

1. Weaning was one of the practices about which data was secured from the large sample of informants. It is discussed in Chapter VI, along with toilet training, punishment, the seclusion of girls, and age of marriage.

For a very detailed description of life crisis rites in Blida, ca. 1913, see the annotated translation from Arabic, by Henri Pérès and G.-H. Bousquet, of J. Desparmet, *Coutumes, Institutions, Croyances des Indigènes de l'Algérie*, Vol. I, *L'Enfance, Le Mariage et la Famille* (2d ed.; Algiers: Imprimeries la Typo-Litho et J. Carbonel réunis, 1948). This material varies considerably in minor detail from that secured in Sidi Khaled. The Kabyle influence in Blida is significantly more evident.

There is no formality about choosing a name for the child. The father selects the name, if the paternal grandfather has not already done so. While names may be chosen before a child is born, they should not be mentioned until later. A boy is never given the name of a living brother but, if a brother has died, his name is reassigned. The names "Mohammed" and its derivative "Ahmed" are used by almost all families. More than a third of the men bear one or the other name, even though their fathers and even their grandfathers may have had the same name. This is not as confusing as one might expect, for a traditional full name simply enumerates the patrilineage of given names. This greatly reduces the chance of duplication, even if it does produce such a name as that of my informant, Mohammed Ben Mohammed Ben Mohammed. Names may be those of other members of the family or they may come from books which indicate appropriate names for children born on certain days of the year. For girls, the name of Fatima, only daughter of Mohammed, is as popular as that of the Prophet for boys.

When the baby is a week old, the paternal relatives assemble at the father's house to celebrate the birth. They learn the name of the child and partake of a feast in its honor. If the father shows the baby to the guests, they are obliged to promise it gifts. One of the kinsmen may also suggest the marriage of one of his own children to the newborn child. The father would find it difficult to avoid giving such a pledge under these circumstances. It is said that the presentation of the baby to the kin is a "nomad custom." In the village it is often omitted because the father does not want to make such an early marriage decision or may wish to avoid obligating poor relatives to give presents.

If, after forty days, the mother shows no hemorrhage, she takes her first bath since delivery. She can, also, now resume sexual relations with her husband. The baby continues to sleep in its parents' bed. In fact, not until puberty will the child sleep entirely apart from them.

Childhood

The life of a small child is bound to his home, his mother, and siblings. Father may occasionally fondle him, but not until the child is three or four years old does this parent begin to show any real desire for his company. Older girls in the household assume maternal responsibilities, protecting and caring for their younger brothers and sisters. If there are quarrels among them, either mother or big sister intervenes. Sister helps see that the children are fed, cleaned, and happy. Like mother, she lavishes affection on her charges and their bonds to her and to their mother are very strong.

In general, children tend to be quiet and restrained. They seldom cry unless hurt and signs of anger quickly subside. There is no nail-biting; thumb-sucking is extremely rare. While vocal among themselves, they are mute and passive in the presence of their fathers and other elders. Rivalry between siblings, which is recognized and guarded against in the birth customs, occasionally breaks into physical conflict. But such displays of anger are frowned upon and quickly stopped.

Around the age of three, children of both sexes experience a brief interlude of closer contact with men. Fathers, and particularly grandfathers, carry them on their shoulders, lead them by the hand, hold them in their laps, and ply them with food between meals. Youngsters receive such attention both at home or in the streets and shops. The presence of other men, either as guests or casual contacts, does not preclude this show of interest in the child, as long as he is quiet and does not interfere with the conversation.

This period also marks the beginning of children's freedom to circulate between the home and streets. Basically, the seclusion of women relates to sex in its functional sense. Prepubescent children and old women, being asexual, are usually free to come and go as they like. Older, but still preadolescent girls, keep a protective eye on younger sisters and very small brothers in the streets. By the time they are five, boys begin to have a life apart from the girls, both in and out of the home.

Most boys are circumcised at about this age. If they are sickly, circumcision may be delayed, but not beyond the age of eight. Children always fear the operation despite the fact that they are generally aware that only the foreskin is severed. A teasing grandfather or other kinsman may scare the child by saying that his penis will be cut off, but the father would be very angry with any child who tried to frighten his son in this way. On the other hand, the father himself may threaten a younger boy for bad behavior, telling him that he will be badly cut and very sick from his circumcision if he does not mend his ways.

A specialist, with two assistants, performs the operation in the father's presence. The foreskin is pulled through a metal ring, tied, and then severed with a single knife or razor stroke. The wound is covered with charcoal dust to stop the bleeding and with the yellow of an egg, so that the scar will not be red. The foreskin is buried, either out of fear or decency. The fearful also secure a *kitab* or written charm for the boy's protection.

The circumcision of a son is an occasion for a feast, but the boy may not be present and must, in fact, fast for two days. He does receive some new clothes, though, in addition to the bright, silk robe (*gandoura*) which he wears for the operation. Relatives from both sides of the family are assembled for the celebration, and *talebs* are invited as an act of piety. To have a feast, one should kill an animal for meat — a sheep or a goat or even, more ostentatiously, a camel. Whatever the meat, every host will feel the religious obligation to share the feast food with some of the community's poor.

The daily eating arrangements of the family provide further recognition of a boy's growing masculinity. Not necessarily after circumcision but when he shows his capacity for self-control, he will be allowed to eat with the men and boys instead of with the women and small children. Each group sits on mats around a common bowl or platter, but the women do not eat until the males have finished. Elder men serve themselves first, conversing freely, but boys who have not reached their late teens may not speak unless addressed. Around the mother's platter, eating is more casual and she favors the smallest children with the best bits of food. In recent years, some returnees from the city have introduced the practice of the family eating together, if the group is not larger than five or six. Under these circumstances, the father is still served first, but otherwise there is less restraint and anyone may talk.

When children are old enough to look after themselves, they receive very little notice from adults, unless they begin to interfere with the activities of the grownups. When this happens, they are shouted at, briskly ordered about, and shoved or struck to get them out of the way. Parents rarely need to resort to these methods, but with other people's children, who throng the streets, adults are harsh indeed. Nevertheless, children find adult life fascinating and get as close as possible to whatever is going on. They make no direct move to interfere, but soon the sheer weight of their numbers brings an adult outburst which temporarily scatters them.

Such an unusual event as the whitewashing of the mosque attracts hundreds of children. As observed in 1950, the special guards, assisted by old crones, tried to keep the crowds from blocking the progress of the parades to and from the mosque. Even so, the children so encircled the drummers that they could hardly walk. Other marchers roughly pushed the youngsters away, knocking one lad to the ground. Scrambling up, he struggled against the crowd to retrieve his fez but was upbraided and pushed at every step.

In addition to the activities of their elders, children have a variety of other amusements. Boys occasionally play an indigenous sort of shinny in the streets. The French school introduced soccer playing, but the game has not spread beyond the school playing field, where it is a focus of adolescent activity. Some adults, however, do come to watch the interschool soccer game with Ouled Djellal. Actually, these contests have had to be policed ever since a match at which the onlookers were inspired to resume the old fued between the oases in a free-for-all fight.

More typically, games are less active. One often sees pairs of boys, surrounded by kibitzers, playing *feldja* or "tent cloth." This is what we would call a "board" game, but the square figure on which it is played is just traced in the sand. The "men" used in the game consist of pebbles and date pits. Following rules resembling a cross between those of tic-tac-toe and checkers, each player tries to take all of the men of the other. Girls were never observed playing *feldja*. They seemed to prefer such make-believe amusements as building little gardens in the sand.

As boys grow older they abandon *feldja* for checkers and dominoes. Men usually gamble on dominoes for small stakes. For this reason, the more religious members of the community disapprove of the game. *Carta*, played with a distinctive deck of cards, is a popular pastime and gambling game in the teahouses of Algiers. Now young men in the oasis also occasionally play it. The noise and excitement of urban card playing, with its shouting and slapping of winning cards on the table, is in marked contrast to the more quiet, but jocular, play of the traditional games.

Animals provide a focus for some amount of childhood activity. In families which have flocks, their grazing occupies young boys throughout the day. Usually, however, only a few animals have to be fed and watered or a loaded donkey be driven by a lad who is assisting his father. The treatment of animals often strikes the Westerner as thoughtless or cruel. While it is true that the Arab is much less prone to suffer vicariously for animals, he does not hold that they are part of the unfeeling world of "things." Just as they differ in their ability to work, they are believed to vary in their sensitivity to pain. In fact, ideas concerning sensitivity are most highly developed concerning beasts of burden.

The ass is considered the least sensitive animal and is ruthlessly kicked, beaten, and goaded. Donkeys are good workers, but what can a caress mean to a beast which will not respond to a kick? Anyone who has ever tried to make a donkey work will know where the mule gets its stubborn qualities. Our "mule skinners" would understand the Arabs' attitude completely. The only real difference is that we believe a donkey to be stubborn, whereas the Arabs consider it insensitive.

The camel is said to be a harder worker than either the mule or donkey but also more sensitive to pain. Horses are the poorest workers and are, in fact, used primarily for riding. They "feel pain more than man" but this does not spare them from free use of whip and spur. It would seem, therefore, that the treatment of animals varies with their sensitivity but also that the beast's feelings may sometimes be disregarded.

Figure 7. Making Palm Gardens in the Sand.

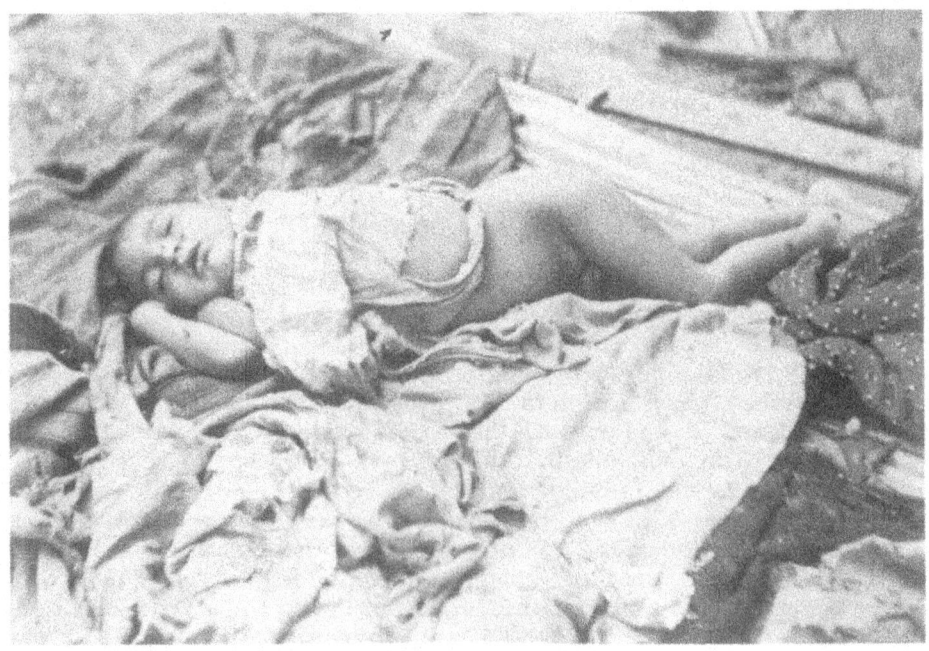

Figure 8. Napping on a Scaffold Bed.

The rough treatment of animals is very evident in the behavior of small boys. When one manages to catch a pigeon, he gleefully carries it about by its wing tips. I inquired of one seventeen-year-old lad what a pigeon felt on being carried thus. He responded with a laugh, "They know that they are caught by the wings, all right." The laugh was perhaps the most revealing part of his response. Boys sometimes amuse themselves by dropping date pits on dung beetles or by dragging a captive chameleon around on a cord until it expires. In general, there seems to be some satisfaction derived from the power to dominate and to hurt.

The almost complete lack of pets is also striking. Rabbits are the only exception, for children do find pleasure in holding them. They are also treated more gently, being carried by the ears, but also being given support under the body so that they do not scream and kick.

Some wild birds are surrounded by sacred lore. Swallows are said to spend the winter in Mecca, from whence, in spring, they flock back to the minaret of the village mosque. Small sparrows frequenting the courtyards are called "marabouts." They are relatively tame and are sometimes caught, but their sacred quality influences their fate. A spot of henna is put on their heads and then they are released.

But there is more than such amusement in a child's life. Girls soon participate in the household chores. While the sweeping of dirt floors, the washing of clothes, and bathing of small children are kept to a minimum, they must all be done. The preparation of food and the supervision of youngsters are more demanding. If there is no well in the family courtyard, someone must carry water from the public well in the Oued. Small boys may help with this task and in running errands between cloistered households, but they tend to have less work to do than their sisters. Koranic schools provide the serious side of the boys' lives before they are big enough to aid the men in their labor.

All fathers are not sufficiently religious or financially able to send their sons to a *taleb* for schooling, but the majority of boys receive a few years of such training. It is started around the age of six or seven, so that they will be able to perform their daily prayers by the time they reach puberty. Then, also, they must assume the obligation of fasting during Ramadan. In addition to learning from the *taleb* the content of the prayers and the postures of the salaam, the lads begin to learn the Koran by heart and to explore the complexities of reading and writing Arabic.

This training consists of copying a section of the Koran which is to be memorized and then chanting it, in unison, until it can be repeated by rote. This continues, sura by sura, but only students who will become *talebs* themselves continue studying long enough to learn all of the chapters of the holy book. The majority simply memorize a small portion of the Koran and go through the motions of reading from their writing boards, without ever really learning to read.

Students gather daily at the house of the *taleb* for two-hour sessions in the early morning, at noon, and in the evening. Several years of such schooling may leave them illiterate, but they do learn discipline and respect for authority. The teacher is a strict and punishing figure, quick to use his rod on the palms or on the soles of a delinquent scholar. Only the regular chanting of orderly boys will satisfy him.

Another lesson learned by every student is respect for the sacred word and even for the alphabet in which it is written. *Baraka* resides in both. The *taleb* not only emphasizes this fact but provides the scholars with written charms for their own protection.[2] Respect for this *baraka* extends even to Arabic script used in secular writing. The Arabic letter mîme or "M" is particularly sacred, as it is Mohammed's initial. For this reason, old correspondence or Arabic newspapers should not be thrown out with dirt and refuse. Great variation exists, however, in the matter of the actual handling of written material. Many ignore or are oblivious of any sanctity in secular writing. At the other extreme, one man objected to a French paper being thrown on the ground because it contained "M's," even though they were in Roman script.

The values emphasized by the *taleb* and the lessons learned from him have continuing influence on the child to the degree that they find support in the behavior of the adult community. Informal tuition by elders is the principal source of knowledge of the spectrum of manners and morals which distinguish the Arab. Everyone does not behave as he should, of course, and breaches of most forms of etiquette were observed, even among adults.

Decency, Modesty, and Shame

A sense of shame is a desirable attribute, as is evident in the statement attributed to Mohammed, "Have shame while taking in food, as you do in passing it out." This linkage of the etiquette of eating and of excretion needs to be understood in terms of the fact that, underlying many facets of Arab culture, there is concern with cleanliness. The rules of cleanliness associated with the five daily prayers are exacting and the etiquette of eating requires cleanliness, even though the Arabs eat with their fingers.

---

2. Chapter VI presents detailed information on prayer, charms, and various other supernatural practices.

Such are the norms, but this is certainly not to say that the people are clean.

The European is usually shocked at the Arab's apparent unconcern over public defecation and urination. It is true that the sandy streets and outskirts of the village are littered with excrement. It is also true that the figure of a squatting Arab, relieving himself, is commonplace. But it is far from true that the Arabs have no modesty concerning such matters. In the first place, one should remember that the out-of-doors is as exclusively men's territory as is a Men's Room in the Western world. But in the oasis men do not congregate to perform their excretory functions; they withdraw from the company of others. Even in their courtyards, there are secluded dungpiles to which they can go. It is said that women do not have the same sense of modesty before other women, but the separation of the sexes is mandatory.

The men do not have the American's feeling of modesty about the fact that they are relieving themselves, but they are much more modest about the exposure of their bodies. The Arab characteristically squats, both to urinate and to defecate, and his flowing robes protect his privacy. Another rationale for this position, so far as such a custom is open to explanation, is that it is easier to keep the clothes clean, and they must be kept so if one is to pray in them. Squatting to urinate is considered to be so characteristic of Islam that an Arab who is not a good Moslem is likely to be ridiculed with the statement, "He stands to urinate." In the French cities, however, where the rare public toilets are dirty and urinals are plentiful, the Arabs quickly adapt the French custom of standing. Mention must be made of the fact that, after defecation, an Arab wipes himself with his left hand, quite literally, although he may use some sand. This is but one aspect of a definite etiquette of handedness.

In the ablutions before the prayer, the mouth is washed out three times with water and it is the right hand which brings the water to the mouth. The right hand carries water to the nose, to be snuffed up and then blown out into the left hand. In eating, only the right hand is used. To offer one's left hand in greeting is an insult.[3] When an Arab picks his nose, he does so with his left hand. These customs clearly involve the use of the right hand for clean things and the left for dirty. The etiquette is followed because it is traditional, however, and not explicitly for reasons of cleanliness.

Although the hands should be washed before eating, the practice is not common. On formal occasions a ewer of water is

---

3. Most Arabs are right-handed. One left-handed man, about whom I heard, shook hands with his right hand and his seventeen-year-old son was unaware of the etiquette of handedness after defecation.

provided guests for this purpose. After eating dates or other sticky foods one uses a towel at the end of the meal to wipe off the hands. In taking food from the common dish, each person should reach into that part directly before him. Thus, when the platter is copiously filled, no man eats what another's fingers have handled. Of course it is different for the women and children who receive the platter when the men have finished.

The separation of the sexes at meals is also associated with a feeling of shame about eating together. This extends to a distaste for eating in public. Except for the drinking of sweet mint tea, which is almost a requirement for any social intercourse, and the between-meal eating of dates, men eat at home. Single men adapt to French restaurant eating in the city, however, and their only concern is over the ritual purity of the food.[4] The following incident provides some feeling for the oasis attitude toward public eating. In Sidi Khaled there was a middle-aged, psychotic woman who was permitted to roam the streets in a dress so badly torn that her pubes was exposed. Neither this nor her demented ranting at passers-by attracted attention. From an interest in the Arabs' perception of her condition, the anthropologist once asked how they knew she was crazy. The immediate response was, "Because she eats in the street." The exposed condition of this woman also points up the fact that the people do not seem to experience vicarious shame unless the shameful behavior reflects on themselves, as it would if the person were closely related.

There is no feeling of inappropriateness about belching. A person may say, "Allah forgive me," after a loud belch, but with about as much feeling as our "God bless you" after a sneeze. Sneezing has its little formalities among the Arabs also. After a sneeze, one should say, "Allah be praised," and anyone present should follow this statement with "Allah be merciful." A yawn requires no comment whatever.

Flatulence is quite a different matter. A feeling of intense shame is associated with the passing of wind in the presence of anyone, even a close relative. Arabic distinguishes between *drat*, which is audible flatulence, and *tish*, which is offensively odoriferous but less likely to identify the offender. Either is so humiliating that, except with children, it almost never occurs in the presence of others. An adult will withdraw from a group, without comment, to pass wind in private and then air out his clothes before returning. The intensity of this taboo is illustrated by a local folktale, which is a variant of one which occurs in *A Thousand and One Nights*. The theme of the story concerns a young man

---

4. Pork products may not be eaten, nor may horsemeat under the Malikite cult. All animals must be slaughtered by having their throats cut.

who passed wind in the presence of his sister. He was so ashamed that he left home. Years later he returned to find his sister grieving over his absence. In her joy at his return, she asked, "Why did you leave, when all that you did was to pass wind?" He was so shamed by this reference to his offense that he left home again, never to return.

This sense of shame is developed in children by their parents, who laugh at the young offenders. In case of a *tish*, the parent asks who is responsible and, usually receiving no admission, proceeds to accuse each child, even young adolescents. Both false accusation and mirth at the expense of the guilty are apt to lead to tears. The matter is so serious that adults would never show awareness of such an offense on the part of another adult, although small children might surreptitiously giggle about it.

The Arab's sense of personal dignity is one aspect of his susceptibility to feelings of shame. Public humiliation is a powerful sanction and it is used to control village deviants as it is to train children. When men are caught stealing from the gardens, they are bedecked with a necklace of stolen produce and drummed through the streets. Several villagers have been punished in this way and subsequently all left the oasis.

The Expression of Emotion

Even though it is painful to be laughed at, few are shielded from such mirth. One should not laugh at one's father or brother or at a stranger. But I have seen men laugh at their father, despite the fact that he was a holy man and a marabout of a *zaouia*. In a somewhat formal situation, the marabout forgot my name and had to ask it. The hilarity which this provoked may have been more open because of my presence, but the situation contains the basic element of much of Arab humor.

People laugh at the caïd because he wraps his turban so badly that the head cords, which are a mark of his status, fall down over his eyes. Other humorous situations are a horseman on a runaway horse, a shepherd in pursuit of a frightened flock, a man tripping over his own cane, a person performing his ritual ablutions in the wrong order, or a cripple stumbling under too heavy a load. The last is not amusing because the man is crippled, but because he overestimated his abilities. Serious misfortunes are not considered funny, but when someone overextends himself or fails to do what may reasonably be expected of anyone in his position, he is the butt of mirth.

Humor, of course, is indulged in for the sheer pleasure involved. While sexual joking, between men who are intimates and not too closely related, is a definite part of Arab culture, the respect the anthropologist was shown cut him off from these jokes. One type of such humor, in which young men engage, is competitive, fictitious bragging about sexual exploits. The humor lies in the extravagance of the sexual claims — the contrast between what one says and wishes were true and what is known to be possible.

Another type of Arab humor is practical joking and mimicry. In one instance, a youth was bet that he was afraid to go into a nearby cave at night. He was then preceded to the cavern and was frightened away with awesome noises. Another villager has quite a reputation for his pranks, in which he even uses disguises and "props." Coming into the market place one night, with a false beard and flowing robes, he claimed to be a caïd from the southern desert. He was accepted by some and shown the deference he pretended to merit until he exposed his identity and roared with laughter at his victims. The retelling of such pranks inevitably embellishes them. It is doubtful that the market-tax collector whom he shot with a popgun, in a fit of pretended rage, really collapsed and had to be carried home.

Similarly, the exploit of another wag is now claimed to have involved a French schoolteacher as well as the German prisoner-of-war who was victimized as he worked on the new school building. In this instance, the joker pretended he was dangerously insane and made his victim salute him and go through various drills. Quite aside from the original incident, the real fun is watching the mimic reproduce the calisthenics he claims to have forced the teacher and prisoner to execute. The grown son of the "popgun murderer" has his own variety of tricks, which he likes to play on children. He puts a frog, snake, or scorpion in a handkerchief and then, after engaging some child in conversation, thrusts the creature at the startled youngster. Such humor is quite consonant with the apparent pleasure we noted among children in bedeviling small animals.

The fact that humor is associated with the discomfiture of others seems related to the social norms which require that man should not expose his emotions. He should never cry because of physical pain. If a small boy cries upon being hurt, he is kissed by his mother or sister and told that he should not cry. He may be encouraged by being told that the pain will disappear or that he is a good boy and handsome. Females, on the other hand, just naturally have to cry. A woman may cry because her husband is going to work in France or just because she has a headache. Other women in the household, hearing her sob, might cry with her. They will not talk about her troubles but some will comfort her. A man may cry in the privacy of his own home at the death of a close relative or friend or even over a great financial loss. To the outside world he will show no sorrow and may even seem unconcerned. Male relatives will try to give a grieving man courage by telling him that his misfortune is just fate, but it would be shameful for them to grieve with him.

Men love those for whom they grieve. Here again the free manifestation of feelings is not permissible. Emotional ties between spouses are not expected to be more than sexual but years of coexistence can lead to more inclusive interdependence. No sign of affection is permissible, though, except in the privacy of the sleeping quarters. While a man's ties to other near kin, both male and female, may be close, he is only permitted to be demonstrative toward small children. After a long absence a man might kiss his mother or sister in the presence of the family but he would be more reserved with his wife. In contrast, women are quite openly affectionate with their children and among themselves. Caressing, kissing, and close body contact are usual in the home. Hand-kissing is an expected gesture of deference between persons of the same sex. Formal kisses on the cheek express a closer relationship and are also permissible among men in public. The only less formal public expression of emotion among males is the practice of holding hands while walking together. This is common behavior between close friends and begins in adolescence. While it may sometimes be associated with homosexuality, which is the interpretation a Westerner is apt to make, the custom is far from being indicative of perversion.

Like his love and sorrow, a man's fears should be kept to himself. He might express them to his brother or close friend, but only a "great fear" would be mentioned to his father. Regarding the sorts of things men fear, it is striking that the examples given of fearful situations were often those which also provoke anger or those in which the situation would indirectly affect the person's reputation. While fear of bodily injury may be important, it receives little comment. The taboo against the showing of pain probably extends to the admission of fear of it. It is said that a man would be afraid if he saw his paternal cousin being beaten by people in the market place; if he heard that the French had put his son in prison; or if his son went to the French because the father had refused to arrange his marriage. Aside from the fact that fear is strikingly associated with the French, these examples have another common characteristic. All involve situations in which the kin bond throws a man into open conflict with forces more powerful than himself. The impending threat to his strong feelings of pride seems to underlie the fears.

When asked in what situations a person might experience fear without any implication of anger or humiliation, the examples given were that of walking through the streets of Ouled Djellal and having everyone look at you (fear of the evil eye) and that of walking alone at night, when one might be struck with a club.

As with laughter, a man may freely vent his anger so long as he avoids retaliation. A father's word is final and he quickly becomes angry with a disobedient child or wife. If the infraction is not major, he screams vituperations and slaps the offender. But if he finds his wife outside the courtyard door or leaning over the wall, he will probably be sufficiently enraged to beat her with a stick. Outside his home, he will meet injustice and affront from his equals with a screaming tirade but physical aggression toward other men is rare. In defense of his home, however, every husband sees a housebreaker as a potential adulterer and shoots without hesitation.

Sexual Knowledge and Values

Women are not only secluded but kinsmen may not even mention their names publicly. Within the kin group, sexual topics are taboo for a man in conversation with practically everyone except brothers of about his own age or similarly aged cousins or brothers-in-law. This restriction is as strong with consanguinal relatives as it is with affinal ones. But there are many males with whom one can joke and brag about sexual matters not affecting one's own kin. In such conversations, the use of euphemisms is usual. Reference to the penis is made with the Arabic words for "pencil" or "knot"; to copulate is to "giggle"; and the vulva becomes the "blind eye."

Despite the rather Puritanical attitude toward the free discussion of such topics or the open display of affection, Arab children learn about sex at an early age. In fact, the contrast between the lively interest in sex and the suppression of public indications of these feelings is one of the striking features of the culture. Children are given no parental instruction in matters of sex but family sleeping arrangements provide what almost amounts to laboratory training.

The Arab home is generally short of bedrooms, beds, and bedding. People sleep in their clothes, the very poor on grass mats on the floor. Most Arabs can afford a bed, however, but blankets are less common. The bed consists of a semirigid panel, crudely woven from the ribs of palm fronds. Such a bed is about four feet wide and eight feet long. As its native name of "scaffolding" implies, the woven panel is supported, two feet or more from the floor, on forked sticks or sawhorses. With the sleepers huddled together and lying diagonally on the bed, it can accommodate as many as six people.

Until they are five years old or more, children sleep on the same bed with their father and mother. Under such intimate circumstances, the children inescapably become aware of their parents' intercourse. The adults are not disturbed by such cognizance of their sex life, but they consider that it is bad for even a baby to witness it. They commonly wait until the middle of the night to copulate when the children are asleep. If a child awakens, the parents will cover themselves or tell the child to turn away so as not to see them.

When children are older, they are moved from the parents' bedroom to one of their own, where brothers and sisters sleep together until they are about thirteen. From this age, the boys and girls should sleep in separate rooms. All of these arrangements are fairly elastic and depend upon the facilities available and the ages of the children. One very reliable and rather prudish informant stated that he had kept his children in his own bed until they were ten years old and had let them sleep together in another room until they were thirteen. This Arab was relatively well off and could easily have afforded as many bedrooms as he needed.

If a man has two wives, each sleeps in a separate room. The wives spend alternate nights with their husband, except when one is menstruating. In monogamous unions, there is no intercourse during the woman's period but she need not leave her husband's bed. In polygynous households, the wife who is not sleeping with the husband may bed with the small children of both unions.

In a poor family in which adolescent brothers and sisters cannot have separate rooms, the parents are "careful to watch them." This caution is not primarily required to inhibit incestuous relations. A boy soon learns that having sexual relations with any girl in the household — sister or cousin — is one of the worst things he can do and that it is punishable by death or, if he is fortunate, by being driven from the home. Further, he learns that it is his responsibility to protect his sister's virginity and to kill, if need be, anyone who seduces her. An adult brother is even likely to assume an absent brother-in-law's duty and punish the adultery of his sister, killing the man and possibly even his sister.

Because married sons may remain in their father's household, extended patrilineal families develop and continue to live together even after the death of the patriarch. This is most apt to be the case in more wealthy families, in which the patrimony holds the group together. While such families are not common, they are far from rare. Even poorer men may take into their homes the children of a deceased brother, if his widow does not remarry. In all such composite families, boys will be reared with their father's brother's daughters, who are considered ideal marriage partners. The only case noted of fornication between children in the same home was between such cousins. In this instance, the girl became pregnant and the young man left home, which is probably what brought the incident to public attention. The total evidence seems to indicate that premarital intercourse is rare for girls. The bragging of some men about their relations with girls from other families is, however, in conflict with the great emphasis placed on virginity and the customs which protect it and expose its loss.

It was said that, in the oasis, the parents of an unmarried girl who became pregnant would arrange an abortion rather than a marriage. It does seem likely that the man involved would flee for his life from the enraged father. The idea of abortion is repellent to the progeny-conscious Arabs. In the city, with its mobility and anonymity, the solution for the unwed mother is adoption of the child and change of residence for the girl and her parents.

While fornication is under heavy taboo, sex play is quite acceptable among siblings, until it becomes too dangerously close to being a prelude to intercourse. The genitals of a baby are stroked by its brothers and sisters "to amuse and please it," but not in public. A small child may practice self-masturbation without reprimand, although later he or she learns that such activity should only be pursued in private. Ultimately he learns that it is not approved adult behavior. Among siblings in the same bed, fondling and mutual masturbation are common practice, both homosexually and heterosexually. Such activity, of course, is restricted to the bed. When early adolescents are first separated in their sleeping arrangements, "they are told that they must no longer play with one another. In touching his sister's breasts, a boy might get ideas."

As a result of this background of early experience, with parents and siblings, the erotic attachments of men to their mothers and sisters are very strong. The Oedipal situation is clear in the usual examples which men give of "Satan's dreams," those in which they have intercourse with their mothers or sisters or fight with their fathers. Nor are these feelings one-sided. A man of thirty-six stated that his mother and sister still liked to have him sleep with them (no euphemism) but that he was "afraid to because of what he might do" when he had dreams.

At a time when a boy's sexuality is becoming increasingly demanding, he is cut off from his sisters and pubescent girls by new sleeping arrangements, paternal vigilance, and the seclusion of girls to their homes. Most of his waking hours he now spends outside of the home, surrounded by unaffectionate, adult males. Homosexual relations with brothers and other boys are extended to include felatio and sodomy. Bestiality with goats, sheep, or camels provides another outlet. These practices are not approved but are recognized as common among boys. They are strongly taboo as adult behavior, although it is not unknown for a *taleb* to practice sodomy with students. It is the passive role in such relations which is most shameful and I heard of one boy of thirteen who received pay for assuming it.

The only heterosexual outlet for an unmarried youth is with a rare, unguarded female or, more usually, with prostitutes in Ouled Djellal. Visits to these women may become the cue to the father to arrange his son's marriage. The customs associated with this will be described shortly. Before doing so, it is relevant to note the kind of sexual instructions provided young married men by an ' âlem (religious savant) of the Great Mosque in Algiers. Part of their significance lies in the necessity for interdicting some practices. The men are told that any sort of sexual contact is permitted between spouses except anal copulation and felatio. *Coitus interruptus* is known and permissible, [5] but deviations from normal sex relations are not usually employed to avoid pregnancy. Charms are written for this purpose by 'âlem or *taleb* and only the most acculturated urbanites know of French methods of contraception.

After the birth of his first child, one young man went to the mufti of the Great Mosque to secure such a charm. He did not want to have another baby too soon after the first, for the women of his family had told him about a six-month old baby which had become so jealous of a three-month old foetus that it sickened and died. They did not think to tell him that the baby had to be weaned at that time because of the mother's pregnancy. The mufti supplied a contraceptive charm and is said to have guaranteed to pay all the expenses of childbirth if the man's wife became pregnant while wearing it. It was further understood that the husband was to take the charm from her at the end of a year, for it would be wrong not to have progeny.

Marriage

By reason of divorce, every Arab may normally expect to be married at least twice. A man's first marriage is arranged by his father, and all those of a woman are arranged by a responsible male kinsman. In the village a young man is not supposed to approach his father directly with a request that his marriage be arranged. While this may occur in the city, in the desert a son communicates his wishes to a close friend of his father, who

---

5. See also G.-H. Bousquet, "L'Islam et la limitation volontaire des naissances," *Annales de l'Institut d'Études Orientales*, VII (1948), 95-104.

informs the parent.[6] If he has not already arranged a match, the father discusses the matter with his wife or, if she is dead or divorced, with his mother. The women have doubtless been considering potential brides for some time, for they have much greater contact with, and knowledge of, the nubile girls of the community. If there is no girl available in the immediate kindred, an old woman will be sent, on some pretext, to the home of a likely prospect to look her over. When the boy's parents agree on a particular girl, a food gift is sent to her parents. More wealthy Arabs will send subsequent gifts but their purpose is not explained nor need it be, for their import is clear. Even though the match may not be desired by the girl's family, these overtures may not be refused.

Several weeks after such initial contact, the father of the boy visits that of the girl. The former is accompanied by some older man of character and distinction who speaks for him. The subject of the proposed match is broached. If the girl's father wishes to refuse, he offers some excuse, such as the extreme youth of the girl or a previously arranged match. Under more auspicious circumstances, the discussion gets down to particulars. The man who speaks for the boy's father states the size of the proposed dowry to be paid to the bride's father. He also communicates what gifts the bride herself will receive. A wealthy father might refuse to accept the initial offer, but haggling is more apt to be involved over the frequency with which the girl is to be allowed to visit her parents. Her father may press for five or six visits a year, against proposals of two or three. He also requires assurances that his daughter will receive good treatment and be well clothed. Finally all differences are compromised and agreement is reached. The couple who are to be married are informed of the match. They have little to say about it and, in fact, are not in a position to question their parents' judgment. The young people may never have seen one another or, more probably, will only have childhood recollections of their future spouses. Such lack of acquaintance even characterizes subsequent marriages.

Marriage constitutes a contract, and the formal witnessing of the agreed conditions and the payment of the dowry constitute

---

6. While in the oasis, an incident occurred which illustrates the general tendency of a son to deal with his father by indirection on important matters. In this instance, a young man had the anthropologist record a conversation with an elder brother in which they expressed their belief that their father should add another room to the house. An evening of entertainment had already been planned in which recorded music was to be played for the whole family. The recorded argument for the new room was introduced along with the music and drew no comment whatever.

its legal implementation. The previously more common and still acceptable form of marriage is "by *djema'a*." This "assembly" of witnesses includes the two fathers and two male witnesses, usually *kebirs*. The presence of the imam of the mosque is also desirable. Paternal agreement to the union before such witnesses establishes the legitimacy of the offspring and their inheritance rights. According to local custom, girls as young as thirteen may be married by *djema'a* .

Marriage by cadi comes under French control and the bride must be at least fifteen years old. In this form of marriage, the cadi conducts a brief ceremony and makes a written record of the contract. Such agreements have long been used by the wealthier families but have become more general as a result of the fact that the French government only recognizes marriage by cadi as a basis for the payment of family allotments. Even in 1950 this was resulting in the remarriage, by cadi, of couples in their sixties who had been previously married by *djema'a*.

It is the ceremonial of wedding, not the legalities of marriage, which make the occasion an exciting one. The festivities continue over a four-day period and draw relatives together even from a distance. The field worker and his wife attended the wedding of a man from the oasis who was in the French army in Oran. The soldier had returned to Sidi Khaled to marry a patrilineal cousin. In order to be present for the wedding, his brother came with his wife and two small children by bus from Algiers. One of the groom's sisters was invited and expected to attend, although she was married to a nomad and lived in the desert. When no camel was sent for her, however, her husband refused to provide her transport. It was a big wedding, for the Zekri lineage to which the principals belonged was a large one. About one hundred people participated in one way or another.

During the days before the consummation of the marriage, the groom was not permitted to see his parents and absented himself from home as much as possible. He amused himself in the streets and in the homes of young men his own age with eating, conversation, and song. As an urbanite, he would have liked to have heard the professional women singers who sometimes enliven these occasions, but his oasis kin looked with disfavor on their ribald jesting. Yet the proceedings were far from dull. Gunfire, drumming, and singing marked the successive nights on which henna was ritually applied to the groom's hands and those of his bride in separate ceremonies.

The climax of the celebration is normally the bringing of the bride to her husband's home and bed. In this case, no new house was being established, so a vacant house was lent for the occasion by a relative. On the third day the borrowed house was appropriately furnished with heirloom rugs for an evening feast attended by the women, girls, and small boys of the groom's family. Following a copious meal, the whole assembly trooped out toward the bride's home, crying out with wavering "you-yous" and singing as they went. The groom and his companions followed at a distance in the shadowy streets. Only the women entered the courtyard of the bride's parents. She was found dressed in finery and seated between two old women in one of the rooms off the court. A sheer veil covering her head was raised by each admiring guest. But through it all, the bride remained motionless and silent, with downcast eyes and a disconsolate expression. A bride is, in fact, expected to be unhappy during the days of her wedding, for she is leaving her home.

The time for her departure having come, her head was completely covered with a white cloth and her two women companions tried to raise her to her feet. After resisting their initial attempts, she finally let herself be led forth. The group flowed back toward the wedding house. This time their singing was punctuated by gunshots fired by the men, who still remained aloof. Within one of the rooms of the wedding house, the bride was installed on cushions between her two protective crones. The white cloth was removed from her head but the veil remained, to be lifted by curious newcomers who had not yet seen the bride. Around her swarmed a compact and excited segment of the women's world. Mothers nursed their swaddled infants and laid them on the carpet to sleep calmly through the hubbub. Small boys pulled and pushed at little girls. Old women swung their canes to clear out the youngsters.

As the heat and the jostling in the small room became intense, most of the crowd moved into the courtyard. A drum was brought and the crowd opened to permit individual women to dance. Even grandmothers came into the cleared circle and performed the Naïl *danse à ventre* with amazing vigor and skill. And so the festivities continued through the night, while the bride sat in glum splendor in the room apart.

Meanwhile, the men had gathered briefly in another room to congratulate the groom and chat among themselves. They soon dispersed, however, to sleep. This was the "women's night" and dawn brought little change. Some slept a few hours when overcome by fatigue, but the festivities were never interrupted. Gifts of gold jewelry were brought to the bride, who tried on the pieces before passing them to an old woman to lock in the coffer by her side. The gifts stirred conversation among the guests, but still the bride remained quiet and downcast.

Facing her sat an unmarried, adolescent sister, richly dressed and jeweled. She did not participate in the festivities but simply stared at the bride and the activities around her. Nearby, an old woman who had been telling prayer beads arose and danced in what appeared to be almost a trance. She was believed to be crazy *(mahboul)* but possessed of *baraka*. After more prayers, she called the sister of the bride to her and blew her blessing thrice into the girl's mouth and each ear, on her forehead, and down the front of her dress. Now a good marriage would come to this girl, as it had to her sister.

The gathering of the men, on the following night, took place at the home of the groom's brother. By contrast with that of the women, it was a drab affair. Yet the slaughter of a sheep and the feast of couscous for some sixty guests was an occasion of importance. Joking, laughter, and song raised it from the mundane, but its essence was that of a banquet. The women too had eaten special platters of couscous covered with sugar "to sweeten their words," but eating had been of secondary interest. The men's feast concluded, the groom was escorted to the marriage house and to the beginning of his life with a bride he had never known.

An Unusual Conflict Over a Marriage

During the field period an episode occurred which was revealing as to a brother's attitude toward his sister's marriage. The incident is also significant as evidence of the local attitude toward Negroes, for it involves a girl who was pledged to marry a wealthy Negroid Arab from one of the southern oasis. The girl's brother, a young married man still living with his father, protested vehemently when the marriage was arranged. He swore he would never permit his sister to marry a Negro and would kill the man before he would let him take his sister. Nevertheless, the legalities of the marriage were concluded and the Negro arrived in a car to get his bride. The brother met him, forcing him to flee at gunpoint. The thwarted groom protested to the administrator, who sent two soldiers to arrest the indignant brother. While the latter sat three days in a cell, the groom collected his bride and returned south. Upon his release from prison, the brother returned home in a fury, threatened his father with death, and moved from his house. Urged against violence by the local *kebirs*, he broodingly refused to have further contact with any of his family.

At least some of the villagers believed that the father must have received an exceedingly high dowry for his daughter. What other reason could there be for marrying her to a Negro? Such racial prejudice is rather striking in view of the fact that it is not general in Islam. Elsewhere, even sons of the same Arab father may vary markedly in racial characteristics. A son born to a Negro concubine has the same legal status as a son born to a legally married wife, whatever her race. Where such miscegenation is common, as in the southern oases, racial discrimination is unknown.

Sidi Khaled has had little contact with Negroes and that only of a very specialized sort. Attached to the family of the caïd is a single family of Negro "slaves," the father of which is the son of a slave of the caïd's father. These are the only Negroes seen in the oasis, except for an occasional *bousaadia* or itinerant entertainer. The status of these Negro "slaves" is such, in the caïd's lineage, that the man, while no eunuch, waits upon the women of the lineage with no restriction. Against this local background, the stereotype of a Negro as a low-status person is quite understandable. Generally comparable situations must be common in Algeria, however, for there is a widely known Arab proverb which runs, "You can no more make a savant of a Negro than you can cut planks from cork."

The End of Life

Death, of course, does not normally follow as precipitously upon marriage as this presentation might suggest. The birth and childhood of new generations, and the work and relaxation of the old, follow the familiar themes already outlined, filling the lives of parents and grandparents until death does remove them. Even this severance is not complete, for women continue to visit family graves, at least to leave annual offerings of food.

Death is only unusual as a personal experience. Every adult has already experienced contact with the death of others and knows that when he too is dying, he will be placed on his right side with his face to the east. Thus, death will overtake him lying as he will in his grave, facing the sacred city toward which his daily prayers have been directed.

Burial should follow death as soon as possible, with the sole limitation that the interment take place during daylight. Thus, a person who dies at night is not buried until dawn. Otherwise, burial occurs within the few hours required to make the necessary arrangements. The preparation of the corpse, the making of the grave clothes, and the digging of a grave go on simultaneously. There are local men and women who specialize in the washing of the dead. Such men know the order in which the body parts must be washed — penis, head, the right side and members, and then the left. The corpse is allowed to dry and then marked with henna on the chest, forehead, and hands. After being perfumed, it is dressed in shirt and pants, completely enshrouded, and laid on a bier brought from the mosque.

Close relatives of the deceased are by now assembling at his house and kinswomen are trying to assuage the misery of their weeping sisters. Unrelated men also gather in the street and accompany the bier to the grave. Moving silently, at a fast walk, they bear the body to the cemetery and set it by the grave. Again proceedings are turned over to specialists who, shielded from onlookers by a cloth over the grave, lower the body into the ground. The shroud is removed from the head, which is laid on a "pillow" of grass and so protected with stones as to shield it from dirt. This finished, the grave is filled and prayers are said either on the spot or during the daily services at the mosque.

That evening, food is prepared and distributed to the gravediggers and to the poor. Some is left at the grave by the women the following day. While such offerings are known to be eaten by the birds, it is felt that they are "good" for the deceased. Three days later, the women again visit the grave and exhaust their misery in tears.

Extreme forms of mourning are not approved. "The dead are *dead*" and it would be wrong for a widow not to eat or to cut herself off from others. She would be lacking in feeling and respect, however, if she wore new clothes or laughed and joked. But the legal limit of her widowhood has its practical side. She may not remarry for four months and ten days, and not then, if the passage of this time has found her to be with child. Before marrying again, she must bear her husband's child. A widower may take a new wife immediately, but a sad heart does not turn so quickly to such thoughts. Marriage is the normal state of man. The press for its reaffirmation derives most clearly from the fact that the task of living in the oasis cannot be carried out alone.

CHAPTER V

CONTACT AND CHANGE

The basic requirements of experimental research are a control group and an initially identical experimental group which is later exposed to the influence of some independent variable. The effect of the latter on the dependent variables is observed by noting differences in the latter between the two groups. The difficulty in applying this research design to human society is not primarily the latter's complexity, but the fact that we cannot manipulate societies like white rats. In addition, many of the most important cultural variables are very slow to change. It is for these reasons that the "natural experiment" is sought.

In such a natural situation, part of a society is known to have been exposed to some influence which has not touched some other segment of the society. The effects of this influence on specific social variables may be discernible through comparison of the two groups. Such a natural experiment, however, never completely fulfills the requirements of the experimental model. The identical origin of the two groups is always open to some question. Inevitably there have also been numerous influences operative on both groups, so the effects of the independent variable are never completely isolated and changes which have occurred in the control group cannot be known with absolute assurance. The problem for the social scientist is to design research so as to make it conform as closely as possible to the ideal. This should not be taken to mean that experimentally designed research is the only, or even the best, method of social investigation. It can be said, however, that it is the best method for testing the validity of hypotheses, no matter how the latter may be derived.

Theoretically oriented research employing naturally "controlled" conditions is relatively new to anthropology.[1] The research design employed in Algeria was an attempt to fit the field situation to the experimental model in a more rigorous way than had theretofore been attempted. It is interesting to note that Professors George Spindler and Walter Goldschmidt developed independently, at virtually the same time, a very comparable design for the study of change among the Menomini

1. See Fred Eggan's excellent paper tracing this development, "Social Anthropology and the Method of Controlled Comparison," *American Anthropologist*, LVI (1954), 743-63.

Indians.[2] The fact that both studies grew out of combined anthropological-psychological-sociological interests doubtless accounts for the parallel.

The Contact Groups

The sixty-four Algerian Arabs who provide the data for the ensuing analyses have a homogeneous background, at least in their common origin, in the oasis of Sidi Khaled. Admittedly there is both cultural and psychological variation within the oasis population, the implications of which will be considered shortly. The Arabs were selected so as to provide a wide range in the degree of contact with French urban centers. Part of them had never been beyond the immediate vicinity of Sidi Khaled. Others had lived most of their lives in French-dominated cities and two informants, it will be recalled, were born in Algiers to parents who were migrants from Sidi Khaled.

The control group, or "oasis group," consists of those twenty Arabs who had not more than six months of urban contact. Of these, nine men had no contact whatever and eleven had visited relatives in Algiers for a week or more. The necessity for including the latter arose from the difficulty of finding persons in the oasis who had never left it and from the desirability of having at least a moderately large number of control cases for statistical treatment. As French-urban contact is our independent variable, the inclusion in the oasis group of some Arabs with a little contact operates against our hypotheses. The same may be said regarding those French influences which have reached the oasis through the local school, through the French administration in Ouled Djellal, and through Arabs who have returned from the city. While these influences are ignored in the research operation, their effect is to decrease any differences found between the control and experimental groups.

The "urban group" is the experimental group. It includes the twenty-eight Arabs who had spent at least a quarter of their lives in Algiers or cities of metropolitan France. All had more than five years of such contact and most of them had been in the city over twenty years.

An intermediate group of sixteen cases (called Group B) was eliminated from the analysis of change, the comparison of extremes being a legitimate procedure. As Group B included nine

---

2. George Spindler and Walter Goldschmidt, "Experimental Design in the Study of Culture Change," *Southwestern Journal of Anthropology*, VIII (1952), 68-83. Also George Spindler, *Sociocultural and Psychological Processes in Menomini Acculturation* (Berkeley: University of California Press, 1955).

men who had returned to the oasis after living as much as five years in the city,[3] they were obviously marginal socially as well as in their length of contact. Group B is included in the over-all analysis of Arab personality but excluded from the oasis-urban comparisons of culture and personality. Culturally the group shows its marginality, sometimes being like the oasis group, sometimes like the urban, as well as showing intermediate characteristics. Psychologically, Group B shows some distinctive features, probably associated with their failure in the city. Aside from noting these features in the ensuing analysis, the marginal group was not subjected to any special study.

The selection of the oasis and urban groups involves the operational definition of the independent variable. Its rather gross delineation involves a number of subvariables, some of which should be indicated, although no attempt was made to treat them separately. The urban group: (a) have had five or more years of contact; (b) tend to have moved to the city before they were twenty years old; (c) have spent at least a quarter of their lives in the city. The relative importance, for change, of these subvariables and of the various factors embraced under the terms "French-urban contact" present problems for further research.

Statistical Treatment of Data

Numbers not only express variation but they can be treated statistically, with due caution, to help clarify their significance. In fact, the concept of "statistical significance" is the only statistical device we shall employ.[4] Of course no formula can tell the investigator whether or not his results are theoretically significant. Such a judgment depends upon his whole research design and methodology, as well as upon his findings. What a measure of statistical significance can do is express the degree

---

3. Two members of the urban group were also returnees, who returned to the oasis after successful stays in the city—the rarely fulfilled ideal of the migrant.

4. With the small numbers involved, almost all the comparisons are made with 2 x 2 tables, dividing the distribution of each variable as nearly as possible into halves. Levels of significance are derived from calculations of Chi square, using a correction for continuity. Hagood and Price, *Statistics for Sociologists* (Rev. ed.; New York: Henry Holt & Co., 1952), pp. 366, 369-70.

In distributions in which any theoretical cell frequency was below five, Fisher's Exact Test was used. See Sidney Siegel, *Nonparametric Statistics for the Behavioral Sciences* (New York: McGraw-Hill Book Co., 1956), p. 96. Tests of hypotheses are one-tailed while exploratory analyses of relationship are two-tailed. Probabilities derived from Fisher's Exact Test are doubled, as Siegel suggests, to approximate a two-tailed test of significance.

Figure 9. A Young Man from Algiers.

of probability that an identical distribution of data could be produced by chance. When this probability (P) is five chances in a hundred or less, the data are generally and arbitrarily regarded as "significant." All this really says is that the more closely two characteristics vary, the less likely it is that their covariation is due to chance. Conceivably, two sets of functionally unrelated data could show a P lower than .05 and a higher P might reflect a quite functional relationship between a partial cause and its effects. So even statistically significant findings must be considered in the light of their general consistency and apparent theoretical significance. All significant values of P are noted in the tables and figures accompanying the text or in the appendices. Relationships which do not reach statistical significance will be referred to in the text as "tendencies" to covariation.

Original Homogeneity of the Control and Experimental Groups

The initial chapter referred to the possibility of sampling bias or of selective migration from the oasis and pointed out the critical nature of this possibility for the interpretation of the research results. Although the forces leading to migration were found to be so general as to make the movement relatively unselective, an analysis of the family and educational backgrounds of the two groups was made to see if there were any significant differences (Table I).

Considering the small numbers involved in the groups and the non-random selection of the samples, the similarities in background are very striking indeed. Only two statistically significant differences appear between the oasis and the urban groups:

1. The oasis Arabs are more likely to have had more than five years of Koranic schooling.[5]

2. The oasis Arabs are more likely to have had polygynous fathers.

A few other differences appear in oasis-urban backgrounds, but they are not statistically significant. The fathers of urban Arabs are somewhat more apt to have had over five years of urban contact themselves. This is to be expected since, in many cases, the fathers moved to the city taking their sons. The more

---

5. There is no oasis-urban difference in whether or not Koranic school was attended. Protracted Koranic schooling is, however, related to whether or not French school was attended ($P = .05$), but there is no tendency for advanced Koranic training to vary with more protracted French schooling. In terms of acculturative influence, the two kinds of education would appear to operate in opposite directions and possibly tend to cancel one another. Advanced Koranic education does not vary significantly with polygyny of the father ($P = .15$). See Appendix B, p. 193.

Table I

COMPARISON OF FAMILY AND EDUCATIONAL BACKGROUNDS OF OASIS AND URBAN SAMPLES

Background Traits	Number of Cases Oasis (20)	Number of Cases Urban (28)	Per Cent of Group Oasis	Per Cent of Group Urban
French schooling				
None	15	20	75	71
1 year or less	1	2	5	7
1–5 years	3	3	15	11
Over 5 years	1	3	5	11
Koranic schooling				
None	6	10	30	36
1 year or less	1	1	5	4
1–5 years	3	12	15	43
Over 5 years	10	5	50	18
Over 5 years / less = P .02				
Urban contact of father				
None	8	10	47	38
1 year or less	2	2	12	8
1–5 years	4	3	24	12
Over 5 years	3	11	18	42
Father's marriage*				
Polygynous	9	5	50	18
Monogamous	9	23	50	82
P = .05				
Those with monogamous fathers*				
Father married only once	2	4	22	17
Divorced and remarried	7	19	78	83
Informant's mother*				
Father's last wife	10	19	56	70
Not last wife	8	8	44	30
Position among siblings				
Only child	1	0	5	0
Eldest	3	2	16	7
Youngest	6	6	32	22
Other	9	19	47	70

	Mean Oasis	Mean Urban	Median Oasis	Median Urban
Those with polygynous fathers				
Number of father's wives	4.9	5.2	5	3
Number of father's co-wives	2.3	2.0	2	2
Number of informant's siblings †	8.8	9.0	10	10
Those with monogamous fathers				
Number of father's marriages	2.8	2.5	3	2
Number of informant's siblings †	4.6	5.0	3	4.5

* Excluding cases in which father died and mother remarried.

† Including only those who lived to maturity.

striking fact is the similarity between the groups in the proportion of fathers who had no urban contact.

The urban group of Arabs are somewhat less likely than the oasis Arabs to have been the youngest, eldest, or only child in the family, but the difference between the groups does not reach significance. It follows, therefore, that any effect that position among siblings might have on personality variables cannot have produced the statistically significant personality differences which were found between the groups. We note, also, that the difference in sibling position is opposed to what one might expect from the mean numbers of siblings (oasis, 6.7; urban, 5.7). This is probably to be accounted for by a tendency to keep eldest and youngest children at home, in the oasis, as helpers or as being too young to migrate.

Economic factors seem to be responsible for the relationship of the father's polygyny and of advanced Koranic education to lack of movement to the city. Men who are more secure economically can afford the luxury of plural wives and can pay for more education for their children. Such fathers are also more likely to be able to establish their sons economically in the oasis, so they do not have to seek work in the city.

No exact measure of the economic status of the Arab informants or of their fathers was secured. An indication of economic position was derived, however, from an appraisal of the degree of security provided by their occupations. These were simply dichotomized into "upper", or more secure, and "lower" economic groups.[6] All of the informants were so categorized but nine of their fathers were omitted because of insufficient information.

The urban group tended to be lower in an economic position but not more unemployed (Table II). The occupational levels of fathers and sons were definitely related in both the oasis and city (Appendix B). Possibly because of the inadequacy of the data on the economic status of the fathers, this variable did not show a significant relationship to the fathers' polygyny or to the amount of education which they gave their sons, although the tendencies were in accord with our expectations.

An alternative explanation of the oasis-urban difference in background is that nomads who settled in Sidi Khaled might be more apt to be polygynous and might be less likely to have sons

---

6. The upper economic group included owners of stores and teahouses, garden owners, *talebs*, a barber, an upholsterer, jewelers, a butcher, a conductor, clerks, government officials, and men on army retirement pay. The lower economic position embraced the unemployed and all unskilled labor or occupations involving little capital:—day laborers in gardens, on the docks, or in stores; food vendors; itinerant merchants; and plasterers, whose economic marginality is well recognized.

going to the city. While the economic level of nomadic fathers was usually classified as low only because of their sedentarization, no such ambiguity existed as to their nomadic origin. Upon analysis, such origin was found to bear no relationship to polygyny.

Our interest in the social factors which might have produced the background differences in our samples is concerned with establishing the degree of similarity between the two groups before the urban migrants left the oasis. The most relevant question is whether or not differences in background are responsible for the oasis-urban contrasts in culture and personality which were found. If so, the contrasts cannot be attributed to change. In order to control for this possibility, the two background variables which showed a significant oasis-urban difference were analyzed in relation to the cultural and psychological variables.[7] None of the eight Rorschach variables [8] upon which oasis-urban comparisons were made showed a significant relationship to either of the background factors.

All sixteen cultural variables which showed significant oasis-urban difference were subjected to comparable analysis.[9] Three traits were found to be significantly related to one or the other of the background characteristics and two traits were related to both of them. These statistical relationships could result either from culture change or from premigration differences between the groups or from both. To determine what was involved, oasis-urban comparisons were made for each of the five traits, controlling the effect of the father's type of marriage and the informant's degree of education. This was done by testing separately for urban change among informants with monogamous fathers and among informants with five years or less of education.

Even with these background differences controlled, the levels of significance of the five oasis-urban cultural differences still fell between .11 and .0001. Only two of the seven tests made produced a P over .05 and these involved different background and culture traits. In both of these instances, the relationship of the background variable to the culture trait was then analyzed, holding constant the degree of urban contact. Neither of these tests revealed a significant relationship.

This necessarily complicated procedure leads to the conclusion that differences in the backgrounds of the oasis and urban samples are minimal and not responsible for the psychological and cultural differences found between them in 1950. These

---

7. See Appendix C for all these analyses.

8. Rigidity, maladjustment, anxiety, hostility, bodily preoccupation, orality, unpleasant content, positive content.

9. In these analyses, however, one-tailed tests of significance were employed because the significance of the oasis-urban difference had been so tested.

differences may, therefore, be interpreted as due to change. While this conclusion is limited by the sorts of background characteristics considered, the degree of control which they provide goes well beyond the assumption that the origin of both groups in the same oasis assures the initial identity of the groups.

Demographic Comparison of the Groups

Another control of the comparability of the oasis and urban groups is in terms of their basic demographic characteristics (Table II). Again they were found to be strikingly similar. The only significant difference was the greater probability of urban Arabs having two or more living children. There is little differential in infant mortality in our samples so the explanation must lie elsewhere. Miscarriages may be more frequent in the oasis, although the existence of a better service for prenatal care in the city is the only evidence on this point. Some of the other demographic data may be relevant to the difference in family size. The slightly higher mean and median age of the urban group is probably an important factor, despite the slightly greater prevalence of bachelors in the city and a tendency for urban men to marry somewhat later. There is no apparent reason why the number of children should be related to either of the two selective migration variables and, in fact, they are not.

Marriage

We turn now to the first group of culture traits which we have chosen to consider as dependent variables. The global hypothesis employed throughout these analyses is that French-urban contact will produce culture changes away from the Arab pattern as expressed in the oasis and toward the Western norms of the French. Table III presents a summary of the ages at first marriage of the oasis and urban Arabs and of their wives. These may be compared with the variation in beliefs concerning the ideal ages for marriage.[10]

The most apparent acculturative changes are with regard to the ideal age of marriage for women and their actual age of marriage. The social factors responsible for the change to later marriage are readily apparent. To be married "by cadi," a girl must be at least fifteen years of age, although she can be married "by *djema'a*" when even younger. For all legal purposes, the French require marriage by a cadi, who keeps formal records.

---

10. During interrogation, data on ideals were always secured initially.

Table II

DEMOGRAPHIC COMPARISON OF OASIS AND URBAN SAMPLES

Demographic Traits	Oasis	Urban		
Age*				
Mean	35.6	36.7		
Median	32.0	34.0		
Number of wives†				
Mean	1.9	1.7		
Median	1.0	1.0		
	Number of Cases		Per Cent of Group	
	Oasis	Urban	Oasis	Urban
Marriage status				
Married	17	20	84	71
Never married	3	8	16	29
Children — living†				
1 or none	12	7	71	35
2 or more	5	13	29	65
	P = .05			
Children — deceased†				
None	9	8	53	40
1 or more	8	12	47	60
Economic level				
Upper	13	11	65	40
Lower	7	17	35	60
	P = .10			
Employment status				
Employed	18	21	90	85
Unemployed	2	7	10	15

* Forty per cent of the oasis group is over 33 years old, compared to 50 per cent of the urban group.

† For married informants only.

Table III

AGE AT FIRST MARRIAGE

	Number of Cases*		Per Cent of Group	
	Oasis(20)	Urban(28)	Oasis	Urban
Actual age at marriage (male)				
20 or less	9	6	60	40
Over 20	6	9	40	60
Ideal age at marriage (male)				
20 or less	15	16	75	89
Over 20	5	2	25	11
Actual age at marriage (female)				
15 or less	8	3	73	27
Over 15	3	8	27	73
	$P = .05$			
Ideal age at marriage (female)				
15 or less	13	11	65	40
Over 15	7	17	35	60
	$P = .05$			

* Variations in totals result from incomplete information.

As payments of family assistance and workers' insurance both necessitate such marriage, the pressure to conform to the required pattern is strongest on the urban Arabs who are more involved in the whole nexus of commercial employment. Along with this, and probably influenced by French marital norms, the Arabs in Algiers have also come to feel that there is something unseemly in the very early marriages of desert girls. In fact, with many Arab urbanites it is an expression of opprobrium to say that any custom is like that in the desert.

The men's actual age of marriage shows some similar tendency, but this is certainly due to the relatively poor economic position of the urban migrant. Compared with their ideals, they clearly had to wait longer to get married than they wanted to. Only two of the informants had made polygynous marriages — one a man from the oasis and the other from Algiers. Arabs say that it is "like a shot in the arm" for an older man to take a young wife. But men generally express the sentiment that plural wives would be desirable except for the fact that co-wives always quarrel, making their husband's life unbearable. Only the wealthy can support multiple broods of offspring and keep co-wives contented. The decline in polygyny is, therefore, probably associated with the decline in per capita income which has occurred with the rapid growth of population.

Reference to Table II discloses the fact that, while divorce is not the rule, the mean number of wives is approximately two, indicative of the commonality of divorce and remarriage. Many of the marriages are still new and fragile and the expectation of two successive wives will probably continue in the city as in the oasis.

Seclusion of Women

Comment has already been made on the fact that women are secluded to the homes of their fathers or husbands or, in the case of a fatherless widow, to the courtyard of a brother or son. Except on limited, specific occasions when women may go out if appropriately veiled and accompanied, they are cut off from the world during their sexually active years. The decision as to when a girl should begin to be kept at home is based on her stature and breast development, rather than on the onset of menstruation, which is reported to be between the ages of twelve and fifteen. A girl who has grown tall will be secluded, even though secondary sex characteristics have not yet appeared. The termination of seclusion is similarly dependent not only upon the climacteric but also upon how long a woman remains physically attractive. The inclusive ideal ages of seclusion portrayed in

Table IV do not simply reflect the estimated ages at which these biological phenomena occur. They also indicate the fact that fathers seclude their daughters by a certain age, irrespective of their maturation. Even more important, the distribution indicates the informants' rigidity or permissiveness regarding seclusion.

The beginning and end of seclusion show no significant differences between the oasis and city, although there is a tendency for later initiation and earlier termination of seclusion in the city. The oasis shows some bimodality with regard to both the beginning and end of seclusion, in contrast to the "normal" distributions in the city. If this bimodal tendency is not simply due to sampling, it may reflect the existence of both traditional and new values in the oasis. By and large these traits show little susceptibility to change.

Some feeling for the seriousness with which the Arabs take seclusion may be derived from an incident which occurred during the field research. On the night of the twenty-sixth of Ramadan, it is customary for families to have a feast of meat. On the morning of this day meat is sold, market-tax free, outside the tomb of Sidi Khaled, located a quarter of a mile south of the village. All of the men of Sidi Khaled, and even of Ouled Djellal, come to buy meat and to participate in the noonday prayers at the saint's tomb. Traditionally, the women of the two communities profited by this occasion to go out into the deserted streets, for a brief moment turning the world of men into one of women. Lookouts were posted to warn of the men's return and, until that time, the women reveled in seeing their relatives and the friends of their childhood.

Some years ago the *djema'a* of Sidi Khaled expressed the men's rigid sentiments regarding seclusion by forbidding the women to leave their homes on this occasion. Ouled Djellal ultimately followed suit and, on this feast day in 1950, a few of the most dour old men made a point of playing checkers in the market place instead of going to Sidi Khaled. Nevertheless, many of the women came out into the market. The caïd, who remained behind in anticipation of trouble, ordered the men to leave, as the only way to avoid trouble with the husbands of the women. The men resisted and fights ensued. The incident became a *cause célèbre*, on the basis of which a group of disgruntled leading families, who were receiving no graft from an honest French administrator, succeeded in having him removed by the Gouvernement Général.

The reasons that men give for the isolation of women include recognition of the fact that the outside world holds an attraction for women. This should not be interpreted to mean that women are generally discontent with their life behind walls. In fact, the

Table IV

LENGTH OF SECLUSION

	Number of Cases		Per Cent of Group	
	Oasis	Urban	Oasis	Urban
Age at beginning of seclusion				
8-10	9	8	45	29
10-12	4	13	20	46
Over 12	7	7	35	25
Age at end of seclusion				
45 or less	1	5	5	19
46-55	9	10	45	37
56-65	1	9	5	33
Over 65	9	3	45	11

Arab argues that one of the purposes of seclusion is to keep women content by not letting them see more attractive men, other women who are better cared for, and the wealth of material goods which their husbands cannot provide.

The principal reason for seclusion is obvious in the factors which determine its duration. Women in the oasis are conceived of as being "like animals, highly sexed and willing to have intercourse with any man. That is all they care about." One Arab supported his lack of confidence in women with the following bit of Islamic lore:

> The old sages selected the four thousand most important rules of living. These they reduced to four hundred, then to forty, and finally they arrived at the four most important rules. These were: Have no confidence in women; do not eat what disagrees with you; do not expect to keep your wealth; seek knowledge from the cradle to the grave.

Several other men referred to these sages, but the only rule they could recall was never to trust a woman.

As may be seen from the confidence ratings in Table V, the urban Arabs are significantly more inclined to recognize individual variation among women and to believe that their character is a matter of training. A husband gains confidence in a wife "by general observation — what she talks about and whether she shows herself at the window." But even the most sophisticated woman cannot go out alone in the streets "or she will be annoyed by Jews, Frenchmen, and ignorant Arabs." Such is doubtless the case in a city in which unaccompanied women are usually hags or prostitutes.

On those occasions when a woman may legitimately leave her home, she is protected and hidden from men. She should be accompanied by a close male relative, of mature years, for the distrust of women extends to their use as chaperones. A woman's mother-in-law, if sufficiently old herself, might accompany her, but many men would not have comparable confidence in their wives' mothers (Table V). Compared with the oasis group, however, the urban Arabs are much more trusting in this regard.

The same table illustrates the fact that in the desert only a deviant will consider allowing a woman out of the courtyard during daylight, except in case of a death in the family. In the city, however, it is the deviant who will not permit his women to go out in daylight. It is normal for the Arab woman in Algiers to go out veiled, with only her eyes exposed. In the oasis, even though she goes only from house to house at night, a woman is often expected to cover her whole head.

In contrast to customs concerning the length of seclusion, these last four traits seem to change as a complex, although the

Table V

SECLUSION CUSTOMS

	Number of Cases		Per Cent of Group	
	Oasis	Urban	Oasis	Urban
Confidence				
In some women	2	12	10	46
In none	17	14	90	54
		$P = .02$		
Chaperonage				
Wife may be accompanied by her mother	8	21	40	75
Wife may not be accompanied by her mother	12	7	60	25
		$P = .02$		
Wife may go out				
Day or night	1	23	5	82
At night only	19	5	95	18
		$P = 7 \times 10^8$		
Veiling				
Both eyes exposed	11	24	55	86
One or both covered	9	4	45	14
		$P = .05$		
Reaction to Adultery				
"Kill"	13	16	69	67
Other responses	6	8	31	33

restriction of a woman's movement to hours of darkness undergoes a more marked alteration than the others. This more radical change results from new situations in the city which require a woman to leave her home. In the desert a woman may legitimately go out to participate in the wedding or funeral of a relative or to join her parents a few times a year. Except for the urgency of funerals, therefore, all visits are planned well in advance and the moves can be made at night.

While these same conditions adhere in the city for the same occasions, there are also new reasons for women to leave their homes. Extended families are less common in the urban community and each elementary family is more dependent upon its own members. People in the oasis are food producers and there are always related men to make the few market purchases and children to run errands. In Algiers, the more rigid work hours of the men and the necessity of shopping for food force some women to do the marketing. In addition, the custom of women bathing periodically at Turkish baths, here called "Moorish baths," has long been a part of the urban Arab culture. Such baths are not available in the desert oasis, where men alone can enjoy the equivalent by burying their bodies in the hot sands.

There are still other occasions when women go out in the city, such as for the family outings which tenement living makes desirable. Mothers also may have to take children to school or clinics. Even for the traditional contacts among kinswomen, daytime transportation is more readily available between their scattered homes.

The increase in men's confidence in women is a commensurate part of the change in seclusion practices. We note that men give up secluding their women during the daytime more readily than they gain confidence in women. This fact and the nature of the social pressures against continuing restrictions suggest that men's confidence is gained from experience with the more lenient seclusion practices which urban life makes inescapable. We shall see later that this change in men's attitude toward women requires rather fundamental psychological reorientation.

Adultery

Table V gives a comparison of oasis and urban reactions to the question, "What would you do if you came home and found a strange man in your house?" Both groups are equally willing to jump to the conclusion of adultery and to react violently to it. Originally a second question had been planned, concerning what the informant would do if he found his wife in adultery. This inquiry never had to be made, for every Arab interpreted the presence of a man in his house as indicative of adultery. The response was usually immediate, clipped, and emotional: "Kill him!" Some would kill both persons and others qualify the response by saying that they should, or would, first investigate why the man was there. One man contended that Islamic law required that a string be drawn between the superimposed bodies of the apparent adulterers to determine whether there had actually been insertion!

The typical violent expressions are not just braggadocio. The following instances of violence, which are not exhaustive, occurred within the last decade around Sidi Khaled:

A nomad near the oasis suspected his wife of having an affair with her youthful paternal cousin. The husband told his wife he was leaving on a trip, but returned, armed, to the camp that night. He saw the cousin enter his wife's tent. Creeping closer and hearing sounds of intercourse, he burst into the tent and shot the adulterer. The wife escaped from the tent in the melee, but the irate husband found her among a group of women and killed her. He was sentenced to five years in prison, purportedly because the wife was not killed *in delicto*.

Another nomad surprised his wife in adultery, killed both offenders, and went free.

A man from the oasis moved to Doucen, where he assumed responsibility for a woman and her nubile daughter. The two lived together in a house behind his garden. One night he found a neighbor crossing his garden toward the women's house and shot the trespasser dead. Although ultimately cleared of murder, his family and that of his victim were never reconciled and each goes armed in the other's territory. The killer keeps a loaded gun on his wall.

In December, 1950, an Arab returned to Sidi Khaled from four years work in France. He found the wife he had left behind living with another man and his children living with kinsmen. The husband twice sent messages to the wife-stealer, telling him to return the wife. Twice refused, the affronted husband broke into the man's house, stabbing him seven times and his wife three. Both were hospitalized and the assailant gave himself up to the authorities. The legal point on which the case would hang was whether or not the woman had divorced him for nonsupport.

Two facts are worthy of special notice in these incidents. First, opportunity for surreptitious adultery and the use of such opportunity seem to be greater among the nomads. Local opinion supports this view. Second, adulterous trespass by a man is met with greater violence than a woman leaving her husband for another man. The latter point is borne out by another incident which occurred in 1950. The brother of an oasis man returned from France, bringing with him the French wife of another Arab.

The latter protested to the offender's family before the kinsman's return. There was a loud altercation when he arrived and he was refused shelter by his brother. This brother happened to be one of two men in the oasis with French wives. The wife may well have taken a hand, for the next day the brothers were reconciled and no further unpleasantness ensued.

Desire for Children

The rapid growth of population Algeria has experienced since the French conquest has gone on despite the very high mortality rate. The background data on the number of our informants' siblings reveal that the average woman has between five and six children who live to maturity. While this number still makes for rapid increase, it represents the biological product of at least twenty-five fertile years of marriage.

The Arabs were asked how many children they desired. As Table VI indicates, a third of them wanted not more than one child. Two oasis men and five from Algiers said they wanted fewer than they already had! While a decline in a desire for children was predicted for the city, only a tendency was found. The generality of the desire for small families is surprising in a culture which has traditionally placed a high value on children. The men are quite explicit in their reasons for wanting few children. They feel very keenly the economic misery to which their offspring are subjected and are quite aware of the economic drain of large families. Another factor, of which they are less aware, is that the traditional large-family values were associated with a general social order in which a large number of sons provided a man with both economic security and political power. These functions have now largely disappeared.

The literature on Islam indicates that men's preference for male offspring is typically so great that the birth of a daughter may even be greeted with signs of disgust. In our sample, however, only half of the men expressed a desire to have just sons. Their reason was the age-old one that a father had to feed and clothe a daughter until she reached economically productive years, and then she got married. Sons, on the other hand, had a continuing economic responsibility toward their fathers. The preference for sons is not associated with lack of urban contact and, although such contact appears to reduce the total number of children desired, the oasis-urban difference is not significant.

Another sort of data was collected to throw light on the relative importance of having: (a) many children, (b) much money, (c) many wives, and (d) many kinsmen. Hypotheses derived from Redfield's comparison of folk and urban peoples led us to expect

Table VI

DESIRE FOR CHILDREN

	Number of Cases		Per Cent of Group	
	Oasis	Urban	Oasis	Urban
Number of children desired				
None or one	5	12	30	44
Two or more	12	15	70	56
Most important in life				
Children	7	2	41	8
Money	7	12	41	50
Many wives	1	1	6	4
Large kindred	2	9	12	38

P = .02*

* "Children" compared with all other choices.

a relative increase of the value of money in the city, in contrast to the family and kin values. The graph of Responses (Table VI) as to which of the four was most important, shows the desire for children to be significantly higher in the oasis, compared to the other three. There is only a tendency toward intensification of monetary values in the city. Men who hold for this value contend that "money will get you all the other things. If you don't have it, your wife can leave you and even your sons depart. In the tribes, if you are poor, your kin may desert you in an emergency."

The tendency to place greater importance on extended kin in the city is contrary to expectation. This trend may be derived from the fact that, being economically less secure, the city dweller feels a need for the security of the assistance which he can claim from kinsmen. In fact, many urban migrants come to live and work for or with their relatives. For those who are not receiving such aid, their lack of kin in the city probably stands in sharp relief against the memories of their extended families in the oasis.

Child Training

The senior author admits to feeling that too much has been made of the influence of toilet training and weaning on character formation. This attitude is apparently reflected in the fact that he was well involved in the Algerian fieldwork before it occurred to him to collect such data. Further loss of data resulted from the difficulty of collecting it from men. Despite the small number of cases, Table VII shows a significant change toward earlier initiation of toilet training in the city.[11] The tests of significance, in this instance, are two-tailed, as there was no obvious theoretical basis for predicting change in either direction. French training practice is unknown to the writer and, more important, it is probably unknown to the Arabs.

The *ex post facto* explanation of the findings seems relatively simple. In the oasis, children grow up on the dirt floors of toiletless houses, on the sand of the courtyard, and on wicker beds. Such carpets as there are remain rolled up except on ceremonial occasions. On those occasions, it should be added, mothers are quite unperturbed by the large wet spots which their babies make on the rugs, despite swaddling. In the city, the infant is on wooden, and often carpeted, floors. His bed is the Western one of his parents. The tenements are equipped with chamberpots and toilets of a sort. The whole physical environment is conducive to earlier training.

11. The expectation that early beginning and early completion of toilet training are related to one another is borne out ($P = .05$).

Table VII

CHILD TRAINING *

	Number of Cases		Per Cent of Group	
	Oasis	Urban	Oasis	Urban
Begins toilet training				
At one year or earlier	0	9	0	64
Later	7	5	100	36
	P = .02			
Ends toilet training				
At one and a half years or earlier	0	8	0	47
Later	5	9	100	53
	P = .16			
Beating of children				
Not preferred punishment	14	27	70	96
Preferred punishment	6	1	30	4
	P = .02			
Isolation of children				
Uses as punishment	7	20	35	71
Never uses	13	8	65	29
	P = .02			
Food deprivation as punishment				
Delays or limits meal	7	18	35	64
Never uses	13	10	65	36
	P = .06			

* Tests of significance are two-tailed except in the case of beating of children.

Urethral and bowel training are concurrent. The mean and median age at which they are started in the oasis is between one and a half and two years. None of the urban informants, however, began training after two. Several indicated that some training started as early as six months, when the child was given "light taps on the bottom" to indicate displeasure at its having soiled its father. Mothers were similarly reported to shake or thrust away a six-month old baby "to make it recall" not to soil her again. For older children, scolding, "making them afraid," and denying them food were given as the methods of teaching retention.

Along with this, from the time a child can sit, its mother periodically holds it, squatting, over the sand or on a pot. She encourages it by grunting and says *kaka*. Anal control is not expected until the child can say *kaka* to indicate its needs to defecate. Urethral control is established earlier. On one occasion I drove my interpreter, with his wife and their year-old child, from Algiers to the desert, a nine-hour trip. The father informed me, with some pride, that his son had not urinated from the time he left Algiers until he reached the oasis.

On the other hand, a child of three or more may wet its bed. One man told me that his four-year-old son had begun to wet his bed upon the birth of the next child. With real insight, the father attributed this reversion to the boy's jealousy of the baby.

Later chapters will show that, despite the early and somewhat rigorous training, the Arabs develop no psychological problems from it. Nor do they develop indications of the meticulousness which personality theory might predict. Such training is, however, the first lesson that unless they withhold self-expression they will be punished. This lesson, reinforced through life, does stamp Arab character.

In contrast to toilet training, weaning is relatively late, occurring between the ages of one and a half and two. There was practically no variation in this regard, all but four of thirty Arabs citing this period. Boys are usually weaned at two and girls at the earlier age. A sickly child may nurse longer and a robust girl somewhat less. The uniformity of this culture trait is accounted for by the fact that the Koran specifies a two-year nursing period, during which a man must support his child's mother even though he has divorced her. The shorter nursing period for girls is apparently due to their more rapid development.

A nursing child receives supplementary food after it is a year old. At first it receives milk from a recently freshened goat. City parents who can afford it may give canned milk. In the desert, dates are soon added, as well as figs, bread, and soft-boiled egg yolks. Milk and potatoes or farina are usual additions in the city. Final weaning is accomplished by painting the mother's nipple with a bitter substance and then offering the breast to the child. "Two or three such experiences wean him," fathers say, as they chortle over the child's unhappy reaction. The Arabs ridicule very protracted nursing and believe it makes the child stupid.

When children begin to understand what is said to them, they learn how to behave by being told, scolded, and punished. Such training of small children and older girls is largely in the hands of their mothers. Detailed information on the mothers' methods of punishment is lacking, but such methods are less severe than those administered by men to boys of six or more. Indirect evidence on this point comes from men's statements that punishments which they impose are apt to be mitigated by the mothers and that parents may have arguments over the severity of punishment. A widowed woman, however, may punish harshly. One Arab, whose father died when he was four, vividly recalled the occasions on which his mother bound his arms and put him in a room by himself for several hours. When he was eight she remarried and the stepfather continued this practice.

Informants were queried concerning three types of punishment—beating, isolation, and food deprivation (Table VII). While none of the relevant French norms was known with any accuracy, it was initially clear that the Arabs were comparatively brutal toward children. An urban decline in beating was, therefore, predicted, but no hypothesis was advanced regarding the other two types of punishment.

Beating, as the preferred punishment for boys, is significantly more characteristic of the oasis. Boys not yet in their teens are usually considered too thin-skinned for severe beating. They are more apt to be struck out of annoyance, sent to their *taleb* for a caning, or punished by nonviolent means. Older boys may be thrashed anywhere on the body, except the head. Children may be slapped but this is frowned on. There is some preference for spanking or beating on the buttocks. The idea that a lad learns from such experience is expressed in the humorous comment that a beating on the buttocks "goes to the head."

The Arabs operate on the principle that sons must be made to fear their fathers. Punishment is intermingled with scolding, shouting, and threatening punishment. When these latter methods fail to change a child's behavior, his father becomes exasperated and punishes him again. The striking of children is rarely a calculated punishment; the parent simply lashes out in anger.

Punishment by isolation increases significantly in the city. Obviously, the urban decline in physical punishment is associated with the increase in other corrective measures. As with the change in toilet training, the physical environment of the city may also contribute to this shift in practice. An oasis child may be kept in the courtyard or made to accompany his father to the fields and thus be kept from play. He is rarely shut in a room, although adequate rooms are actually available. The Arabs show a real dislike for incarceration and have, historically, maimed and executed malefactors but not imprisoned them. Only that worst of all offenses, a wife's adultery, was subject to punishment by immuring. Significantly, the Algerians refer to the isolation of a child in a room as "putting him in prison."

The difference between the oasis and the city, in this connection, may turn on a subtle difference in the perception of living space. Family life in the oasis takes place in the courtyard. The few unwindowed rooms built against the courtyard wall give shelter and privacy while sleeping, or isolate visitors from the family court. In a word, the courtyard *is* the living space.

The tenement, broken up into rooms with specialized functions, involves a different view of the relation of family living to its physical surroundings. Activities in different parts of the home are more cut off from one another and the unitary aspect of living space is lost. With it may go some of the distaste for being separated from the group.

Punishment by food deprivation is not significantly different in the city, as shown by the two-tailed test necessitated by the lack of prediction of change. A marked tendency toward greater use of such punishment in the city, however, is apparent. The idea of depriving a child of food is so foreign to the oasis group that several of them reacted with astonishment, "But the child would get hungry!" Those Arabs who do employ such punishment usually make the child wait only an hour or more after mealtime for its food or refuse it sweets and other tidbits. The men say that they actually cannot deprive a child of food, for the mother always manages to feed it.

Individual and Personal Characteristics

During the interviews with informants, direct observations were made of a number of their characteristics. These included a subjective evaluation of the cleanliness of their persons and clothes, on a scale from "filthy" to "meticulous." At first there appeared to be only a slight trend toward the expected greater cleanliness of the urban group. The analysis of cleanliness in conjunction with economic status, for the total sample, revealed a significant direct relationship between the two ($P = .01$; Appendix B). As the economic position of the urban group had been found to be markedly lower than the oasis group ($P = .10$), analyses were made to isolate the effect of economic position on cleanliness. Table VIII shows that it is only in the

Table VIII

INDIVIDUAL AND PERSONAL CHARACTERISTICS

	Number of Cases		Per Cent of Group	
	Oasis	Urban	Oasis	Urban
Cleanliness (upper economic group)				
Meticulous to clean	6	7	50	87
Dirty to filthy	6	1	50	13
		P = .10		
Cleanliness (lower economic group				
Meticulous to clean	1	2	17	15
Dirty to filthy	5	11	83	85
Knowledge of French				
Some	4	22	20	88
None	16	3	80	12
		P = .0001		
Clothes				
European	0	16	0	57
Arab or mixed	20	12	100	43
		P = .0001		
Cigarette smoking				
Yes	5	16	38	89
No	8	2	62	11
		P = .005		

upper economic group that urban living tends to create greater cleanliness.

During the discussion of the control of selective migration factors, we saw that urban Arabs had acquired some knowledge of the French language and had adopted Western dress. They also acquired the cigarette habit. Sheer contact and interaction with the French and with already acculturated Arabs are the obvious channels for these changes.

Summary of Change Predictions

We have thus far considered the effect of French-urban life on twenty-six Arab culture traits. The general expectation of culture change toward French norms was only tested with twenty-one of these. Eleven showed the predicted change at statistically significant levels and five more showed trends toward such change. In only five instances was there no such evidence and there were no significant reversals.

An attempt has been made to point up the important social conditions responsible for each of the findings. Aside from these comments, the failure to find the predicted change in five of the traits is, with one exception, probably due to the failure of the interviews to reveal the change, or due to the fact that the amount of acculturative contact has been insufficient to produce change. Even the apparent exception of the trend toward greater importance of kin in the city may well be limited to the first-generation migrants. The lack of change in some supernatural beliefs requires detailed consideration and is reserved for the following section.

CHAPTER VI

THE SUPERNATURAL

Every society has some sort of belief in supernatural powers and some way of using them to meet its mundane or spiritual needs. Societies with the simplest cultures seem to employ such powers only to meet practical problems. The emergence of complex civilizations is characterized by the increasing elaboration of the role of the supernatural and the growing importance of its spiritual significance. But, with the break in feudally organized societies which comes with industrial revolution, an intensely pragmatic approach to life has a secularizing effect which increasingly forces supernatural concerns into the realm of the moral and the spiritual.

The Arabs of Sidi Khaled live in a world of supernatural intensity but, when they move to Algiers, they step into a modern Western climate of thought and activity. The experience would be more shattering were it not for the buttress to belief which is afforded by the urban Moslem community. The legal definition of "Moslem French citizens" forces second-class privileges upon them which they can only escape by renouncing their own group and their rights under Islamic law. The effect is to make the Arabs more aware of their religious bonds. In this situation, the supernatural beliefs which are peripheral to the dogma of Islam would seem to be more exposed to erosion by Western customs.

The omnipresence of the supernatural in the oasis is vividly evident in the following extract from a history of Sidi Khaled written by the marabout of the local *zaouia* and substantiated by numerous residents:

> The savants and witnesses are the most reliable sources concerning what appears in the cemeteries. Neither history nor any science refers to that which happens in the cemeteries of this region. The light which glowed on the tombs, such as that on the tomb of the Prophet of Allah, Sidi Khaled, was visible to those chosen by Allah. This light, produced by the bones, varied in the forms it took. It moved by itself. It ascended and was visible at the crest of the mountains of this region. It was also seen behind these mountains. Sometimes it flew and went toward the graves of members of his sect. Then a noise like that of a cannon was heard. These facts are transmitted from generation to generation. Sometimes this light was less strong and was only visible to those who were in his mosque.

In the year 1945, a great light appeared at three o'clock in the morning and it was seen by numerous people. Shots were heard coming from the upper part of the village. Allah does as He desires in His realm and He arranges all. If He wishes, He makes it rain; if He wishes, the rain stops. He calms the winds or makes them blow into storms. He makes the day and the night.

The power of Allah can be called upon by individuals or even whole communities, in times of catastrophe, and miracles wrought. On one occasion the great light appeared, as a portent of salvation, at the Prophet's tomb, while all the men were gathered to pray for relief from a plague of grasshoppers. Another time a severe drought was broken by communal prayer accompanied by the magical pouring of a bucket of water from the minaret of the village mosque. Every man has similarly used supernatural powers to protect his family, to cure illness, to help his affairs, or to foretell the future.

Prayer

The religious obligation to perform five daily prayers rests on all men. Boys who do not go to Koranic school should be taught how to pray by their fathers. It is extremely rare for women to pray, however, and only the occasional devout *taleb* undertakes the religious instruction of his wife or daughters.

The age of nine is the youngest at which a male may be considered an adult Moslem, and then only when he shows signs of puberty. Malikite law, which governs Islam for most of Algeria, prefers eighteen as the age of manhood.[1] Local tradition, on the other hand, permits marriage and requires the fulfillment of religious duties closer to the onset of puberty.

Prayers should only be executed in a state of physical cleanliness. After intercourse or a nocturnal emission, a bath is required before the salaam, which itself involves ritual ablutions. Prayers are performed on a clean mat or rug and slippers are removed on entering a mosque to avoid the desecration from the filth which is inevitably brought in from the street. Clothes should be washed, if defiled by urine or excrement, before being worn during prayers.

Prayer involves a formal series of body movements, including the prostration which we call a salaam. Three specific prayers are repeated during these movements. In addition, the individual may address personal supplications to Allah. The most effective time to make such requests during formal prayer is said to be

---

1. Ruben Levy, *An Introduction to the Sociology of Islam* (London: Williams and Norgate, Ltd., 1930), I, 201-202.

while the forehead is touching the ground during the salaam or after the verbal prayers are finished.

The appropriate times of day for prayers are explicit in the dogma,[2] but, if by force of circumstances, they cannot be performed, they may be "made up" at the first possible prayertime. The afternoon prayer, for example, conflicts with working hours in the city. Arab shops once closed at this time, but the French work schedule now predominates. A man who has missed this prayer can go through the salaam twice at sunset and fulfill his religious duty. In a much more unusual case, a young man who returned to active religious life after a year and a half of apostasy thus made up all of the prayers he had neglected.

The performance of daily prayers was the only aspect of adherence to the dogma which was investigated. All of the Arabs were so vehement in their identification with Islam and so aware of its basic requirements that it did not seem advisable to approach them directly to discover whether or not they fulfilled their obligations. While prayer can be, and often is, executed in private, a man's intimates invariably know whether or not he prays. This information was, therefore, secured about the informants only from their acquaintances.

Two very striking findings resulted. Only half of the Arabs perform the salaam and there is no difference between the oasis and urban groups in this regard. It seemed probable that those who had gone to school with a *taleb* would be more likely to pray as they should. This was substantiated by analysis of the total sample ($P = .01$).[3]

In addition to prayer, six areas of supernatural belief which were peripheral to the dogma were investigated.[4] This is not to say that these beliefs are unimportant in the culture. In fact, judging from their degree of use, some of the traits are more significant to the average Arab than is prayer. The general customs associated with each of these supernatural powers will be considered before treating the effects of urban contact.

Written Charms

The efficacy of written charms lies in the *baraka*, or supernatural power, inherent in certain Arabic words and phrases.

2. Before sunrise, after high noon, in the later afternoon before sunset, just after sunset, before retiring.
3. Of 34 Arabs with schooling, 22 prayed; only 3 of the 16 without schooling did so.
4. The best general work on such beliefs in Algeria is Edmond Doutté's, *Magie et Religion dans l'Afrique du Nord* (Algiers: Adolphe Jourdan, 1909).

Many of these are derived from the Koran, such as suras 113 and 114, which are widely used as protective charms. Other powerful expressions are said to be pre-Islamic. The *baraka* which lies in words can be employed in a transitory way by simply repeating them. Very prevalent is the Arab practice of murmuring *Bismillah* "In the name of Allah" to ward off evil in everyday situations.

The writing of charms is dependent upon the principle that *baraka* can be transferred from words to objects by writing the words on the objects. Subsequent transferral of *baraka* from objects to persons can be accomplished by contagion through contact. To this statement should be added the fact that there is an increment in the *baraka* of words when they are written, for Arabic script, itself, has *baraka*.

A *taleb* or savant *(taleb 'ālem)* writes the charms. The natives recognize that the power of charms varies according to the person who writes them. This results not only from the different levels of education of the teachers, some of whom are recognized as charlatans, but the degree of sanctity of the teacher also involves *baraka*. A truly saintly man does not charge for a charm but accepts any gift he is offered. The charms produced by the man who is clearly out to make money are suspect.

Most charms are protective or curative, although some natives believe in their efficacy to bring about some positive end, such as success in business or love. Protective charms often depend, for their effect, on less intimate contact between the person and the charm than is the case in curative charms. The most prevalent written charm is the "book" *(kitab)*. In this type, the words are simply written on a small piece of paper, which is usually encased in cloth, leather, or metal and worn on the person. Some Arabs feel that simple ownership of a *kitab* provides them protection even if the charm is not worn but left at home. Similarly, charms may be built into the doorframe of a house or written on the outside of a doorway. The protection which charms provide is primarily against the dangers of the evil eye and genii. Only one person was found who used charms but did not believe in either the evil eye or genii. In this case, the man had kept a *kitab* which he had been given as a child to protect him from sickness.

A *kitab* is often employed to cure illness or the charm may be written on the patient's skin. There are also more ingenious devices for bringing the *baraka* of the written word into close contact with the afflicted person. The *taleb* may write the charm on the inside of a small bowl, which is then filled with water and the writing washed off of the bowl and into the water. The *baraka*-bearing water is then drunk by the patient or the afflicted parts of his body are washed with it. Water in the form of steam may also be used to transmit the power of the words. For eye diseases, the charm may be written on a pebble, which is then placed on a charcoal fire. A funnel is held, inverted, over the fire and the patient places his eye well above the small end of the funnel. Water is then thrown on the fire, washing the inscription off of the pebble and causing *baraka-* filled steam to rise to the person's eye. Another method is to burn a paper charm under a squatting patient and the power of the words is conveyed by the smoke. Most curative charms, like protective ones, are directed at the effects of the evil eye and genii.

Genii

The existence of genii is substantiated by the Koran, which also teaches that some genii were converted to Islam. This conversion is the basis of a common belief that there are both harmless and harmful genii. The most dangerous are sometimes distinguished as "afreet." Some people believe that Solomon rid the world of afreet, but others contend that they have been seen in recent days. They are described as gigantic forms with huge heads and flame and smoke issuing from their mouths. They are so malevolent that "if a thousand people had contact with afreet, only two, with the help of Allah, could survive." Sudden death from an unknown cause is often attributed to the work of afreet. Particularly when the head is twisted at death, an afreet is believed to have been responsible.

Although afreet are the most dreadful, they are not the only dangerous genii. Less dangerous ones may cause trouble by entering a person's body. The symptoms of such seizures are epileptic in nature, involving muscle spasms and loss of muscular control. Attacks may occur only once or they may be recurrent. The victim of such seizures is considered to be "married" to a genie and the attack is interpreted as intercourse between the person and the genie. The sex of the genie is appropriately believed to be opposite to that of its human paramour. One man who had experienced such an attack recalls it as follows:

> One night after my father died, I was attacked by genii. My head was twisted around and I could not talk. The genii jumped on me and jabbed me. I could see them and tried to show them to the people about me, but they couldn't see the genii. My arms and legs got stiff and I could not hear what was being said except for the directions which were given to place me with my head to the south and face to the east, as one does with dying people.

The words which people sometimes speak during such attacks are believed to be uttered by the genie. They speak in "strange tongues" or say unusual things which are held to be prophetic.

In some cases, the genie may even be interrogated through the medium of its victim. Here we seem to be dealing with a different kind of phenomenon. Only women prophesy in this way and they may "call genii to them" (become possessed) by smelling benzoin, executing certain dances, or eating sheep's stomach. People who ask questions of such a medium pay her with money or gifts. This type of possession is uncommon compared to the seizures previously discussed and was not encountered in Sidi Khaled.

A person may evidence seizure by a genie[5] in other ways, such as tearing off his clothes and throwing them in the fire, breaking glass, or attacking people without cause. The thing which distinguishes the effects of genii from other abnormal behavior seems to be the transient character of the seizure. The Arabs see no relationship between these attacks and the behavior of people whom they recognize as "crazy" *(mahboul)*. The latter wander aimlessly about, cannot talk coherently, but sit and babble to themselves or revile passers-by, allow their clothes to fall into shreds, and have no modesty about their excretory functions or the exposure of their genitalia. The psychotic behavior of such people is accepted by the population for what it is and they are tolerated and kept alive by charity.[6] Another form of abnormal behavior is characterized as being "saintly" *(mrabotin)*. No deviants of this sort were observed, but they are said never to wash and to sit for hours in the market place, speaking to no one.

Evil genii are credited with still more mischief. The continued crying or misbehavior of a child is probably genie-induced. Even a sheep may be attacked by a genie so that it turns continuously all day long. Such an animal is butchered, but the human victims of genii are treated with supernatural cures. Written charms are commonly employed to exorcise a genie and avoid continuing attacks. Alternatively, a *taleb* may place a pot of water below the right foot of the genie victim and then incant a Koranic passage which makes the genie come out, by way of the nail of the big toe, and fall into the water. The most common method of treating a man in the actual throes of an epileptic-type attack is to force a "male" key[7] into his hand, "even though

---

5. While seizures are interpreted as being the result of encounter with a single genie, the two personal accounts of such attacks both referred to "seeing genii." The other account is given in Chapter IX.

6. Three such psychotics were seen in Sidi Khaled, one a woman of about forty. Her case is particularly interesting, as she was permitted to move freely about the town in virtual nudity, despite the strength of belief concerning the seclusion of women. Like children and crones, she was simply regarded as sexless.

7. A key whose shaft is solid, in contrast to the tubular shaft of a "female" key.

he tries to reject it." The sexual symbolism of this cure is in accord with the sexual interpretation of the attack itself.

Firsthand accounts of encounters with genii are rare, in contrast to the wide knowledge of hearsay stories. One such personal experience was recounted by a middle-aged man and places a different interpretation on the mysterious lights which appear in the desert:

> One night, twenty-five years ago, I went to one of the two houses of prostitution in Ouled Djellal. I stayed very late. It was an overcast night and, as I was walking back to Sidi Khaled, I saw a light which rose about six meters in the air and then descended again. It reappeared several times in different places. I pulled out my knife and ran home. When I got there, I told Meghazi Mohammed about it and he said, "It was an afreet and you are lucky still to be alive."

Many of the secondhand stories concern a very well-known female genie called Betdjellal. She has been attacking local men for over fifty years, although she has not appeared for the last fifteen. The old men say that a quarter of the village saw her at one time or another and, when they recognized her, they would drop everything and run. She appeared to men because she wanted to have intercourse—"It's the only thing men and women have in common." She might appear as a well-dressed, attractive woman and would importune a man in his garden. Having led him away from his companions with sweet speeches, she would change her form, growing to great size or becoming an old hag with long teeth and shining eyes. Then she would seize the man and copulate with him until he lost consciousness.

One informant who "knew a nomad who was married to Betdjellal" tells the story thus:

> One night he was sleeping in the desert and a snake crawled around him. He rose up and saw a strange woman take hold of the snake by its neck. He was frightened by her appearance. She had a flat nose and slant eyes and light came out of her eyes and mouth. He emptied his purse, threw her the money, and ran off. She followed him and told him not to be afraid and became his wife. He was already married and when he slept with his human wife, the genie would tear him away from her. The genie would feed him for two or three days out in the desert. He had intercourse with the genie and only got rid of her by burning a written charm secured from his *taleb*.

The Sahhara

A *sahhara* is a sorceress who specializes in love magic. The power of such sorcery is verified by the Koran (II:96), but it is also clear in the dogma that recourse to sorcery is forbidden.

A *sahhara* can weaken sexual desire or intensify it. She can make a woman desire a particular man, can make a man impotent with any woman other than his wife, or make a woman leave her husband for another man. Such magic can soften a brutal husband or even make him disregard his wife's adultery. Women are said to use sorceresses more than men. The latter most commonly experience the effects of a *sahhara* by being bound to one woman.

Many sorceresses are said to be Jews and some to be Negroes, although others are white Arabs. Their usual method of operation is to work magic upon some substance which is introduced into the victim's food or, more rarely, into his bed or house. The materials used are commonly exuviae of the person upon whom the magic is to operate. The magical substances are often referred to as "poisoning" the victim, and general debility or continuing gastric or pulmonary trouble may be interpreted as the result of love magic.

Such sorceresses are found in both Sidi Khaled and Algiers. One young man recounted how he had tried for four years to gain access to a particular girl in the oasis. Finally, with the help of a *sahhara*, he got into her courtyard and achieved his desire. A city Arab describes, in the following words, his wife's partially successful attempt to use such sorcery on him:

> My wife was always sending food to her parents. I told her we were poor and could not afford to do this. She would even complain that there was little in the house to eat and we were on bad terms. She sent to a *sahhara* and got a meter of red cloth and a meter of another color and put them under our sleeping-mat. I lay with my wife. Then I found the cloths and she denied any knowledge of them. I beat her and sent her back to her parents. Afterward, I had a pain in my heart for several days. For several years, on the anniversary of the event, I had the pain for two or three days. A *taleb* cured me with a charm which I wear.

Evil Eye

It is common knowledge among the Arabs that Mohammed said, "The evil eye exists." The mischief caused thereby stems from the look of an envious person and, in this sense, there is even Koranic reference to it (CXIII:5).[8] There are Mohammedan "rationalists" who do not believe in its power, but for most Algerian Arabs "the eye" is a real source of danger. Any misfortune, accident, or malady is apt to be attributed to the effects of the evil eye. The basic principle of the belief is that the

---

8. Early Near Eastern belief in the destructive quality of covetousness also accounts for the Mosaic commandment against it.

malignant power of the envious glance destroys the thing which is coveted. For example, during World War II, Zaked was shopping with the ration cards of his large family when he met an older man who had only one daughter. This man looked at all Zaked's cards enviously and jokingly remarked, "I ought to take you to my wife to copulate with her." The following day, all of Zaked's children were vaccinated and one of them died two days later, the victim of the old man's evil eye.

It is sinful thus to accuse an individual of having the evil eye and such accusation is never made directly. Still, certain people who have it may be recognized by their envious sighs or covetous glances. Protective measures, in addition to verbal and written charms, include the specific protection of the khâmsa (five). The five fingers of the human hand, or its representation in any form, arrests the influence of the evil eye. A gold or silver khâmsa is frequently worn by women and children for this purpose. Extending the open hand, palm foremost, toward a person is the grossest insult, for it is a direct accusation that he has "the eye."

There is a polite ruse which is employed to secure protection and still avoid insult. It consists of wiping the forehead with the back of the open hand, a natural gesture, but one which directs the khâmsa at the feared eye. A whole household may be protected by placing gazelle horns, a horseshoe, or the impression of a hand over the doorway of a house. Iron door knockers in the shape of a woman's hand, which became popular among Europeans at the end of the last century, were widely adopted by the Algerians as both charms and knockers.

Another means of escaping the evil eye is to avoid exposure to it. The isolation of a newborn child and the covering of a bride's head have this function. Likewise, the seclusion of women is not solely a question of propriety and physical protection but is also a safeguard against "the eye." Market places, with their crowds of strangers and idle observers, are particularly dangerous. A young city man who was visiting his father in the oasis absolutely refused to go into the market for this reason.

Dream Interpretation

The Koran refers to Mohammed receiving revelation of future events in a dream (XLVIII:27) and this power of dreams to foretell events may be utilized by ordinary men today. When one sleeps, his soul may wander from him and its experiences are the content of dreams. Some of these experiences are prophetic, but not all. Even for prophetic dreams, the significance is not always readily apparent.

People widely believe that "Satan's dreams," or dreams of intercourse, are "false" and have no meaning. One informant, however, recalled that the day after he had dreamed of having intercourse with his sister, a man asked to marry her. If a person is ritually clean upon retiring, he is not likely to have Satan's dreams, but even if he has dreams of incest they will be "true" and of good portent. Dreams caused by indigestion are generally considered to be false. The time of night that a dream occurs is significant in evaluating it. Dreams in the early morning, before one rises, are true. Those before midnight are either false or will take years to come true. Some believe that dreams on Friday and Monday nights are the best.[9]

Dreams are rarely a direct representation of events as they will occur. Dreams of receiving money and of finding work were, however, reported as having come true. In the latter instance, the man acted on his dream and went to Algiers in search of work. Often a dream's significance is symbolic, as in the case of a man who dreamed that he saw the name "Ali" written on his wife's breast. Shortly afterwards, he refused to sell a piece of land, saying that he was keeping it for his second son, Ali. As he had but one son and as his wife was not pregnant, people derided him for his belief. But, "ten months later Ali was born."

As dreams are a preview of fated events, they cannot usually be a basis of action. The fascination of knowing what the future holds, however, remains great. The significance of dreams generally lies in the interpretation of their symbolism. The meanings of some symbolic dream events are widely known. Dreaming of losing a tooth or seeing a toothless person means a death in the family. Lightning and head shaving have the same significance. A bareheaded man portends misfortune. A howling dog means that the evil eye will strike the dreamer. The receipt of fruit indicates the securing of work. A dream of straw signifies a gift of money.

In the search for the meaning of dreams, people usually try to interpret their dreams themselves. If the significance is obscure, the dream may be discussed with relatives and friends, or the person may go to a *taleb* to learn its meaning. Only *talebs* generally use "dream books" to assist in interpretation.

Analysis was made of the effect of Koranic education upon all of the supernatural traits. In addition to the relationship of such schooling to prayer, education is related to dream interpretation but to none of the other beliefs. Seven of the eight disbelievers in the significance of dreams had never been to Koranic school, while all thirty-seven of the Arabs who had received more than a year of such education believed in dream interpretation and all but two practiced it.

9. The Arab day begins at sunset.

Guezzana

A *guezzana* is a woman fortuneteller. Such seers claim to divine both the past and future. Their methods vary greatly. One uses a mirror in a basin of water; others use cowrie shells, sand, or flour. The pouring of molten lead into water and interpreting the resultant leaden forms is not only employed by *guezzanas* but also by some *talebs*. A *taleb*, however, is more apt to use magical letter systems, numeration, or books of divination. Most men do not take the *guezzanas* seriously and many express the belief that it is forbidden to go to one, although no such opinion attaches to having one's fortune told by a *taleb*. The divination of causes of sickness and other misfortune is largely the work of *talebs*, who can also provide the magical remedies.

There are two *guezzanas* among the sedentarized nomads of Sidi Khaled. There are also *guezzanas* in a nomadic Tunisian tribe which camps annually near the oasis. While its men are herding, these women come into the village and tell fortunes. Aside from satisfying general curiosity about the future, resort to a *guezzana* is most common for the purpose of determining whether or not a particular marriage match is propitious.

Urban Change

When analysis of the effect of urban contact upon supernatural belief was undertaken, it was considered most probable that there would be some decline in all of the characteristically Arab traits. If differential change was discovered among the traits, however, we believed that it might be accounted for either by (1) the degree to which the various traits were integrated into Moslem dogma, or (2) an urban increase in magic associated with the greater insecurity of city life. The last tentative hypothesis was based on a smattering of evidence from as widely separated areas as Africa and Central America. Professor Redfield has stated this hypothesis specifically for Yucatan and its theoretical basis conforms to Malinowski's ideas concerning the function of magic.[10]

Table IX presents the oasis-urban comparison of the six supernatural traits just discussed. It is readily apparent that there is a significant change in three of the traits (charms, genii, and *sahhara*) and that the other three remain unaltered. We are

---

10. Robert Redfield, *The Folk Culture of Yucatan* (Chicago: University of Chicago Press, 1941), p. 334; Bronislaw Malinowski, *Magic Science and Religion* (Glencoe, Ill.: The Free Press, 1948).

Table IX

SUPERNATURAL BELIEFS

	Number of Cases		Per Cent of Group	
	Oasis	Urban	Oasis	Urban
Charms				
Does not believe in	3	13	16	46
Only believes in	5	8	26	29
Uses	11	7	58	25
	Belief/Disbelief $P = .04$			
	Use/Non-use $P = .005$			
Genii				
Does not believe in	1	10	5	36
Only believes in	16	17	80	61
Personal experience with	3	1	15	4
	Belief/Disbelief $P = .01$			
Sahhara				
Does not believe in	1	14	8	54
Only believes in	9	11	69	42
Affected by	3	1	23	4
	Belief/Disbelief $P = .005$			
Evil Eye				
Does not believe in	2	6	10	21
Only believes in	7	9	35	32
Protects against	8	10	40	36
Affected by	3	3	15	11
Dream interpretation				
Does not believe in	2	3	10	11
Only believes in	5	4	25	15
Interprets his dreams	13	20	65	74
Guezzana				
Does not believe in	12	19	60	68
Believes in	8	9	40	32

forced by the lack of evidence of a general secularizing effect of urban life to examine the secondary hypothesis regarding differential change.

If we rank the traits in terms of their relationship to Moslem dogma, we note that all of the powers except those of charms and the *guezzana* find some specific support in the Koran. But while the use of written charms was not advocated by Mohammed, such charms are literally portions of the Koran itself, prepared by the religious leaders of the society. The beliefs in charms and genii seem, in fact, to be the most closely tied to the dogma. The significance of dreams and the existence of the evil eye find support in the Book, but tradition states that Mohammed taught the faithful to disregard the danger of the evil eye. Finally, while the power of sorcery is admitted by the Koran, the use of either a *sahhara* or a *guezzana* is adjured by religious teachers, citing Mohammed. When we compare this rough rank ordering of traits with the changes which took place in the beliefs, there is no evidence that close formal relationship to the dogma creates resistance to change. Actually the two traits which we would expect, on this basis, to be most change-resistant (charms and genii) both decline in importance in the city.

Examining the second alternative hypothesis, we note that charms, *sahhara*, and evil eye are clearly magical, in the sense that supernaturally induced effects are produced in a mechanical, nonpropitiatory, manner. Belief in two of these three declines in the city, clearly failing to support the hypothesis of urban increase in magic.[11]

At this point in the analysis, the original interviews were reexamined to try to determine what was responsible for the differential change in the supernatural traits. It should be understood, however, that the explanations thus developed *ex post facto* cannot be considered as having been adequately tested with the Algerian material. They do, however, appear to be theoretically acceptable and statistically significant.

One fact quickly becomes apparent from the interviews. Arabs who disavowed belief in charms, genii, and the *sahhara* made frequent reference to science and medicine as the source of their beliefs concerning the phenomena which others interpreted supernaturally. For example, one such semi-sophisticate remarks concerning charms, "If a doctor claims to be able to cure and if a person has confidence in the doctor, the cure can be effected. If the person lacks faith, there can be no cure. It is like hypnotism used medically. Charms work the same way."

---

11. There is some suggestion in the data both from Algeria and Yucatan that the predicted change may occur among women, who, in the more fluid urban social order, use magic to hold their men.

If we tabulate separately the primary reason given by each person for his disbeliefs regarding the traits which change and those which do not, we find the following: [12]

Reason for Disbelief	Charms Genii *Sahhara*	Evil Eye Dreams *Guezzana*
Science and medicine	11	0
Religion	1	13
Other	4	7
No reason given	24	27

Of those who gave explanations for their disbeliefs, scientific and medical reasons are associated with disbelief in charms, genii, and the *sahhara* at the .002 level of significance; and religious reasons are related to disbelief in evil eye, dream interpretation, and *guezzana* at better than the .0001 level. The use of religious reasons for disbelief roughly substantiates the analysis of the relations of the various beliefs to the dogma. No one disbelieved in charms or genii solely for religious reasons, only one each made such reference in denying the power in dreams and of the *sahhara,* but four used religious arguments in rejecting the evil eye and ten did so for the *guezzana.*

Pursuing the idea that beliefs in charms, genii, and *sahhara* were displaced by the competing concepts of science and medicine, we note that two of the traits which did not change (dream interpretation and the *guezzana*) involve prognostication. French culture provides no competing trait and many Westerners actually believe at least in dream interpretation. The only aspect of the differential change which remains unexplained is why belief in the evil eye remains stable despite its linkage to the use of charms and the fact that many of the effects attributed to the evil eye are open to scientific or medical explanation.[13] Only a more intensive study of the functional role of the evil eye in Algerian culture can clarify why the Arabs cling to Mohammed's dictum that the evil eye exists, while they ignore his teaching that its effects should be disregarded.

---

12. No individual's reason for disbelief was counted more than once in either column, even though he may have cited that as the reason for disbelief of all three traits. Different reasons for the disbelief of different traits in the same column were, however, tabulated.

13. Later analysis of the relation of personality traits to supernatural traits (Chapter X) also indicates that belief in the evil eye has similar personality implications to those of charms, genii, and *sahhara.*

CHAPTER VII

CULTURE, PERSONALITY, AND PREDICTION

Up to this point our attention has focused on Arab culture and its change under the influence of French contact. We turn now to a consideration of Arab personality and pose once more the question set forth at the outset of the study: Is the relationship between specific culture traits and personality traits predictable, or only discernible in *ex post facto* examination of their interaction? To provide evidence on this question, we proposed to invite a psychological specialist in the analysis of personality to develop a set of hypotheses which would predict expected relationships between various personality traits and Arab cultural practices. The hypotheses were then to be tested with Rorschach and cultural data, both collected from the same sample of Algerian Arabs.

Professor Max Hutt agreed to develop the hypotheses and to make the blind interpretations of the Arab Rorschachs which would provide personality data on each individual, uncontaminated by any knowledge of his cultural practices. It was not proposed that Hutt should describe Arab culture from a knowledge of Arab personality. He was set the more reasonable task of trying to predict what personality characteristics would find expression in the various cultural forms evident among the oasis and urban Arabs. As the culture permits a variety of behavior in any given situation, could a knowledge of the personalities involved permit us to say which individuals would select any particular form of behavior? If we could not predict, on personality grounds, which individuals would employ which cultural alternatives, the case for the prediction of cultural form from a knowledge of personality type would be considerably weakened.

The initial step was to describe to Professor Hutt the kinds of cultural data which had been secured and to indicate the sort of variation which existed. With no other knowledge of the culture and no knowledge of the individual Arabs involved, Hutt then proposed ten hypotheses, stating the theoretical expectations of relationship between the culture traits and personality variables which he felt could be measured from the Rorschach. The test protocols were then turned over to him and he rated each on the various psychological dimensions involved in the hypotheses.[1]

---

1. Analysis involved only 57 cases as 7 were lost before being scored. By the time they were recovered, Hutt was too well informed for further interpretation to be considered as blind.

When he received the Rorschach material, he was told that it included the protocol of a Frenchman-turned-Arab and was invited to try to identify this "ringer." This he attempted to do, making three choices. None was correct, but his first choice was a very acculturated Arab who was also one of the two men in the sample who had been born in Algiers. His second choice was a young Arab who had come to the city at fourteen and had lived there for eight years. The third choice, however, had never been beyond the desert oases.

Validity of Blind Rorschach Ratings

An attempt was made to test the validity of Hutt's psychological ratings by comparing them with evaluations based on personal acquaintance with the individuals concerned. Taking the seven Arabs [2] best known to the field worker and five psychological traits [3] which he felt he could evaluate, fifteen ratings were made. They represented, therefore, the judgments about which he was the most sure. Of the fifteen ratings, thirteen were in conformity with those of Hutt, which is comfortably within the limits of statistical significance. The three judgments which were at variance were of different psychological dimensions, so weakness in judging any particular dimension was not involved. We conclude that the ratings made from the blind Rorschach analysis conform fairly closely to ratings which one might make on the basis of personal acquaintance with the persons tested, *even though they be from another culture.* This finding is particularly interesting in view of the fact that three of the seven Arabs used in this test spoke no French and contact with them had involved an interpreter.

Possible Translator Influence on the Rorschach

In addition to the above modest evidence that the use of an interpreter did not hamper the appraisal of personality, a more rigorous attempt was made to evaluate the possible effect of the administration of the test through a translator. Although the accuracy of translation in the test situation was validated by checking the wire-recorded test responses with a second interpreter, the possibility remained that subtle influences from the intervening personality of the translator might have affected the results of the test.

---

2. Cases 1, 2, 9, 25, 35, 36B, 50—all of which are discussed in detail in Chapter IX.

3. Maturity, cathexis, anality, anxiety, and overt hostility.

Eighteen of the tests were administered in French, without an interpreter, and five different interpreters were used for the other forty-six respondents. One interpreter translated for only two informants, so it is primarily the influence of the other four translators which is of concern. Two of these (designated A and B) translated in the oasis and two (C and D) in the city.[4] If one of these pairs differed from the other in personality and if these differences were reflected in the test results of the Arabs for whom they translated, this might account for, and invalidate, any oasis-urban differences in Rorschach responses.

All of the translators had taken the test, so it was possible to compare their Rorschach results with those of the Arabs for whom they translated (see Table X). Professor Hutt was asked which of the psychological variables would be the most likely to show interpreter influence and he suggested three—R (total number of responses), mYV total (inanimate movement, shading, and vista responses), and the ratings on overt hostility.

Statistical analysis of the data on R shows no general interpreter influence, although for one urban translator (D), who gave only seventeen responses himself, seven of the eight Arab respondents for whom he interpreted gave fifteen or fewer responses. The other urban interpreter gave well over twice as many responses to the test as D, whose R was about average for the Arabs. Yet the R's obtained through the two translators were not markedly different. We conclude that the low number of responses given by the individuals for whom D translated is probably fortuitous. In any event, no difference was found between the number of responses given by the oasis and urban groups.

The mYV total is a significant factor in the appraisal of psychic tension and anxiety. The oasis and urban groups did differ on this dimension. Analysis of interpreter effect with regard to this measure showed no significant relationship between the scores of the translators and those of the Arabs for whom they interpreted. What trend there was in the data was in the *reverse* direction from that which would be expected if an anxious interpreter created anxiety in the test situation. The mYV scores of the respondents with whom interpreter A worked are significantly lower than those of the respondents of the other three interpreters ($P = .05$). Yet one of these other interpreters (C) had an mYV score equal to that of A, next to the highest score in the whole Arab group. But interpreter C translated for Arabs whose scores showed no tendency to be in a reverse direction from his own. The lack of statistical significance of the data

---

4. One should remember that not all of the Arabs who were tested in the oasis fall into the "oasis group" in terms of lack of urban contact. In addition, almost half of the tests of the "urban group" were administered without an interpreter.

Table X
COMPARISON OF RORSCHACH RESULTS OF INTERPRETERS AND OF THEIR RESPONDENTS*

	TOTAL R		
	Interpreter's Total R	Number of Each Interpreter's Respondents Who Had	
		8-15 R	16-43 R
Interpreter's designation			
A	62	7	6
C	45	6	4
B	43	3	10
D	17	7	1
	TOTAL mYV		
	Interpreter's Total mYV	Number of Each Interpreter's Respondents Whose mYV Totals Were	
		0-1	2-10
Interpreter's designation			
A	16	9	4
C	16	4	6
D	4	2	6
B	3	5	8
	OVERT HOSTILITY RATING		
	Interpreter's Hostility Rating	Number of Each Interpreter's Respondents Whose Ratings Were	
		1-1.5	2-4.5
Interpreter's designation			
B	4	8	5
C	3	5	5
D	1	5	3
A	1	2	11

*"Respondents" means Arabs for whom the interpreter translated. For each Rorschach variable, the interpreters are grouped and ranked according to their similarity in terms of that variable.

grouped on a theoretical basis, plus the fact that the only relationship found was a reversal of the theoretical expectation, indicate that the low mYV scores secured through interpreter A did not result from interpreter influence.

The same sort of finding was revealed in the analysis of the overt hostility. A nonstatistically significant trend was found, whose direction was the *reverse* of that which would be expected if overtly hostile interpreters brought out hostility in the tests of the Arabs for whom they translated. Despite his own low rating in overt hostility, interpreter A translated for Arabs whose hostility ratings are significantly higher than those who were tested through the other oasis interpreter (P = .05). This difference is probably not due to the influence of the interpreter but, whatever the cause, the bias in the facts just enumerated is in a direction which would raise the relative hostility rating of the oasis group. The analysis presented in the next chapter, however, will reveal that the oasis group was still found to show less Rorschach evidence of hostility than the urban group.

Summarizing the total evidence, it indicates that the personality of the interpreters did not tend to influence the sort of Rorschach responses given by the people for whom they translated, at least with regard to the three psychological traits considered most likely to show such an effect. The respondents who worked through translators A and D do seem to have been distinctively different, but in ways which do not account for the oasis-urban differences in personality revealed in the subsequent Rorschach analysis.

The Test of Hypotheses

The cultural data for testing Hutt's hypotheses was coded onto cards before the hypotheses and psychological ratings were made available. The coded material was then analyzed in conjunction with the ratings, the cases being identified by number only. The comparison, therefore, was free from contaminating knowledge of the expected relationships to be tested.

Professor Hutt's statement of hypotheses follows. After each, there is inserted a brief discussion of the manner in which the variables were operationalized and the results of the tests.

Only statistically significant relationships are reported in this section, but trends are discussed in the final summary. Appendix D presents the data as grouped in the tests. Hutt's statement begins:

Certain areas of supernatural belief (charms, evil eye, genii, and love magic) show variation among individuals in terms of whether the individuals: (a) have personally experienced the effects of these forces; (b) only anticipate danger from supernatural sources and act accordingly; (c) believe in these powers but do not concern themselves about them; (d) do not believe in them.

It is postulated that these variables will vary directly with certain personality variables shown by the same individuals, these direct relationships being as follows:

I. Highly anxious individuals will tend to show behaviors (a) or (b) above.

Those Arabs who gave Rorschach evidence of anxiety neurosis, neurasthenia, hysteria, physiological tension, or phobia were rated as "highly anxious."

(a) Eleven individuals had experienced the effects of one or more of the following: genii, evil eye, and *sahhara* (dealer in love magic). Such experience was not found to be related to high anxiety.

(b) Those who employed any sort of supernatural protection against the evil eye or who used written charms for any protective purpose were compared with all others with respect to anxiety level. No relationship was found between the variables.

II. Nonanxious, spontaneous individuals will tend to show behaviors (c) and (d).

The categories employed for the psychological variable were cases showing: low anxiety and high maturity (spontaneity), those with high anxiety and low maturity, and a residual midgroup. In terms of the cultural variable, those who, for a majority of the supernatural traits, showed behaviors (c) and (d) were compared with all others. Analysis revealed the personality variables to be unrelated to the cultural ones.

III. Highly anxious individuals who may be characterized as converted will tend to show behavior (b).

The Rorschach material indicated that four-fifths of the more anxious Arabs tended to displace (convert) their anxiety. When these were compared with all others and analyzed in conjunction with the supernatural beliefs, divided as in I(b) above, no relationship emerged.

IV. Nonanxious, constricted individuals will tend to show behavior (d).

The whole group was so constricted that the hypothesis had to be altered to express simply a direct relationship between anxiety and belief in the supernatural power of charms, genii, and the evil eye. Love magic was omitted as the data was incomplete and its inclusion would lower the already small number of cases. Anxiety ratings were dichotomized and analyzed in conjunction with three levels of belief in the supernatural powers considered: no disbelief; disbelief in one power only; and disbelief in two or three of the supernatural forces. The data did not confirm the hypothesis at an acceptable level of significance.

Further Observations on Anxiety and Supernatural Belief

We noted earlier the erosive effect of urban contact on supernatural beliefs, so it is no surprise to find that three-quarters of the oasis group believes in all three of the forces just considered, while only two-fifths of the urban group do so (P = .01). Theoretically, we would also have every reason to believe that the rapid acculturation experienced in the city would increase anxiety. An oasis-urban comparison of anxiety ratings indicates such a tendency, but it does not reach significance. It is noteworthy, however, that we found a tendency for high anxiety to be related to high supernatural belief. This tendency cannot be a product of oasis-urban differences in the two characteristics, for they vary in opposite directions.

Despite our general expectation that acculturation in French cities involves a decrease in Arab supernatural beliefs, reference has been made to evidence from other societies that the use of magic actually increases in the city. Redfield attributed the greater use of magic in Merida than in the villages of Yucatan to the increased insecurity of urban life, and magic is frequently conceptualized as a means of handling anxiety-producing situations. In our earlier analysis, however, we found that in Algeria magic was more prone to decline in the city than were other supernatural beliefs.

We also saw, in the test of hypothesis I(b), that the *use* of magical protection against the evil eye and the *use* of charms was not related to Rorschach indications of extreme anxiety. Tests were also made of the relationship of *belief* in charms and love magic to high and low anxiety rating (dichotomized). Some relationship was found between high anxiety and belief in charms, but again not at a significant level. No comparable tendency appeared with regard to love magic. We must, therefore, conclude that anxiety, as reflected in this analysis of Algerian Rorschachs, gives no clear indication of increase in the city or relationship to magical or other supernatural beliefs.

V. Within groups of relatively homogeneous cultural experience, those individuals who express greatest dependence upon dream interpretation and soothsayers will be most likely to show Rorschach indications of hysteria.

Only sixteen individuals showed such signs of hysteria—five in the oasis group, four in the midgroup B, and seven in the urban group. In order to increase the number of cases which could be used, the urban group was extended to include all individuals who had five or more years of urban contact, irrespective of the portion of their lives which this length of time constituted. This redefinition of the city group added six cases to it, including two who showed indications of hysteria.

(a) None of the five oasis Arabs who showed hysteria used dream interpretation, while all but one of the other oasis Arabs interpreted their dreams. This complete reversal of the hypothesis was significant at the .002 level.

(b) The same reversal was found in the urban group but not at a significant level. The significance of the reverse relationship for the total Arab sample was .03.

Of the six supernatural traits studied, there was greater uniformity of practice among the Arabs with regard to dream interpretation than with regard to any other trait. Nor was there any difference between the oasis and the city. Those Arabs who show signs of hysteria are certainly nonconformists so far as dream interpretation is concerned.

(c) With regard to the use of a soothsayer *(guezzana)*, such practice is under religious interdiction and virtually no one admits to it. The hypothesis, therefore, was tested on belief in the efficacy of such prognostication, about which there is a difference of opinion. No relationship to hysteria was found in the oasis or city groups.

VI. Of the individuals with marked anal characteristics, those with Rorschach indications of hostility will be the most inclined, of the total population, to punish their children by severe physical means.

This prediction was tested using the rating on overt and latent hostility separately. In each instance, those Arabs with high ratings on both anality and hostility were compared with all others. With regard to punishment, those who believed in beating and slapping their children or who considered physical punishment the best method of discipline were contrasted with the milder disciplinarians. Neither type of hostility combined with anality varied significantly with severity of punishment. An alternative hypothesis, suggested by Hutt after these findings, predicted that the combined hostility ratings, taken alone, would show such a relationship. This alternative was no better than the original hypothesis.

VII. (a) The degree to which individuals have assimilated French culture traits is positively related to Rorschach changes in either or both psychogram and content.

(b) The length of time individuals have been in French-urban contact is positively related to Rorschach changes as above.

The Rorschach-derived variables employed in hypotheses VII and VIII are somewhat less determined by personality factors than those used in the other hypotheses. In making the ratings on assimilation and interest in the supernatural, all relevant content in the test protocols was employed. For instance, with regard to hypothesis VII, if an Arab saw urban phenomena in the ink blots, this fact would be considered along with the degree to which the formal determinants were "Western" in character.

The degree to which the Arabs had assimilated French culture was measured by means of an "assimilation index," based on the type of clothes worn, knowledge of French, amount of supernatural disbelief, smoking of cigarettes, and degree of confidence expressed in women. The relationship of this index to length of urban residence was highly significant ($P = .001$), but neither degree of assimilation nor length of city contact was related to the Rorschach ratings.

VIII. The degree to which individuals believe in certain supernatural phenomena and use these beliefs in their daily lives is positively related to the degree to which there will be projected content and symbolic content in this area in their Rorschach responses.

The Rorschach ratings on supernatural concern were not found to be related to a general index of actual supernatural belief and practice. The Rorschach ratings were, therefore, also compared with the various degrees of involvement which the individuals showed in each of the six supernatural traits. Of the twelve possible comparisons, the psychological ratings were found to be related to only one supernatural belief—that in charms ($P = .05$). Among believers in the power of charms, however, the use of charms showed no relationship whatever to the ratings. The theoretical significance of the finding with regard to belief in charms is further limited by the realization that, on a pure chance basis, one would expect to find one such statistically significant relationship in every twenty analyses. Of the twelve analyses made, five showed trends in the hypothesized direction, two were in the opposite direction, and five indicated no relation at all.

IX. Marked anality as determined from Rorschach protocols will vary directly with (a) the marked use of food deprivation as punishment; (b) high evaluation of money as compared with other things in life; (c) personal cleanliness; (d) preference for early toilet training.

Test of these four predictions demonstrated that anality was related only to cleanliness ($P = .05$). Even the prediction with regard to preference for early toilet training was not borne out.

X. The degree to which men favor more restrictive practices with regard to the seclusion of women is positively related to their degree of inability to develop mature and intense human relationships, as judged from Rorschach responses.

The hypothesis was tested with two separate measures of ability to develop good human relationships. Both maturity and cathexis ratings were made from the test protocols. Each type of rating was analyzed in conjunction with the Arabs' beliefs as to the age at which girls should be secluded and the age at which women could be permitted to emerge from seclusion. Maturity ratings were significantly related, in the predicted direction, to the preferred age for ending seclusion ($P = .01$) and cathexis showed a similar tendency. Analyzed in conjunction with the preferred age for beginning seclusion, however, the maturity ratings showed no relationship whatever and high cathexis ratings were inversely related to late initiation of seclusion ($P = .05$). The obvious conflict between the two significant findings presents an interesting problem.

Most likely, in responding to the query concerning the end of seclusion, Arab men had their wives in mind, for it is their wives' seclusion over which they have control. With regard to the beginning of seclusion, they would be more likely to think in terms of daughters. If we re-examine the findings with this distinction in mind, the apparent contradictions disappear.

It is not easy for a man to have confidence in his wife in a society in which women are considered to be highly sexed and amoral, particularly when men have little capacity for establishing secure rapport with anyone[5] and marriages never result from previous emotional ties. It is only through long periods of interdependence, and then only for men with greater psychological maturity, that such confidence can be established. We would also expect greater cathexis to provide an alternative to incarceration as a means of maintaining such a marriage relationship.

Following the same line of reasoning, an explanation can also be offered for the reversal of the hypothesis, so far as cathexis and the preferred age for beginning seclusion are concerned. If the reference of seclusion in this instance is to daughters, even an emotionally mature Arab has no experience upon which to base a belief that his daughter is an exception and will not succumb to her sexual urges. But the stronger the father's emotional ties to his daughter, the more he will be interested in her welfare and virginity, and the earlier he would seclude her.

---

5. See Chapter VIII for evidence on this point.

While these *ex post facto* observations help us understand the relationships which were uncovered by the statistical analysis, this analysis does not, of course, demonstrate the validity of the explanations.

Summary of the Findings

With the evidence before us (Table XI), we return to the original question of whether or not individual cultural behavior can be predicted from a knowledge of the personality. Obviously some of the hypotheses were born out by some of the analyses, but many were not. Of the thirty-four tests made, five relationships were found to be statistically significant. These involved only four of the hypotheses and were reversals of the predictions in two cases.

Another way of looking at the results is to consider the total evidence with regard to each hypothesis, including the tendencies for variables to be associated, even though the degrees of association do not reach the level of significance. On this basis, only revised hypothesis IV is unequivocally supported, but only one test of the prediction was made and the results did not reach statistical significance. Hypotheses I, VII, and IX seem to find some support in the evidence.

On the other hand, reversals of predictions are about as numerous and somewhat better substantiated. The reversal of hypothesis V is significantly and consistently supported, and the data incline toward reversals of hypotheses II and VI as well. The evidence on the remaining three predictions fails to support them, either consistently or at all.

The purport of the above is clear. Although relationships were found between the psychological and cultural variables, success in predicting the relationships was no better than chance. It may, of course, be argued that the failure results from methodological inadequacies. Evidence has been presented, however, which indicates that the techniques involved have been generally found to produce reliable results. As to whether or not they did so in this specific instance, it can be said that, at least with regard to the adequacy of the blind interpretation and the lack of interpreter bias, our control studies give us confidence in the procedures. Additional evidence as to the adequacy of the data derives from the succeeding stage of analysis.

Following the blind interpretation of the Rorschach protocols, all available information was used to delineate the nature of Arab personality and its relationship to cultural norms in the acculturative situation. Dr. George De Vos was the psychological collaborator in this task and the Rorschach test results were

Table XI

SUMMARY OF TESTS OF HYPOTHESES

Hypothesis		Result	Hypothesis	Result
I	(a)	0	VIII (cont.)	
	(b)	+	*Sahhara*	
			belief	0
II		−	effects	+
			Evil eye	
III		0	belief	+
			protection	
IV		+	or effects	−
			effects only	0
V	(a)	− P = .002	Dream interpre-	
	(b)	−	tation	
	(c)		belief	0
	Oasis	0	use	0
	Urban	−	*Guezzana*	−
VI	Latent	−	IX (a)	−
	Overt	0	(b)	+
			(c)	+ P = .05
VII	(a)	+	(d)	−
	(b)	+		
			X Maturity and	
VIII	Index	+	begin se-	
	Charms		clusion	0
	belief	+ P = .05	end seclusion	+ P = .01
	use	0	Cathexis and	
	Genii		begin se-	
	belief	+	clusion	− P = .05
	effects	+	end seclusion	+

Key: P Statistically significant relationship.

+ Variables show a tendency for relationship in hypothesized direction.

0 Variables unrelated or so little related that a shift of one case would eliminate the tendency.

− Variables show a tendency toward a reverse relationship from that hypothesized.

rescored and interpreted in the light of Miner's personal knowledge of the individual Arabs and their culture. As might be expected, Rorschach scoring is so standardized that there was little variation between the results of the two psychologists.[6] When De Vos' individual personality evaluations were compared with the data on individual variation in cultural norms, numerous statistically significant relationships emerged which, while not predictable, were meaningful in both psychological and cultural terms. Had the data been unreliable, it is difficult to see why these relationships should appear.

If, then, the test of Dr. Hutt's hypotheses was a valid one, how should we interpret the failure to predict cultural norms from personality traits? To understand the failure, we shall refer to a distinction which Kardiner makes between two types of "reality systems" found in culture.[7] "Empirical" reality systems embrace such cultural areas as technology and science. The rationale for such systems lies in the lawful relationships among things in the natural world. Kardiner sees "projective" reality systems, on the other hand, as derived from the personality structure and the cultural forms which they involve as predictable from personality data. He indicates that religion and folklore are the most clearly projective, presumably because these systems are the most lacking in empirical basis.

In his concentration on the extreme contrast between scientific and religious reality systems, what escapes attention is that reality systems related to the structure and function of society can be based on empirical evidence comparable to that concerning the physical properties of matter. It is, of course, only by reference to the culture that one can hope to determine what these regularities are and, therefore, what remaining areas of culture may be projective and predictable from personality.

To use our interpretation of the findings on Hutt's hypothesis X as a case in point,[8] cultural prediction failed because there was no basis in personality theory for believing that Arab men's maturity would be positively related to the earlier termination of their women's seclusion but unrelated to the later initiation of seclusion. The explanation of the findings lies in the social

---

6. De Vos' cumulative data on Rorschach determinants are not directly comparable with Hutt's results, as one is expressed in terms of mean scores and the other in terms of medians. Despite this fact they are very similar, as can be seen in Appendix E.

7. Abram Kardiner, (New York: Columbia University Press, 1945), pp. 38 ff.

8. The validity of this particular interpretation is irrelevant here. The correlations of cultural and personality data in Chapter X show many other instances of cultural forms which would appear to have similar personality implications but which, in fact, do not.

structure and in the relation of men to various sorts of female relatives. The fact that men control the end of seclusion for their wives but only the beginning of seclusion for their daughters derives from biological and cultural factors. The concepts of "wife," "daughter," and "seclusion" may have their projective aspects but they are also based on empirical reality. Not until that reality is understood can one isolate the projective aspect of the associated behavior.

Because personality and culture are by definition related in consistent ways, the nature of one will indicate something about the general nature of the other. But to predict the complex manner in which the two are related in specific areas of behavior requires that one know what particular personality traits will be relevant and predominant in each cultural situation. The analysis of the Algerian data in our final chapter shows, for example, that culture traits which have particular personality concomitants in the oasis may change in the city without commensurate changes in these personality traits. In other words, acculturative social forces in the city can force behavioral adaptations despite the personality implications of the earlier behaviors. We must conclude that factors external to the basic personality structure contribute so much to the determination of specific cultural forms that prediction of the latter becomes impossible on the basis of a knowledge of general behavioral predispositions.

CHAPTER VIII

PSYCHOLOGICAL CHARACTERISTICS OF THE ALGERIANS

There is no argument concerning the existence of manifest differences between Arab and Western culture. More difficult, however, is the collecting of evidence on subtle differences in personality structure. Our purpose in these chapters is to examine how the Algerian Arabs perceive Rorschach ink blots and to infer, from this and other evidence, how their personalities compare with those of normal and maladjusted Americans. Moreover, it will be possible to demonstrate that variations in Algerian Rorschach responses are related to the respondents' residence in the city or in the oasis and to show how these variations reflect acculturative changes in cultural beliefs and practices.

The following is not intended as a complete analysis of Algerian personality. It is an attempt to describe the prevalence of certain characteristics which Arabs show in coping with the perceptual task involved in the test. The frame of reference used is an application of the psychoanalytic theory of "ego defenses" to Rorschach interpretation. The psychologist will find familiar phrases handled as though they were novel, in an attempt to make their interpretation more meaningful to the interested nonspecialist.

There has been only one comparable study to assess Arab personality.[1] This was published in 1935 by Bleuler and Bleuler and was one of the pioneering efforts in the use of the newly developed Rorschach technique cross-culturally. The subjects were Moroccans, who may have come from a population element more closely tied to Berber origins than were the Algerian Arabs.

As becomes evident through the following presentation, our results, in regard to Algerian personality configurations, substantiate in some respects certain findings of the Bleulers. When compared with their results, ours were most similar in regard to the prevalence of particular illogical, arbitrary habits of thought, well described by the Bleulers as follows:

---

1. M. Bleuler and R. Bleuler, "Rorschach's Ink-Blot Test and Racial Psychology: Mental Peculiarities of Moroccans," *Character and Personality*. IV (1935), 97-114.

According to the principles of the Rorschach Test, the peculiarities which we find in the records of our Moroccan subjects would indicate, in the first place, a good power of observation of a person who notices all sorts of things and retains a very exact impression of them in his memory. We should, however, not credit such a person with the capacity of picking out that which is important and essential in all these detailed observations. To put it bluntly, he could not see the wood for the trees. His thought would lack purposive directness, and his logic would be poor. Purposeful, methodical thinking would be impaired; his abstractive faculty, his aptitude for co-ordination and subsumption of thoughts, his ability to think in a systematic, well-organized way would be very defective. Still, he would not merely be a narrow-minded pedant; for his peculiar power of combination, though self-centered, undisciplined, and illogical, would be conditioned by his emotions. From his observations he would not abstract what is important to him, but rather what he likes and what pleases him; he would combine them together in a fantastic or artistic manner, unreal but full of personal sentiment. He would be a man who observes details sharply and distinctly, and weaves them into semi-artistic and semi-fantastic wholes. He would be a fussy, nagging fellow and a romantic dreamer at the same time.[2]

The evidence we find to substantiate the above differs somewhat from that which the Bleulers cited. They emphasized the Moroccans' lack of "whole" responses and a tendency to use many small details. Our records, generally, show no such imbalance, when compared with American samples. Nevertheless, our analysis of the quality of thought expressed by Algerians is in full accord with that reported in the Bleulers' quotation. Some Algerians also fit the description of the Moroccans with regard to the nature of their responsiveness to the social environment. The Bleulers described a marked extroverted interest and enthusiasm for momentary events but, underlying this, a more deep-seated, self-centered seclusiveness. These characteristics will be discussed in detail.

While the Bleulers' description fits the personality configurations found in many of the Algerian records, it is by no means characteristic for all. This chapter will also deal with typical Arab traits but in the next chapter individual differences will be discussed insofar as they are related to varying patterns of acculturation. In addition, the records of deviant individuals will be examined in the joint light of Rorschach and other behavioral data. Finally, in a third chapter, the relation between specific personality factors and cultural beliefs will be explored.

Some of the Rorschach measures used herein were developed by De Vos and have not been widely employed in "culture and personality" work. Much less emphasis is placed on Rorschach determinants than is customary in clinical summaries. Instead,

---

2. *Op. cit.,* pp. 107-08.

measures of affective symbolic content and the logic of thought processes are stressed, as are over-all indices of rigidity and maladjustment.

Rigidity and Maladjustment[3]

Psychological rigidity, as here inferred from Rorschach data, refers to the habitual tendency of an individual to avoid anxiety through inflexibility in perception and behavior. Rigidity is a characteristic of people who cannot react or adapt freely to new situations but who tend to react, instead, with set patterns of behavior and ways of thinking developed in the past. A rigid person often reacts to a new situation only in response to some partial resemblance which that situation has to his past experience. The more rigid an individual, the more limited and invariant his patterns of responses. Rigid behavior naturally differs, in its components and integration, from person to person and from culture to culture.

The Algerian Arabs, as a group,[4] score extremely high on the rigidity scale (Table XII), their mean score being significantly different from that of a sample of normal Americans.[5] Only a minority of the Arab records have scores comparable to those characteristic of these Americans. The difference between the scores of the oasis and urban Arabs is not significant, but the difference in the standard deviations of the two sets of scores reaches significance, the urban group showing greater variability.

---

3. The rigidity and maladjustment scales here employed were developed by Seymour Fisher in a study of Americans described in "Pattern of Personality Rigidity and Some of Their Determinants," *Psychological Monographs: General and Applied,* LXIV (1950), No. 1. They have since been applied in Japan and in a study of Japanese American Acculturation. See G. De Vos, "A Quantitative Rorschach Assessment of Maladjustment and Rigidity in Acculturating Japanese Americans," *Genetic Psychology Monographs,* LII (1955), 51-87.

4. In the following analysis, oasis-urban comparisons omit the subsample of 16 cases (Group B) which was intermediate between the two extremes in amount of urban contact. Generalizations about the Arabs, as a group, are based on the total sample of 64 cases.

The statistical analyses were conducted by De Vos. Levels of significance were computed by Chi square, except in some instances where low marginal totals required the use of Fisher's Exact Test of Probability. When the term "significant" is used in the discussion, statistical significance is meant.

5. The primary materials of the American samples used as controls in this study were kindly made available by Dr. Samuel J. Beck who has used them in his normative studies of the Rorschach Test. S.J. Beck, A. Rabin, *et. al.,* "The Normal Personality as Projected in the Rorschach Test," *Journal of Psychology,* XXX (1950), 141-98.

Table XII

RORSCHACH INDICES OF RIGIDITY AND MALADJUSTMENT
IN ARAB AND AMERICAN SAMPLES

		Arab			American		
		Oasis	Urban	Total Sample	Normal	Neurotic	Schizophrenic
	N	20	28	64	60	30	30
Rigidity	Mean	51.0[a]	46.3[a]	50.1[a]	27.7	30.8	32.2[a]
	S.D.	10.3[c]	20.2[c]	14.0	15.3	15.3	16.8
Maladjustment	Mean	63.3[a]	61.8[a]	62.2[a]	34.0	65.8[a\ b]	80.6[a\ b]
	S.D.	19.8	26.1	20.2	16.2	31.7	23.8

Key to significance of differences at the .05 level or better:

a. Compared with Normal American.
b. Comparison between Neurotic and Schizophrenic Americans.
c. Comparison between Oasis and Urban Arabs (no other statistical comparison of standard deviations was made).

The maladjustment scale is composed of various Rorschach indications of deviation from the "ideal" ranges of Rorschach indices of intellectual and emotional functioning. It is a quantitative measure in which high scores indicate severe imbalance in a number of these indices. Most individuals show some variations from the ideal so that it is extremely rare to find a record with no score at all. It is noteworthy that the mean score for the Arabs on the maladjustment scale is markedly higher than that for Normal Americans and is comparable to that obtained from a sample of American Neurotic records. Such results suggest that Algerians, as a group, develop types of personality integration which make for potential psychic tension and distortion, by ideal standards of adjustment. The lack of significant difference between the oasis and urban Arabs on their mean scores in either of these measures attests to a basic similarity in their personality structure. One striking difference between the groups does occur, however, in this connection. While the rigidity and maladjustment scores are unrelated to one another in the oasis group, they show a significant correlation in the city.[6] This relationship is apparently associated with an increase in stress reactions in the urban group, which will be discussed later.

Mental Approach: Perceptual Elaboration and Organization

Contrasting Rorschach responses indicate considerable difference between Algerians and Americans in their mental approach to the world about them.[7] The utility of the test rests, of course, on the tendency for an individual's orientation to life situations to be reflected in the way he perceives the ten ink-blot cards. For example, a reaction to the total blot area, in a "whole" or W response, suggests a more global or abstract orientation, whereas attention to large detail is more indicative of a pragmatic or concrete orientation. On the average, whole responses constitute 42 per cent of all the responses given by an Arab, while members of the Normal American group have a mean of about 19 per cent. The total number of responses given by Algerians (mean 19), however, is much less than for Americans (mean 31). Nevertheless, the average number of the Algerians' whole responses is slightly higher than that of the American group. These results contrast with the Bleulers' report of a mean of 2.7 W for the Moroccans. A qualitative examination of the whole responses given by the Arabs reveals differences from those found in the

---

6. Kendall's Tau = .28, significantly different from zero at the .05 level.

7. See Appendix F for detailed comparison of Arab and American Rorschach results, relevant to this and subsequent sections.

American records. The Algerian W's are usually vaguely perceived things of indefinite shape, such as mountains, or trees, or various sorts of "additive" or arbitrarily constructed combinations of items. The tendency of the Moroccans toward illogical, rather than systematic, thought, as noted by the Bleulers, is readily apparent in these Algerian responses. Arbitrary juxtaposition of elements, rather than logical, carefully checked objectivity, seems to guide the selection and combination of the percepts given in many instances.

The proportion of small or unusual details (Dd) is quite similar between the Algerian and the Normal American groups, contrary to the Bleulers' findings of a high proportion of Dd responses in the Moroccans. Large detail responses are notably infrequent among the Algerians, implying a less matter-of-fact approach to problems.

The low response total does not indicate lack of mental activity on the part of the Algerian Arabs in meeting the Rorschach task. The responses are elaborated, albeit with arbitrary and illogical modes of thought which will be discussed later. The Algerians actually show a great deal of intellectual push, in terms of a drive to organize their percepts into complex configurations. They obtain a mean Z score (a measure of organizational drive, developed by Beck,[8]) quite similar to that of the American sample, with its much higher response total.

Fluidity, Blocking, or Constriction in Associative Processes

The Algerian Arabs show considerably more associative blocking than do the Americans. In addition to the rather low mean response total, they also evidence blocking in their long delays before giving an initial response (46" as compared to 32" for Normal Americans on Card I). In respect to a third measure of associative blocking—that of "rejection" or refusal to respond appropriately to individual cards—the Algerians are not significantly different from the American sample. These measures of associative blocking contribute considerably, however, to the group's high rigidity and high maladjustment scores reported above.

Other measures of psychic constriction are also significantly higher among the Algerians. They tend to withdraw responses or to deny previous responses during the subsequent inquiry. One notes extreme tendencies to constrict percepts, especially among the rural group, in the appearance of so-called "oligophrenic" responses, in which only one part of a percept usually seen as a

---

8. Samuel J. Beck, *Rorschach's Test* (Revised; New York: Grune and Stratton, 1950), Vol. I, 58. ff.

totality is given as an answer. This sort of response occurs most frequently on Card III, where a number of individuals see only human heads rather than total human figures.

When a large proportion of the responses relate only to the form of the blots (F%), this strongly indicates psychic constriction as there is a relative lack of the use of color, movement, and other determinants. The Arabs generally show no measurable difference from the Normal American group in F%, except for the urban group, which is significantly lower. In both American and Arab groups, a large proportion of individuals receive high scores on the rigidity scale for constriction of this measure.

The prevalence of a great number of rigid and constricted records would presuppose stereotypic thinking in a fairly large number of cases. This presupposition is borne out. Unlike Western records, it is not solely a high percentage of animal responses that indicates stereotypy in this group. Rather, it is through the additional pervasive use of botany and landscape content that some individuals reveal the narrowness of their range of interests and their lack of free use of imagination. As in the Normal American sample, one must consider variations in intelligence in accounting for some of the more stereotyped records. Nevertheless, on the average, the Algerians do show a greater tendency toward stereotypy than the American sample.

Communality of Thought

The popular or "P" responses are those given most frequently to the various specific blot areas on the cards. The number of popular responses which an individual gives is a measure of participation in the common thought of the group. In previous reports by Hallowell,[9] on certain acculturating American Indian groups, and in previous work of De Vos with the Japanese, much similarity was found between the popular responses of these groups and those of Americans. To assess the relative use of populars in Algeria, the twenty-one American populars reported by Beck were slightly modified to produce a list of Western P's.[10] Then a list was made of the twenty most popular Arab responses. The two lists overlap in only eight of the responses (Table XIII). The Algerians produce P's of a sort not previously reported as popular for any group. "Mountains in the distance," architectural features (mostly mosques) seen at a distance, and a number of

---

9. A. I. Hallowell, " 'Popular Responses and Cultural Differences: An Analysis Based on Frequencies in a Group of American Indian Subjects," *Rorschach Research Exchange,* IX (1945), 153-68.

10. See Appendix G for details and bases of this modification.

"tree" responses are commonly seen. Such responses, particularly those involving distance, suggest that the desert environment affects perceptual habits. Human and animal life are also sometimes seen as being far off. Actually, the only mountains visible from Sidi Khaled are the Atlas, thirty miles to the north. Some of the human figure percepts reported for the Moroccans were also perceived as being distant or possibly hiding behind trees.

It seemed probable that the use of popular responses would be influenced by acculturative processes. To test this hypothesis, the occurrence of the twelve, uniquely American popular responses was compared with the occurrence of the twelve, uniquely Arab populars. Analyses were made of the effect of urban residence and of Koranic and French education on the type of popular responses given. There seems no reason to doubt the assumption involved that French P's are more like those of Americans than are those of the Arabs. In the urban group, eighteen of twenty-eight individuals saw one or more uniquely American P's. Only two of the twenty oasis Arabs saw any of these P's. This difference is significant beyond the .001 level. As to the number who saw one or more uniquely Arab P's, there were twenty of twenty-eight in the urban group and nineteen of twenty in the oasis. This difference does not reach statistical significance but is in the hypothesized direction.

Continued French schooling is influential in the production of popular responses, as witnessed by the following results: Of thirteen individuals with more than one year of French education, seven used uniquely American P's, as compared with fifteen of the remaining fifty-one Arabs (P = .10). The analysis also indicates that those without either French or Koranic education, which co-vary, tend more toward the production of uniquely Arab populars, but these trends do not reach significance.

In summary, the evidence indicates quite clearly that one result of moving from the oasis to the city is some development of Western ways of looking at things. The loss of distinctively Arab types of percepts is less marked and, presumably, more gradual. The impact of formal French education in the oasis shows similar effects. The fact that those who have some French education usually have gone also to Koranic school may be related to the relatively slight loss of uniquely Arab perceptual norms among the educated men. These findings with regard to popular responses and education were the only instance in which French schooling was found to be related to a Rorschach variable.

The Arabs, as a whole, produce a very low average number of popular responses, even in terms of "Arab" populars (3.9 as compared with 6.8 for Normal Americans). This relative lack of communality in P responses suggests a tendency for Algerian

Arabs to be idiosyncratic in their perceptions, to think egocentrically, to be relatively insensitive to group pressures, and to be low in the need to conform. The inner-directed nature of the Moroccan psyche, as described by the Bleulers, and the individualism often mentioned as a component in Arab personality are both supported by this Algerian Rorschach evidence.

Subjective, Illogical, or Arbitrary Thought Patterns

In addition to the above modes of constriction, the Algerian records deviate from the Normal American sample in terms of various ideal standards of logical, accurate, and objective thinking.[11] In some ways the Arabs show similarities to the thought patterns of the sample of Neurotic Americans. It is to be noted that the Rorschach signs of thought disorder are not, in themselves, diagnostic of specific pathology. As a matter of fact, the Neurotic and Schizophrenic American samples used in this report cannot be clearly distinguished from one another by the frequencies of these disorders. In only a few cases can they be differentiated from the Normal group. For adequate diagnosis an intensive clinical analysis of an entire record is necessary. Most individuals using the test have abandoned a "sign" approach to diagnosis in Rorschach work. We revert to tabulating signs only to demonstrate cultural differences in frequencies.

The accuracy with which the Arabs use the form of the test blots in arriving at their percepts, as measured by Beck's F + %, is significantly lower for the Algerians than for the Normal American group and even somewhat below that of the Neurotic Americans. Diffuse, unclear, and confused responses lower the scores on form accuracy. Poorly perceived trees or animals are not infrequent. Such responses alternate, in some records, with quibbling over details or arbitrarily distinguishing differences between the two sides of the symmetrical blots. Among the urban Arabs, especially, poorly perceived anatomy contributes to very low F + %.

The oasis group is somewhat more prone to give a direct affective impression of the blot, such as, "It's frightening," "It's very pretty," or "This one is much worse." In this group especially, there is much illogical elaboration of responses, in an attempt to justify them. There is some tendency to derive responses from a personal association or experience which is called to mind by a portion of the area included in the response.

---

11. See Appendix F, Parts II and III, for comparative scores and method of scoring.

Table XIII

LIST OF THE 20 MOST POPULAR RORSCHACH RESPONSES OF AMERICANS AND ARABS

		American Populars (revised Beck)		
Card	Location	Responses	Rank	Per cent of Respondents
I	W	*bat, butterfly	3	75.7
	D4, D3	human figure	8	31.7
II	D1, D6	*animal	4	64.3
	W, D	human figure	18	15.9
III	W, D1, D9	human figure	5	59.2
	D3	tie or ribbon	14	19.7
IV	W	animal skin or furred animal	11	23.0
V	W	*bat, butterfly, bird	1	89.2
	d1	leg	15	19.1
VI	W, D1	*animal skin	6	43.2
VII	W, D9, D2, D1	human head	16	17.2
VIII	D1	*animal	2	88.4
	D3	bones, ribs	18	15.9
	D4, D8	*tree	12	22.3
IX	D3	human figure	9.5	26.7
	D4	*human head	9.5	26.7
X	D1	*crab, lobster, or spider	7	40.7
	D2	dog	13	21.7
	d5	rabbit face	18	15.9
	D4	vermiform animal	20	—

*Common to both groups.

Table XIII (Cont.)

Arab Populars

Card	Location	Responses	Rank	Per cent of Respondents
I	W	*bat, butterfly	11.5	12.5
	W, D2, D7, d8 D5	mountain	7	20.4
II	D1, D6	*animal	14.5	10.9
	Ws, Ds6, Ds5	landscape	7	20.4
	d4	architecture	9.5	14.0
	D2	bird	11.5	12.5
III	W, D1, D9 D11, d6	human figure, human head	5	21.0
	D1	tree	18.5	9.4
	D5	fish	4	21.9
IV	W	sea animal	9.5	14.0
V	W	*bat, butterfly, bird	2	70.0
VI	W, D	*animal skin	14.5	10.9
	W	architecture	7	20.4
	D3	winged animal	18.5	9.4
VII	W	mountain	14.5	10.9
VIII	D1	*animal	1	75.0
	D4, D8	*tree	3	31.3
IX	D4	*human head	18.5	9.4
	W, D9	tree	14.5	10.9
X	D1	*crab, lobster, or spider	18.5	9.4

*Common to both groups.

A forced quality of thinking is revealed in the Arabs' tendency to give "whole" responses, no matter how distorted, to every card or, compulsively, to include every area of the blots by giving detailed responses. Often these details are then arbitrarily united. Vague, ill-defined responses are sometimes followed by others which contain meticulous attention to detail, parts of the blot being eliminated to improve the accuracy of the percept. Occasionally, alternate percepts are given in an attempt to make the answer more precise but the individual feels compelled to decide between the alternatives even though he cannot do so.

The Arab records may be best characterized as different from the Normal American sample in their pronounced tendency to display modes of thought usually categorized as obsessive-compulsive and "projective" ego defenses. The types of thought disorder listed under "Obsessive and Arbitrary Thinking" in Appendix F, Part II, show a striking degree of prevalence in both the oasis and urban Arab records. On some of these indices, almost half the records manifest at least one occurrence of such thinking. Such thought processes are somewhat more common in the Neurotic American group than among the Schizophrenics. Notably present in the Arab records are evidences of arbitrary, projective thinking of a type found in paranoid clinical cases in which the ego structure is still fairly intact. The Arabs are also more like the abnormal American samples in indications of "Impaired Logic" (Appendix F, Part II).

Patterns of Organization and Expression of Emotions

A quantitative analysis of the symbolic meaning of the content of Rorschach responses, as well as the use of color, movement, shading, and form, permits us to infer a great deal about the nature of emotional structure. Percepts such as animals, humans, plants, and the like, when approached from a psychoanalytic standpoint, are often sufficiently suggestive or are elaborated in such a way as to give clues to underlying attitudes or affective states. Cultural differences in symbolism may be important and must be taken into consideration, but the types of symbols considered are largely common to both Arabs and Americans. By analyzing the content and determinants one can also make certain inferences both as to the nature of the psychic mechanisms used to control inner impulses and as to the nature of reactivity to outer stimuli.

There are various factors involved in such analysis of underlying personality patterns. In our method five aspects are considered: [12]

[12]. The method is described in G. De Vos, "A Quantitative Approach to Affective Symbolism in Rorschach Responses," *Journal of Projective Techniques*, XVI (1952), 134-50.

1. Certain responses throughout a record can give clues to underlying *affective tone*, whether it is disproportionately negative, with undue emphasis on unpleasant content, or sufficiently positive in nature to signify good intrapsychic adjustment. For example, two men can be seen as fighting or can be seen as skating or playing a game.

2. The *attitudinal stance* or "set" taken toward the environment and toward other individuals is revealed in the content of human and animal responses. Content can help assess whether affective relationship to the outside world is structured in active or passive terms or whether it is related to it in terms of dependent needs or in terms of active interests. For example, "a baby chick with its mouth open" would symbolize a receptive dependent orientation, whereas "a lion stalking its prey" is more active and assertive in context. "Two men bowling" is a type of action which is more nearly passive than "two men tugging at a rope."

3. In certain instances the content can be revealing as to the nature of *cathexis* involved in affective drives. Content sometimes helps reveal whether the strongest emotional focus is basically on other persons or on the self. Sometimes a self-orientation is positively toned in an eroticized defensive narcissism. Or, as is true in more malignant instances, narcissism can involve a destructively toned, more primitive conversion of aggressive feelings toward others into excessive bodily preoccupation. Such a negative withdrawal into bodily preoccupation does occur in a minority of the Arabs living in the Casbah but it is almost totally lacking in the oasis.

4. Immaturities in *psychosexual development* are indirectly represented in certain types of responses. In some records one finds content that strongly suggests fixation at, or regression to, earlier stages of psychosexual development. These Rorschach protocols give some clue to the relative amount of interest directed toward pregenital oral, anal, or phallic developmental stages. As will be noted below, the oasis Arabs, for reasons which are not clear, give more "oral" content, whereas the urban group shows a shift toward "anal" and "sexual" responses.

5. Another aspect of personality structure is the nature of the *ego defenses* controlling the emotions. In addition to the content of a response, one can also analyze the formal structure of a response (the nature of the determinants of a percept: its form, movement, color, shading, perspective) and learn much concerning the "socialization" of the ego as a mediator between outer pressures and inner needs. Defenses such as repression, denial, projection, and displacement become apparent.[13]

13. Bruno Klopfer and D. M. Kelley, *The Rorschach Technique* (Yonkers-on-Hudson: World Book Co., 1942), pp. 226-39.

Depending on the nature of the ego controls, anxiety can be experienced as diffuse, readily aroused feeling or it can be bound up in various defensive maneuvers. An individual can be explosive and volatile in his affective responsiveness on the one hand, or incapable of easy, spontaneous expression of emotion on the other. In Rorschach analysis the manner in which the various determinants in a record are combined with the basic form of a percept is used to shed light on ego functions in regard to the emotions. For example, one can note statistically, by analyzing the relation of color to form in the responses, that the urban Arabs are more prone to explosive release of affect, whereas such potential volatility is less in evidence in the rural records.

Affective Tone in Rorschach Content

The great psychic stress experienced by the Arabs in Algiers appears in the significant differences in the affective tone of the urban group when compared with the oasis group, as well as when compared with samples of Normal and maladjusted Americans[14] (Table XIV). Comparison of the total Arab group with the Normal Americans brought out a significant tendency on the part of the Arabs to produce a higher proportion of "anxious" content. The average amount of anxious content, however, did not reach that obtaining for the Neurotic Americans. The oasis and urban groups show no difference from one another in this regard but are markedly different with respect to other types of "unpleasant" content.

The oasis group gives somewhat less "hostile" content and much less "bodily-preoccupation" material. The proportion of all content scored as unpleasant among oasis Arabs is almost identical with that of the Normal Americans. It is significantly lower than that of the urban Arabs, who closely approach the control group of Neurotics. The similarity of the total Arab group to the Normal Americans, on these measures, masks the wide oasis-urban differences.

The data on "positive" (pleasant and constructive) content show the Arabs, generally, to be significantly lower in this dimension than the Normal American sample and even slightly below the Neurotics. As might be expected from the data on unpleasant content, the oasis Arabs give more positive content than the city group, but the difference does not reach the level of statistical significance.

---

14. Appendix H presents the occurrence of percepts in various subcategories of all of these indices. These data show more marked differences between the Arabs and Normal Americans than the percentage categories in Table XIV.

Table XIV

COMPARISON OF INDICES OF AFFECTIVE SYMBOLISM

	Arab						American					
	Oasis		Urban		Total Sample		Normal		Neurotic		Schizophrenic	
N	20		28		64		60		30		30	
	Mean	S.D.	Mean	S.D.	Mean	S.D.	Mean	S.D.	Mean	S.D.	Mean	S.D.
Hostility %	6.8	8.6	10.0	7.9	8.5	7.4	9.4	7.1	11.6	6.9	8.3	7.7
Anxiety %	19.1b	14.2	18.7	14.9	18.3a	14.1	13.8	7.6	22.6a	11.8	23.7a	14.1
Body preoccupation %	2.0b	3.6	10.1b	19.0	5.7	12.4	4.1	4.9	9.3ac	12.8	19.3ac	23.2
Total unpleasant	27.9b	17.5	38.8b	23.8	32.5	22.8	27.3	12.0	43.5ac	13.2	51.3ac	20.0
Dependent %	7.1	7.1	6.1	8.0	7.0	8.3	4.6	4.6	7.0	7.4	6.0	6.8
Positive %	13.2	10.7	9.4	9.2	10.4a	9.4	17.2	10.9	11.9ac	9.8	6.9ac	5.8
Neutral %	49.3	19.6	43.0	37.5	45.3	29.0	49.3	15.6	35.3a	19.2	34.6a	19.1

Categories do not total 100% because of omission of "Miscellaneous."
Key to significance of differences at the .05 level or better (calculated for means only):

a. Compared with Normal American.
b. Comparison between Oasis and Urban Arabs.
c. Comparison between Neurotic and Schizophrenic Americans.

There is a larger amount of dependent affect in the total Arab sample than in the Normal Americans. As is true for the comparable rise in dependency responses in the Neurotic Americans, the difference is too slight, with such small samples, to be certain of its significance. In short, the evidence on the affective tone of responses is consistent with that from the rigidity and maladjustment scales and indicates some definite differences in intrapsychic stress between the oasis and the urban groups.

Attitudes Toward People Expressed in Rorschach Content

The specific nature of human and animal content in the protocols can be used as a key to respondents' underlying attitudes toward people. Aggressive, deprecatory, submissive, anxious, and other attitudes are revealed through the types of animals or humans seen and the action or inaction attributed to them.

In their animal responses the Arabs showed no indication of active or passive orientation through a preference for small, weak animals or large, fierce ones. There were distinct differences among the individuals in this regard, however, as will be brought out in the individual sketches presented in the following chapter. The records do manifest some very distinctive characteristics in the way the Arabs handle human percepts.[15] Rarely do they see human figures involved in some form of movement or engaging in positive activities. When very active movement appears, it is frequently attributed to a foreign or supernatural figure. A high proportion of responses involving humans present them as incomplete or mutilated. The incidence of such responses is higher in the city. They usually involve bodies without heads or legs or, conversely, heads are seen in blot areas where Americans perceive whole figures. In connection with a large number of mutilated figures, specific reference is made to the genital area. Such attention to mutilation and to genital organs is also characteristic of the frequent internal anatomy responses found only in the records of those Arabs who have lived in the city.

The Arab men are not prone to see women among their human percepts. Only 12 of 82 such responses are women. In three of the six female percepts given by the oasis Arabs and those in the intermediate group B, attention is drawn to sexual parts. In only one response is a woman perceived as associated with children. In a single instance, that of an Egyptian woman washing clothes, is there active movement. The general impression one gains is that men do not tend to relate to women as social beings but rather as sexual objects. There are no responses that might possibly be

---

15. See Appendix J.

interpreted as symbolic of a hated-but-feared woman even indirectly representative of feminine authority.

In the oasis there is a tendency to see strange humans or humanoid figures as supernatural in nature, particularly as devils and genii. In the urban group there is only one such reference to "a savage or devil." When fantastic figures are seen by this group, the percepts are described as "monsters," "invisible men," or a "Negro king who is half animal." Quasi-political figures make their appearance: "capitalist," "communist leaders," "enemies," and "Russian dancers." These trends are minor indices of acculturative change.

In all, there are eight references to Negroes. These percepts generally suggest a deprecatory attitude, even though two responses are fairly positive ones of Negro dancers in the role of comic entertainers. As was pointed out earlier, the Algerian population, for Moslems, is rather unusual in its disdainful attitude toward Moslem Negroes. There are a few non-Arab human percepts, but only one is designated as a Frenchman and he is described by an oasis Arab as hiding in a tree. A number of the responses given by the urban group are humans perceived in extremely small segments of the blots. These responses seem to be related to the use of other indications of projective defenses in the same records.

Another peculiarity noted in a few of these percepts is the occurrence of figures attached to each other in some way. They include enemies entwined, two genii bound together, Siamese twins, and women tied to posts. One can speculate that such figures somehow symbolize a helpless dependency on a hated object, from which one cannot break away. In general, the human-like percepts are described as being relatively passive or immobile, whereas those of animals show a greater range of activity. It is clear that living things, which the Arabs perceive as different or distant from themselves, are more readily imbued with activity. The impression one gains from such results is that the Arabs may be affectively reactive, but they do not readily express their inner states nor are they capable of easily entering into rapport with one another. Instead, they are prone to project hostile and threatening attitudes into others and therefore tend to be defensively hostile, rather than spontaneous, in their basic attitudes. The numerous responses depicting bodies with missing parts may be interpreted as reflecting a fear of emasculation not too deeply buried from consciousness.

Certain Inferences Concerning Cathexis

As previously mentioned in connection with a comparison of rigidity and maladjustment, the most striking relevant difference between the urban and oasis Arabs is the correlation of these measures in the urban group. Those who are high on both measures tend also to be those who show the greater amount of bodily preoccupation content, which also distinguishes this group. In most of these cases anal and sexual content is included with other anatomical concerns. The over-all impression given by these records is such that it seems relatively safe to assume that such results have a similar meaning, whether derived from the protocol of an Arab or from that of a maladjusted American.

Records high in anatomical preoccupation are usually produced by individuals having severe hypochondriacal concerns or, in some instances, by individuals having homosexual problems. In the most severe cases, such responses are found in psychotic reactions of various sorts. Moreover, hypochondriasis, as such, is more readily found in borderline paranoid cases, where projective defenses are strongly indicated. Body parts become the focus of hostile destructive projections. In individuals concerned over perverse sexual practices, such as homosexuality, anal percepts or percepts of diseased tissues are forthcoming. In this connection, the increased number of anal responses among the urban Arabs is especially significant.

In the urban group, an alternative pattern to the high anatomical preoccupation of those with high maladjustment and rigidity scores is the significantly high proportion of percepts with hostile implications found in the records of those with low scores on both the rigidity and maladjustment measures. A great number of these percepts are of a type which sees bodies with parts missing or otherwise distorted or multilated. This sort of response is usually found in individuals with sadomasochistic concerns or those preoccupied with castration fears. Such responses are significantly more prevalent among the Arabs than in the Normal American sample. Responses indicative of tension over the expression of hostile impulses [16] are significantly more common in the urban Arab group than in the oasis group, but such responses appear in one out of six of the American records as well.

Many of the sadomasochistic responses fit the type which

---

16. Paul Kane, on the basis of a study of American prisoners, concludes that hostility is part of a defensive reaction to a more basic feeling of inadequacy. This sort of individual does not necessarily recognize his own behavior as hostile but tends to deny it and project such feeling into others. See Kane, "Availability of Hostile Fantasy Related to Overt Behavior," *Illinois Medical Journal*, III (1957), No. 3.

Fisher and Cleveland describe as "permeable."[17] These responses suggest some penetration into an object through an opening or by violence. Also soft, amorphous substances, such as smoke or clouds, are high in "penetrability." Such penetration responses, either in connection with anatomical content or in more indirect symbols, suggest that some of the Arabs have an unconscious fear of penetration, in passive homosexuality. Such fear is probably being warded off, as unacceptable to the adult ego, through hypochondriacal displacement and particularly through the projection of hostility into others. Such hostility would be most apt to be projected into authority figures toward whose power the Arabs feel vulnerable, such as the French. We note that on Fisher's and Cleveland's "Penetration Score" the urban Arabs score significantly higher (2.8) than the oasis group (2.1; P = .05). The former are also significantly higher in amount of hostile anxiety reflected in their Rorschachs.

Sadomasochistic preoccupations are in evidence in about half of the urban Arabs. The degree to which such concerns are disruptive of general ego functioning must be determined from the perspective of an analysis of the whole record. In some cases to be presented in the next chapter, there is some assessment of how such orientations are integrated into the total personality.

In comparing the relationship of hostile and bodily preoccupation responses with supernatural beliefs, a very striking relationship appears. The use of Koranic charms is found to be inversely related, in a very significant fashion, to such Rorschach content.[18] For the entire group, there is but a single case of an individual who both gives such responses and uses charms. This suggests that a culturally approved concern with this magical practice is, in some measure, an alternative to more internalized, intrapsychic methods of handling aggression. The increased stress apparent in the Rorschachs of the urbanized Arabs is concomitant with a drop in the use of such beliefs.[19] Those in the

---

17. The recent work of S. Fisher and S. E. Cleveland with the relation of "soft" and "hard"· or "permeable" and "impermeable" Rorschach content to body image and psychosomatic involvement is a most promising approach. See their "Behavior and Unconscious Fantasies of Patients with Rheumatoid Arthritis," *Psychosomatic Medicine*, XVI (1954), 327-33; also "Body-Image Boundaries and Styles of Life," *Journal of Abnormal and Social Psychology*, LII (1956), 373-79.

18. See Chapter X.

19. The study of flying personnel under stress reported by L. Alexander and A. F. Ax also demonstrates a significant increase in what we have categorized as hostile symbolism concerned with mutilation and body anatomy in those individuals showing psychic breakdown under stress of continual air raids over Germany. "Rorschach Studies in Combat Flying Personnel," in P. Hoch and J. Zubin (eds.), *Relation of Psychological Tests to Psychiatry*, (New York: Grune & Stratton, Inc., 1951), pp. 219-44.

Casbah who maintain them, albeit with a tendency to be fairly high in rigidity, do not show either of the alternative indicators of intrapsychic stress.

The relation of hostile content to externalized projection was supported in part by comparing belief in genii with belief in charms. As indicated, only one Arab with a strong belief in charms gave Rorschach responses indicative of hostility and none gave bodily preoccupation responses. But of the ten individuals who had a strong belief in genii and who did not believe strongly in charms, four had markedly high scores on hostile affect. In these instances, strong belief in genii may be inferred to be related to a readiness to project hostility into human or humanoid beings.

Content As Related to Psychosexual Stages of Development[20]

In spite of a tendency to give fewer responses in most affective subcategories, the oasis Arabs give significantly more oral responses than the urban group. This difference exists in hostile oral responses, usually represented by biting, aggressive animals; in positive oral responses, such as food or food preparation seen in a positive affective light; and a miscellany of responses suggesting oral concerns in an indirect fashion, as, for example, unusual attention paid to the mouths of animals or humans, food utensils, and the like. Neither group produces dependent oral responses, such as sucking or licking animals (one oral-dependent record did appear in the intermediate contact group, B).

The reason for the lower number of oral responses in the urban group is not clear. There is concern with food production in the oasis, since it is an agricultural community; but, at best, such an explanation cannot account for the greater number of specifically hostile oral responses in the oasis. A highly conjectural possibility is that those who remain in the oasis may have somewhat stronger primary ties to maternal figures. While the amount of oral content is high in the oasis, the total Algerian material is not so characterized. The Arabs show about the same amount of most types of oral content as the Normal American sample.

A few of the urban Arabs give anal and sexual content in the test. Six city Arabs gave two or more such responses, while no oasis Arab did so. Especially when the thinking processes and other subsidiary data are also considered, some of these and other individuals show a general regression to, or fixation at, what is described in psychoanalytic terms as the "anal" stage. Whereas

---

20. See Appendix H for relevant data.

it is doubtful that every case of severe castration threat is necessarily related to anal-sexual preoccupation, many of the records give strong indication of retreat from genital sexuality, with a great deal of castration threat in evidence. Moreover, it is interesting that the Arabs are significantly higher than the Americans in the type of response called "anxiety gloom," a category for scoring the respondent's concern with dead or dying things and suggesting a depressive, dysphoric mood. In American records, such responses are found quite often among men concerned with their potency as well as with aging generally.

The data suggest that fear of impotence is not rare among the Arabs, in spite of their polygyny and cultural norms overtly expressive of high virility among men. It might be argued that if the sexual expectations from men are great, the fear of impotence would be commensurately great. While this is probably true, the Arabs' mental preoccupation with sex, as well as such hypersexual activity as does occur, is commonly interpreted, psychoanalytically, as stemming from deep-seated fear of impotence. The fear of retreating into passive homosexuality is one of the dangers besetting an individual who retreats from genital masculinity in the face of subconscious castration threat.

Ego Defenses Used in Controlling Emotions

Other aspects of Rorschach responses which provide evidence about personality are the type of reaction to the color in some blots, the use of shading or tones of grey, and the perception of three-dimensional "vista" in the blots. These determinants are considered in conjunction with the role of form and movement in the responses.[21] The generally low response total and the high incidence of responses which are determined solely by form must be taken as the frame of reference within which the other determinants are analyzed. The over-all rigidity, thus revealed, characterizes many of the records and influences the interpretation of the occurrence of other determinants.

We note first that the proportion of Arab responses involving human movement is significantly lower than that of the Normal American group but the percentage of color responses is about the same. The ratio of movement to color responses is thus

---

21. See Appendix K, which varies somewhat from the usual presentation of the statistics on Rorschach determinants. The table gives both the mean frequency of the determinants and the proportion of all responses which they constitute. It also indicates the proportion of the color responses which are form-dominated or color-dominated and whether they are accurate as to form. Data from both Arab and American groups are included.

heavily weighted in an extratensive direction by the relative lack of M. The conclusion would be that the Arabs are prone to be reactive to outer stimuli rather than to avoid such influences. In addition, there is a significantly higher proportion of shading responses among the Arabs than in the American group, which supports the above conclusion. In some individual cases where shading predominates, however, it indicates a more passive attitude toward environmental stimuli than the active one implied by color. Vista responses in some records suggest a tendency toward personal isolation as a defense against reactivity to the environment, but to a degree no greater than that in the American records.

Differences between oasis and urban Arabs suggest some acculturative shifts in the nature of the controls exercised over emotional reactions.[22] There is some tendency for the city group to show less over-all constriction (lower F%) and a somewhat greater loosening of outer controls as evidenced in an increase in the proportion of poorly controlled color responses. Similarly, there is a significant increase in shading responses, with poorly controlled shading showing a greater increase than the more controlled responses. This trend toward less controlled shading responses is consistent with that of the color responses but it does not reach the level of statistical significance.

Whereas the urban Arabs differ from the oasis group in the proportion of uncontrolled color responses, they do not differ much from the Normal American group in this respect. They do show, however, markedly fewer well-modulated color responses (FC+). Both in the lack of movement as a balance against color and in the lack of well-modulated color, one finds indications of less emotional control than among Normal Americans.

In spite of the lower F% in the urban group, there is no striking difference from the oasis Arabs in the use of human movement, which is quite low in both. Animal movement, as scored by Klopfer's system, shows no difference between the groups. There is, however, an almost fivefold increase in the number of inanimate movement responses in the urban sample. In many respects these responses are indicative of internal tension, especially when they occur in such content as "explosions."

---

22. The sixteen Arabs who are intermediate between the oasis and urban groups in amount of acculturative contact are considered in the analysis of the Arabs, as a whole, but were not analyzed separately. The marginality of this group, noted in Chapter V, is apparent in their Rorschach protocols.

Nine of them had gone back to the oasis from the city and it is probable that there is psychological selectivity in this return movement. They are markedly higher than either of the other groups in R, F%, and Dd%, and are much lower in C than either.

It seems safe to generalize that, compared to the oasis group, the urban Arabs show definite tendencies toward more poorly controlled responsiveness to outer stimuli, combined with a greater conscious experience of inner feelings of anxiety and tension. Whereas such tendencies can be easily related to observable emotional outbursts which occur in both groups, a problem still remains with regard to how such behavior is held in check in situations where it might produce reprisal. In some cases high rigidity is perhaps a defense against the unsanctioned display of affectivity, perhaps leading to retribution. In other cases anxiety and feelings of potential threat from the environment may help individuals to control their reactive behavior. This latter, more open, affective pattern seems to occur more frequently in the urban group. Whatever the conscious controls, the potential for open emotional expression is there. When the individual feels safe from reprisal, his inner tensions can seek release. When openly emotional behavior does occur, it is usually a momentary display. There is insufficient control of the potentially reactive affectivity to utilize it in the accomplishment of long-range goals.

As for the sort of behavior one might expect with this labile emotionality, the content of the color responses is not characteristically violent or negative in tone. The many flowers and colorful trees do not suggest hostile reactivity. It is the distorted and dismembered human figures which indicate that hostilely perceived outside stimuli will be violently reacted to when it is felt safe to do so. The Arab is also capable of strong emotional expressions of a positive sort when moved by friendly feelings. Distrust of others, however, is a frequent barrier to such responsiveness.

Impression Gained from the Records of Three Arab Women

Three Arab women were tested by Dr. Agnes Miner through an interpreter. These few records offer no real basis for generalization but certain similar characteristics in them are interesting enough to bear some comment.[23] Two of the three records show very high rigidity scores and the maladjustment scores are also high due to a variety of factors essentially like those of the men. In the amount of positive affective symbolism, all three women are higher than most of the men. Two of the three records have more than the male average for dependent and submissive content. Combining positive and dependent affect in each of the three cases, we find 72 per cent, 40 per cent, and 44 per cent of

---

23. See Appendix L for the tabulation of determinants.

their responses so characterized. There is not a single bodily preoccupation response nor any hostile response.

Affectively, these women could be classified as content within the narrow scope of their world. There is emphasis in their records on architectural responses (arches and mosques), on flowers and trees and, for two of the women, on ornaments and pretty clothes. The other woman stereotypically sees practically nothing but fruit trees or flowers. Human content is almost lacking in these records, with only one movement response given to a tiny detail area. The color area, in contrast, is relatively free and positively used, albeit with some insufficiency of control. The one record with thirty-one responses shows very adequate use of intellectual functions.

These results, briefly considered, support the anthropologist's impression of lack of dissatisfaction among the Arab women over their subordinate lot in life and of their rather easygoing adjustment, sometimes in terms of over-all stereotypic and rigid behavior, but essentially without much inner turmoil. There is, in these three cases at least, no suggestion of suppressed or diffuse hostile feelings. Field observations also characterize the women as expressing affect more freely than the men.

It may be speculated that the men, in not assuming much conscience on the part of women, take an additional burden on themselves. The expectations directed toward a woman are not so great. She is not forced into a role full of stress and tension. The man, on the other hand, is much more subject to internal tension. While growing up he must overcome severe feelings of threat from an aggressively perceived father.

Some Observations on the Cross-cultural Use of Rorschachs

The question may arise as to whether the so-called indices of thought disorder and emotional control are related to psychopathology in the Arabs. Obviously the Arabs function adequately in their society, but it is still meaningful to inquire whether the Arab Rorschachs imply the same things about the nature of Arab personality structure as would similar evidence from Americans.

The collaborating psychologist ventures the opinion that the internal consistency of the Arab evidence points to the conclusion that the prevalent personality mechanisms among Arabs are related to syndromes recognized by psychologists and psychiatrists among Americans. The patterning of Arab personality is understandable in these familiar terms.

It might be argued that certain of the statistically significant differences in Rorschach responses between Arabs and Americans have more to do with culturally conditioned differences in

Figure 10. Women Openly Express Their Emotions

perception and less to do with personality vectors inferred on the basis of the usual assumptions in Rorschach interpretation. The importance of such conditioning is suggested by the fact that it is human movement responses that are most lacking among the Arabs. Cloaked humans may not be as easily discernible as are humans whose limbs are emphasized by Western dress. Moreover, the human form receives little representation in Arab art.

Likewise, as noted earlier, the large number of vista responses, some of them reaching popular levels for the group, may be related to the habit of scanning the desert horizon. The figures in hiding and the emphasis on trees, with specific attention paid to the relative denseness of the leaves, may also reflect patterns of oasis life. The culture, therefore, may well influence the absolute number of these responses found in the group as a whole. Granting some such influence, one questions if the relative prevalence of these responses in certain individuals in comparison with others does not still indicate interpretable personality differences. In addition, certain ways of handling the blots, even though they be fairly common, may still have interpretable significance for the group as a whole, although one must be wary of the cultural factors involved.

The Arabs give many animal responses, but animals are no more portrayed in art than are humans. There is likewise no apparent reason for the human head to be seen more readily than the entire body on Card III. Seeing only the human head suggests constriction of a severe sort, substantiated by other accompanying signs. The tendency to see genii and afreet or, if humans are seen, to see them in antagonistic situations still has a specific psychological significance. All of these things are suggestive of difficulties in human rapport.

Some determinants, such as the color responses, were occasionally misleading unless offset by specific knowledge of Arab culture and general modes of expected behavior. In the beginning, when inferences were made from color responses, the Rorschach analyst rather consistently tended to underrate the Arabs on their affective reactivity as compared to behavioral expression of emotion observed in the field. The color responses did not suggest to the analyst the ebullient, almost histrionic outbursts of affect that were reported. Comparable American records would imply a more controlled display of emotion. It became apparent that cultural sanctions about affective display were involved. The fact that, among the Arabs under some circumstances, there is less check on sudden, relatively uncontrolled expression of aggressive feelings was important to the interpretation.

The amount of shading in some of the records was at first interpreted as indicative of a proneness to anxiety that would tend to inhibit affective display and make the individual outwardly compliant. While this characterization is generally accurate, it does not suggest the emotionality which the Arabs sometimes display.

Other interpretations held up well. For example, the amount of reversal of figure and ground in the records, in the form of "space responses," tied in best with what could be interpreted as antagonistic, aggressive, oppositional behavior. In two such instances of individuals with a large number of space responses, the men were found to be active in anti-French political movements, which gave them an outlet for their oppositional feelings.

The case analyses given in the next chapter illustrate how Rorschach data can contribute to an integrated picture of personalities in change, even when applied to individuals outside the context of Western culture. Finally, the significant relationships which were found between certain Rorschach results and cultural beliefs will give rather conclusive proof of the validity of the use of the Rorschach test to differentiate, meaningfully, among Arabs with regard to their personalities.

CHAPTER IX

SOME INDIVIDUAL PATTERNS OF ADJUSTMENT

Having presented a frame of reference derived from a general consideration of the projective materials, we turn to some specific cases illustrative of personality variation.[1] They fall into two categories. The first six individuals were selected by the anthropologist, from among the people best known to him, as representing varieties of acculturation. They vary from a youth who seeks to identify with the French to a member of the nationalist underground movement. Also included is the Islamized young man of French extraction, who was not in the Arab sample but whose Rorschach protocol was much like those of the Arabs.

The second group of five cases was chosen either because they were deviants in the community or because their Rorschach protocols presented unusual characteristics or both. They range from psychotics to one man whose spontaneous, happy character stands out from the others.

Methodologically, these case studies initiated the collaborative effort of the authors. Each case was prepared independently on the basis of field observation and the Rorschach protocol. Then the two appraisals were brought together. In some instances (Nos. 1, 2, 9, 25), personality estimates had been written in the field, before the Rorschach test was administered. The other cases were worked up by the anthropologist from field notes and memory. As all that he knew about Rorschach interpretation was learned after the fieldwork and no reference was made to the protocols in preparing the field observational sketches, his appraisal may be considered to be independent of the test results.

The psychologist, at this stage, knew little or nothing about Arab culture or personality and had no knowledge of the individuals concerned. In the collaboration, the Rorschach sketch was presented first and then points of convergence or disagreement with the field observations were brought out. All of the available material was then used, as in the clinical use of the Rorschach, to bring understanding to the apparent discrepancies. Through this process, the psychologist gained progressive understanding of Arab personality and its particular reflection in the protocols.

---

1. The names are fictitious and some personal histories have been altered in minor ways so as to protect identity.

Some limitations found in the blind, cross-cultural use of the test have been commented upon. The ensuing cases present the integrated pictures of the individuals, with remarks as to the problems involved in their derivation.

A. PATTERNS OF ACCULTURATIVE ADJUSTMENT

Case No. 1: A Young Man Who Wants to Be Like the French

Ali once spent four months in France as a personal servant to a Frenchman and we see him as a teen-aged, oasis youth who intensely desires to identify with the French way of life. He uses a mixture of European and Arab dress and is vain about his wristwatch, a certain mark of French contact. He wears a fez like an Arab urbanite and swears that he will never wear the more rural turban. His command of French is fair and, in general, he shows a surprising degree of superficial assimilation for one who has spent so little time outside the oasis. Apart from his sojourn in France, he has lived only two months in Algiers with his uncles. Beneath the clothes and speech, however, we find a core of cultural belief which is characteristically like that of the unacculturated oasis Arabs.

Ali's father worked for many years in Algiers before marrying and returning to Sidi Khaled, where he operates a store. While in the city, he learned very little French, but he did learn to respect the position of the French. He saw to it that Ali secured all the education possible at the French school in the oasis. While the father was not generally punitive towards the boy, he did initially force Ali to attend school. These six years of training stand in contrast to Ali's two years of Koranic schooling.

Ali is the youngest of the three children his mother bore. His elder brother is now living in France and his sister is married. After his mother died, his father married two women with whom he now lives. Ali has a half brother and two half sisters from these unions. His relations with his stepmothers apparently have been good, but they are local women and he tends to deprecate some of their practices, such as tattooing, which his mother did not follow.

Ali is a constant braggard. He expresses his supposed superiority both verbally and actively in his arrogant behavior toward others, even when they are his seniors. Occasionally he does this even with his father but never with non-Arabs or Ahmed (Case No. 2) who is his hero. In other relationships, however, his arrogance was so marked that the anthropologist could not employ him as an interpreter. He was sometimes unable to live up to his boasts of superior ability, as when he claimed he was a good cook and sought such employment. When given the opportunity to cook for the anthropologist, Ali had to bring the cooked food from his own home, where his stepmother had actually prepared it!

This sort of deceit, with its concomitant suspicion of others, is not unusual among the Arabs, but Ali is particularly marked by it. He is the only person who saw the possiblity of using the anthropologist's wire-recorder as a device to discover what people said about him in his absence. In the same vein, he maintains that, were he married, he would test his wife's fidelity by pretending to leave the house and observing what happened when she thought him gone.

There are marked compulsive traits in his behavior, particularly with respect to keeping himself and his clothes clean. Whenever there is a possibility of his outer robe becoming soiled, he removes it, as he is unusually meticulous in his dress. While he was a servant, Ali was trustworthy but lazy, avoiding any exertion as being beneath him.

While generally voluble, Ali is somewhat restrained in talking about sexual matters. There are some strong indications that he may have been the active partner in sodomy with his half brother, three years his junior. This brother is known to have been severely beaten by the father for having had such relations with other young men. The two brothers now have separate sleeping rooms, in spite of crowded living conditions in the father's house.

Ali's Rorschach protocol is characterized most readily as an obsessive-compulsive one in an individual of not much more than average intelligence. He demonstrates strong achievement push without much indication of real ability, emphasizing his somewhat shallow nature. Of 45 responses only one is a whole response. Responses to rare details constitute 22 per cent of the total. Another 9 per cent are given to the smallest of the more common areas used on the cards. He is extremely constrictive, both in the use of his intellect in any but a stereotyped manner and in the repression of inner awareness, but he shows less constriction in an extraversive direction, producing three color-dominant responses. He attempts to approach tasks in a rote manner, not integrating but enumerating. He counts off his percepts with exaggerated exactness, carefully noting "two rats," "two silkworms," "two bats," "two cocks," and so on. Since the symmetrical nature of the blots allows for two of each percept, this type of response is found only in compulsively organized individuals. The content reveals very little symbolic material. There is no human or animal movement. The only two percepts that may involve force in any way are "falling snow" and "two killed rabbits fastened to a tree trunk." The latter response suggests some passive fear of mutilation. Most of his animals are small rodents or burrowing creatures, suggesting a rather feckless self-image underlying his exterior braggadocio. A number of Ali's responses, consisting of small faces and protrusions such as sticks, legs, and the like, are scored as indicative of obsessive anxiety. Nothing else is noteworthy in the record.

The ego controls are basically sound and the thinking processes show nothing exceptional aside from the compulsive structuring of thinking generally. The rigidity and maladjustment scores are close to the means for the entire group. He gives a total of four Arab popular responses in addition to four populars found in both Western and Arab records. These indicate perceptions fundamentally in conformity with the Arab group.

The general impression one gains of Ali is that his pro-French attitude is derived initially from his father's positive orientation toward the French and the fact that his mother represented the French-Arab cultural mixture of Algiers, in contrast to the rural Arab attributes of his stepmothers. He has been able to meet his achievement needs, in the face of his somewhat limited abilities, by mild deceit and compulsive striving to conform to the external symbols of French identity. By application to his studies in the French school, by attention to French standards of cleanliness and speech, by attaching himself to the highly acculturated Ahmed, and by securing a position with a Frenchman, he has been able to outstrip even his father. There may be some basic hostility to his father, but Ali's extremely superior air probably also reflects his adolescence.

Case No. 2: A Man Who Can Live In Two Worlds

Tall and somewhat more heavy-set than the average Arab, Ahmed is a handsome man in his late thirties. His white turban and *gandoura* are scrupulously clean, his nails well-tended and his face close-shaven every Friday. He lives in a house adjacent to that of his parents. His father had two wives in polygynous marriage. Ahmed's mother was the second wife and he is the youngest of her children. Ahmed has had but one wife, and only six of their children are still alive. His household, however, also includes two nephews and a male servant who sleeps in the courtyard.

One wife is all he desires, he says, for he gets along well with her and has no liking for the inevitable quarreling which polygyny produces. Primarily, though, Ahmed does not want the additional children another marriage would entail. He has no daughters and concedes that a girl would be desirable. His attitude toward women generally is conservative. He contends that he has confidence in their morality but he is very restrictive concerning the movements of his wife, not even permitting her to visit his garden.

Ahmed's father worked a year in Algiers, but he devoted most of his life to his gardens in Sidi Khaled and to the teahouse which he established in the village. For brief periods he also held a minor official position to which he was appointed by the French. His contact with the French led him to enter Ahmed in the local French school. The boy was a bright scholar, completing six years' training with distinction. In addition, Ahmed had a year's Koranic training from which he derived maximal benefit. Not only did he memorize a quarter of the Koran, but he became remarkably literate in Arabic.

In his youth Ahmed went to France, where he worked for two years in a factory. While there he dressed as a Frenchman but, on returning to the oasis, he assumed Arab clothes except for sweater, shirt, socks, and bedroom slippers, which are not uncommon "street wear." His wristwatch remains the most obvious symbol of French contact. The effects of his acculturation are, however, much more marked than this.

He has been an outstanding innovator in the community. Both economically and politically he has benefited from his dual cultural role. In addition to managing his large garden, irrigated with water from a gasoline-driven pump, he runs the teahouse which his father started, operates a trucking service, and has served as a member of the elected *djema'a*. He seems to be quite conscious of his bicultural role and aware of its advantages and disadvantages in different situations.

Ahmed's attitude of poise and composure, toward both French and Arabs, is so controlled that he never appears entirely relaxed. The only real indication of inner strain is his habit of cracking his knuckles. Apparently a very pliant individual, he accepts suggestions with no show of insecurity or threat. But, even in a situation of mutual exchange of confidences, he is careful never to express hostility. He is not prudish and will speak freely on any topic other than his wife and his own feelings.

In spite of his close association with the anthropologist and his readiness to converse, Ahmed never invited him to his home, although other Arabs were not as reserved or defensive in this regard. Much contact took place at Ahmed's teahouse, where his generosity toward others was often apparent. In the affective area he is generally reserved, except with his youngest son who is three but still has a wetnurse, although he is beyond the normal time for weaning. The boy is frequently brought to the teahouse where Ahmed holds him on his knee and plies him with sweets.

Ahmed shows himself to be quite reactive to sensory stimulation. He loves his gardens and will put rose petals in his nostrils to savor them long and fully. In this sensitivity he is not unique among the perfume-loving Arabs. But he is unusual in that, during the hot, thirsty days of Ramadan, he frequently bathes in his garden pool and will gargle the fresh, cool water. In so doing, he remains within the letter of the religious proscriptions, but he maximizes his comfort. His supernatural beliefs adhere to Islamic dogma, but he does not hold the elaborate beliefs about dream interpretation, the evil eye, and genii which characterize others in the oasis.

Although the Rorschach picture of Ahmed is generally in accord with the behavioral impression, it also reveals some surprising internal stresses. He is a flexible (rigidity score 32), extratensively oriented person with eight color responses out of a total of 45 responses (five of them form-dominated). He shows extremely good outer control and can be pleasantly compliant whenever necessary. The nature of the emphasis on shading reinforces this picture. Positive affect is expressed in eight of his responses with a quantitative percentage of 15, close to the mean for the American group. Symbolically, these responses show an esthetic approach emphasizing clothing and ornamentation as well as the beauty of nature.

A strong achievement orientation is indicated by the high response total and the emphasis on whole responses, which is found throughout the record including the more difficult color cards. As is true for the Arabs generally, he is not systematic or methodical but shows his intelligence best when stimulated affectively in a positive way. What seems lacking, somehow, is a mature inner life. His inner satisfaction still seems basically bound to childish or infantile motives, but these wishes seem to be strongly held back and repressed. The Rorschach suggests, therefore, that Ahmed's capacity to relate well socially does not carry over into deeper, more meaningful responsiveness as far as inner attitudes are concerned. In his deeper relationships he may have no inner peace. There are strong sadomasochist tendencies related to an unresolved authority threat. His attention to anality is suggestive of strong latent homosexual submissiveness. In no quantitative score, however, does he suggest strong maladjustment, remaining within the low range.

The nature of his human content and an obsessive preoccupation with butterflies suffering various forms of destruction give the record an unhappy tone, full of concern with sadomasochistic mutilation, until his mood shifts to a pleasurable one on the last three cards. Card I starts with depressive content, "An animal carcass." Also seen is a person without a head. There is some preoccupation with the bones of the legs protruding without any feet. He decides they must be made of stone because, if they were flesh, they would bloat up and rot. On Card III the usual humans are perceived as skeletons. On Card IV he produces his only human movement. On the tower of a mosque seen at a distance are two marabouts, described as arguing. Card VII is a poorly perceived body of a person. The center of Card IX is a woman dressed in a long gown revealing the form of her breasts.

A theme of butterfly percepts is interesting to follow from card to card, for Ahmed sees butterflies on almost every card. They are not seen perceveratively, but rather in a different context and expressing different underlying affect from card to card. He unconsciously uses the butterfly percept to express symbolically various fears and pleasures. One has the impression that he believes himself to be like a butterfly, basically rather soft and defenseless. To defend himself he has developed firm outer controls. His harder, outer social roles are represented by such shelled animals as snails and tortoises. On Card II the butterfly makes its first appearance "ready to eat," lighting on a thumb. The remains of the butterfly are found "torn in several pieces" on Card III. On Card IV there is the stomach of a butterfly that has been "burned by a candle." On Card V a butterfly appears without elaboration and carries no special meaning. Only the head of a butterfly appears on Card VI, followed by the mouth of a grasshopper. The butterfly has big wings on Card VII. Under the stimulation of color on Card VIII two butterflies are seen stuck together by their "back ends," clinging to a tree and copulating "to make little ones." The butterfly again appears on Card IX but in a neutral tone. On Card X there are two butterflies. One response is the "back end" of a butterfly and the other a butterfly in pretty colors.

This preoccupation with oral, anal, and genital sexuality centering around butterflies suggests a time of experience in childhood or youth when Ahmed felt weak and vulnerable but nevertheless sought gratification as a favored and beloved child. He was probably considered attractive and was indulged. Later in life, he has developed more mature outer controls and no longer has resorted to the earlier passive techniques of gaining attention and indulgence. But passive narcissistic feelings, as well as a feeling vulnerability to attack because of his passivity, remain as strong but hidden, currents underneath the surface poise and maturity.

It is noteworthy how his particular personality development suits him for a bicultural role. In addition to his obvious intelligence, his poise, flexibility, and underlying "permeability" to others in social situations make him easily acceptable. It is doubtful that many individuals can maintain such a delicate balance between the French and Arabs without arousing animosity in one or the other, or even both groups.

Case No. 35: A Successful Business Man

Rachid exemplifies an Arab who seeks to achieve business and social success in terms of modern industrial society without giving up his strong identity as an Arab. He lives within Moslem family and marital ethics but in a manner which, by Western standards, emphasizes their virtues rather than their deficiencies.

He is a well-nourished, strong-looking, middle-aged man. Energetic, intelligent, and sociable, he uses these characteristics to further his business success and to establish and maintain an extended family in Algiers. He lives in an apartment in a mixed Arab-French quarter of the city. His wife is his father's brother's daughter, the preferred Arab match. There are two other families closely related to him by similar marriages in the same apartment house and Rachid thinks of the whole group as "his" household. Despite their separate apartments, their lives are closely intertwined, particularly as the women can visit one another without leaving the building.

Rachid speaks very good French, dresses meticulously in Western clothes, owns a car, and refers to himself as an "industrialist." Actually, he runs a small leather-goods shop, associated with which is a leather-working establishment in which he employs three young men.

Like most Arabs, he is antagonistic to French domination, but he does not engage actively in politics. Normally a calm person, only unusual emotional strain may cause him to lose his equanimity. Such a situation was produced when all six children in the extended family had whooping cough and one died. Rachid, who buried the child, was much more upset over the death than the child's own father. The following day he burst into a tirade against economic conditions in Algeria. While these conditions were not directly related to the child's death, they were rationally couched criticisms against the lack of public health care provided by the French. On other occasions, Rachid is less rational in attributing to French domination the continuation of Arab customs of which he disapproves, such as the seclusion of women.

His supernatural beliefs conform to Koranic dogma, but he has little belief in, or concern about, most of the peripheral areas of magic and prognostication. He interprets "seizures by genii" in Western terms. In marked contrast is his firm belief in the power of a sorceress to make a man impotent with all but one woman. He is full of detailed information about such practices.

Rachid's father, a slipper-maker in the oasis, married three women. He divorced his first wife because all her children died in infancy. Then he married again and Rachid was the first child. Later he took a younger wife in polygynous marriage. As Rachid's mother grew older, she lost her place in her husband's bed but remained in his household.

As a child, Rachid had six years' training in the local French school and five years' Koranic schooling. Then he came to Algiers to work for relatives and later went to France as a worker. Upon his return to Algiers, he was an unskilled laborer until he was able to start his own leather-goods business. Married in his late twenties, he has had seven children, only three still alive. But these three suffice. In his struggle for economic security, he is one of the few Arabs in the sample who use contraceptives. His belief that money is the most important thing in life is unequivocal.

His father and mother journey annually to Algiers to stay with him and to escape the desert heat in summer. On their last trip to Algiers his mother remained when his father returned to the oasis. Toward his father Rachid is respectful and deferential. Since there is a tradition against smoking in the family, he will hide and snuff out a cigarette in his pocket rather than have his father find him smoking. The father is proud of his son's success, which has certainly helped Rachid's mother's position in the family.

The psychological picture presented by Rachid is fully in keeping with the overt picture and substantiates the strong identification with a paternal family role and strong achievement orientation. It also suggests, however, a propensity to use projective defences, to connect and integrate thoughts in an arbitrary manner, and to feel vulnerable and threatened by potential dangers from outside. He also shows a somewhat volatile, affective potential possibly related to the type of emotional outburst described by the anthropologist. In general, however, introversive propensities are much more in the foreground on the Rorschach. He also shows a greater degree of personal flexibility than most Arabs (rigidity score of 25) and a stronger achievement orientation, albeit in pragmatic terms ($D\% = 76$) rather than global ($W\% = 18$). This high $D\%$ contrasts with the Arab mean of 51.

There is no doubt, when we approach the material from the standpoint of intellectual functioning, that Rachid is of superior intellectual caliber. In his 26 Rorschach responses he does not emphasize inclusive whole responses. Nevertheless, he attempts to organize and elaborate his highly imaginative responses to a great extent. Although well defined in accuracy, their arbitrary and fanciful nature is sometimes removed from realistic concerns, especially in respect to human percepts. He symbolizes a great deal so that the pressure of various affective promptings are very much in evidence. Considerable potential inner difficulty, which must be overcome in maintaining outer equilibrium, is also apparent in these responses.

The record is full of symbolic expression of a highly fabulized nature. Included are eleven responses with human or humanoid content, five of them having movement as a determinant. This amount of human content with movement is in sharp contrast to the Arab records as a whole although fabulization of a similar nature in man-movement responses is found in other records. Many are original in nature, some even containing a certain bizarre quality. For example, on Card II he sees, "Two monsters arguing. They're connected by their hands. Their hands are tied together." "The body is like a monster and the head isn't human. The body's belted...." On Card III he sees two poor, emaciated figures arguing either about something they both want or about which direction they should take "because of the blood between and in back of them." "The blood shows they're in danger in front and behind; perhaps robbers." On Card IV he sees the head of a bearded Negro king whose body is that of an animal with a tail; also on this card, "Someone hiding in the shadow, with a big nose and beard." He sees on Card V "A person with his head in the ground." On Card VI there are "Two veiled women. Their hands are tied to a lamp-post. You could say they look like ghosts arguing." On Card VII he describes "the body of a person with a belt. It's a body without head or legs." He sees on Card X "A person coming down from the sky with very long wings." At the inquiry, "It's coming down... like a parachutist, with two arms and two wings, which don't look much like wings." He also sees on Card X "Two Alpinists... touching hands."

These responses are overdetermined by affect in a number of ways. Argumentation appears in three of them. Being tied together or touching appears in another three. Parts of bodies or bodies in unusual positions are seen. He pays special attention, in these responses, to the "belted" nature of bodies. The figures are covered with coats or hair, and a bearded face appears out of the shadow. One animal percept, on Card VII, involves animals "rearing back their heads as though to protect themselves." The humans on Card III not only argue about dividing some gain, but they are afraid, arguing about which way to go to avoid the danger symbolized by blood. This content suggests a basic suspicious, defensive attitude at the present time, with a readiness to project hostility and feel threatened from the outside. The symbolic use of blood on Card III is the only use of bright color in the record. As is general for the Arabs, Rachid produces vista responses as well as demonstrating interest in the shading aspects of the cards. His 5 FM and 3 Fm show, as in the case of his 5 M, suggestions of fabulization, but to a lesser degree.

His attitude to coverings and containers causes him to produce the highest score of the Arab group on Fisher's Barrier Score, a scale that correlated highly with achievement drive in research with American subjects. In Rachid's case, it is coupled with a high "penetration" score, suggesting a vulnerability to authority and a capacity to assume compliant roles.

The fabulized nature of his responses does suggest a tendency to paranoia-like defenses, despite his more rational capacities. His belief in the evil eye and in the ability of a sorceress to inflict impotence contrasts with his rejection of allied Arab supernatural beliefs in favor of Western concepts. The retention of some of the beliefs may come from very personal feelings in these areas, so that these beliefs resist change in the face of a generally fairly rational attitude. Also his blaming the French for the Arab practice of secluding women may stem from some personal feelings of ambivalence about this custom.

His assumption of a paternal role and establishing himself as a family head, with other relatives dependent on him, provide him with an outward show of success as a man. The anthropologist notes that, at one time when Rachid was talking about his mother, he made a "Freudian" slip and called her his "wife." His Rorschach response of the Negro king with the body and tail of an animal and his percept of the bearded patriarch hiding in the shadow suggest a lack of complete security in this identity as a successful male. He feels himself prone to attack and destruction. He still idolizes the father but has not resolved his susceptibility to attack from power and authority, first represented by his father. The figures tied together represent a fear of submission and restriction. He sees "two sheep, killed and hung up...on a tree" on Card X; "a hide cut in two" (Card V); "legs without feet" (Card V); and "a body without head or legs" (Card VII). Concern over potency is suggested by the lamp (Card II), the two women tied to a lamppost (Card VI), and the lighted candle whose light is dim in the daytime (Card IX).

In summary, although Rachid has identified with a patriarchal figure, he still has not fully resolved his Oedipal conflict. His special attention to a belief that a female sorceress can make men impotent with all except one woman suggests that a basic tie to the mother may prevent polygynous marriage like that of his father. In spite of underlying fears of threat to his potency and manliness, he has developed self-assertive strivings toward social accomplishment consonant with his superior intellectual abilities.

Case No. 50: An Overtly Aggressive Young Man

Mohammed was a difficult case for the psychologist to understand, for certain of his manifest behaviors are in apparent opposition to characteristics suggested by analysis of the Rorschach material. The two sets of data are reconciled by inferring that his overtly assertive and aggressive behavior are a reaction against an underlying passive-oral orientation.

In his youth Mohammed made several trips to Algiers, where he stayed with his brother. At eighteen, when he left the oasis permanently, he was rather wild and undisciplined. He had received a little training in carpentry from his father but even less formal education when he came to Algiers to work under his brother's tutelage. Neglectful of his duties, however, he quarreled with and insulted the other workers and continually expressed a desire to go to France. Thinking that the experience of making his own way might be good for Mohammed, his brother paid his passage to the continent.

In France, Mohammed worked in a number of menial capacities. Finally, out of a job at the end of a year, he returned to Algiers but not to his brother. Again he found no work and was a bicycle racer for a time. Finally, his brother persuaded a friend to take the youth into his shop. This time he settled down, married his father's brother's daughter, and drew close to his brother whom he now holds in respect.

His alertness suggests fairly high intelligence and, despite his lack of schooling, he has learned to speak French rather well. He wears European clothes and, while still liking native food, his preference is for a generally Western diet. His supernatural beliefs, however, are still like those of the oasis population and his recently reformed behavior includes a return to active religious life.

Mohammed expresses negative attitudes toward the French and toward those Arabs whose submissiveness stamps them as *Beni Oui Oui's*. In the oasis, he identifies with a group of "young Turks" who oppose the older leaders of the village council and the dominant families of the community.

He seemed to form a rather close friendship with the anthropologist and was relatively free of reticence and suspicion toward him. One reason for the positive relationship may have been his actively expressed desire to emigrate to the United States.

Some indication of his underlying personality is available, both in regard to expression of aggression and to the nature of his concern with sexuality. According to his own account, he manifests at certain times highly explosive aggressive behavior. He tells how he once hit a younger brother in "punishment" so hard that his jaw was swollen for days. When he was fourteen he hit a man in the head with a rock, leaving him unconscious "in a pool of blood." To punish him, his father beat him with a stick. While Mohammed was in France he had a fight with a Corsican co-worker, who was bothering him, and beat the Corsican over the head with an iron bar.

Mohammed discussed sexual matters rather freely with the anthropologist. In this regard, the subject gave inferential evidence of homosexual play during childhood and expressed his adult interest in forms of heterosexual satisfaction other than intercourse. There are certain other impressions concerning his sexual behavior, the possible meaning of which is better considered after a presentation of the Rorschach data.

Mohammed's Rorschach is very complex, with a great deal of affective material in his 57 responses. It is, first, a record full of attention to the small details of the cards, with a meticulousness of approach and at times an exactness about trifling matters. There is a total of eight space responses, five of them to relatively rare areas. This reversal of figure and ground suggests the oppositional traits noted in his behavior. There is a certain intellectual querulousness evident in such an approach. Like many of the Arabs, he is not attentive to the popularly perceived blot areas but is idiosyncratic in his percepts.

This is the record of a highly extratensive person. He is stimulated from without (M:Σ C = 0:4; and a total of ten shading responses: 4YF, 4FT, 2FC$'$), but there is a lack of more mature fantasy (M: FM = 0:5). His thinking exemplifies the obsessive and arbitrary patterns noted earlier as being so general in the Arab records. He has six responses in which elements are arbitrarily united, even to the extent of being somewhat bizarre: a bat with a crocodile head; a rare mosquito with big ears; two pigs holding a scarf; a mosquito on a fig; a bird on the belly of a woman; and a toad with a tail like a goat. He shows responses that are highly overvalenced with affect: "A head—big head—empty eyes—closed mouth—empty cheeks—much hair on the sides—a bone in the middle of the forehead." "It is from olden times—dead, but not long dead. It still has some flesh on it."

There are a number of mosquitoes in the responses but it is not clear whether they are perceived as small, jabbing insects or as sucking ones. A great deal of attention is paid to the mouths in his percepts and he also sees a human throat and the "neck" of a guitar. Three responses are the bellies of women. In two cases the inner anatomy is perceived as cut open. In other responses, he is particularly sensitive to musculature, seeing the strong shoulders of American bison and the shoulder of a camel, "in good condition, because it is muscular and thick." Hair is described with great detail as in "a jackal's tail." At the inquiry: "It's full of hair, the hair like cotton...full of hairs like wool"; "An open sweater with a zipper"; "It's knitted wool..."

Since all these responses have an original flavor and are not suggested to others by the blots, they have special significance for him. They can be reconstructed into a picture of a person who has strong underlying oral dependent needs that can at times be sadistically perceived. The need for tactual contact is strong. The attention to musculature and soft qualities suggests strong body narcissism and needs for physical skin contact. Yet there is something repellent involved, as witnessed by the percept of the head with a bony front and closed eyes.

To interpret how these needs might be expressed in relation to a wife, one must know that "fig" is the expression for "vulva" in the colloquial French in which the Rorschach responses were given. With this knowledge, the "mosquito on a fig" response suggests indulgence in oral sexual behavior on Mohammed's part or some feeling of inadequacy with regard to his penis. He contends that he is inconvenienced by the ritual necessity of bathing after intercourse, to purify himself for prayer. To this he attributes the diminution of the frequency with which he has intercourse with his wife. He states that early in marriage he had daily sexual relations but that this now occurs only three times weekly. From his wife it was learned that during one month they only had intercourse once and then at her request.

The examples which he gives of "Satan's dreams" consist of beating up his father and sleeping with his mother. Reports of such dreams are not uncommon, but he adds an idiosyncratic one which consists of walking naked through the streets. This dream, it must be noted, is related to the suggestions of body narcissism found in the Rorschach content. He enjoys showing pictures, which he keeps with him, of himself as a bicycle racer. He openly discusses "variety" in intercourse but adds that sodomy is forbidden. Nevertheless, he says that homosexual sodomy is frequent among boys and acknowledges the existence of animal contacts.

Relating the observational data to that of the Rorschach, one reaches the conclusion that much of his aggressive surface behavior, of which he proudly boasts, and his exhibition of his masculine prowess and physique are counterpoised to underlying infantile, pregenital needs in which orality, both in the form of feelings of deprivation and of aggressiveness, plays a very strong part. His masculine identification is therefore not a secure one. His belligerency and negativism are more acceptable to him than open passivity and dependency. His aggressiveness can be coupled with anti-French feelings and he can vent anger on others who seem submissive, as in the case of the *Beni Oui Oui's*. His change in conduct, after his trip to France, from a belligerent obstreperous attitude toward his successful older brother to one of seriousness and respect may be explained in his shift of hatred toward authority to hatred of the French.

His close relationship to the anthropologist seems to contain certain dependent attitudes. It is to be noted, however, that these attitudes are well controlled and not intrusive. The relatively high number of Rorschach responses with positive affect suggests that, in spite of internal strain and defensive feelings, his over-all attitude toward life is not lacking in a certain basic optimism.

Case No. 32: A Young Nationalist

Now that Algeria is in open revolt, Benazouz is probably either dead, imprisoned, or in hiding. When he consented to work as an interpreter for the anthropologist, the latter was curious as to why such an obviously capable and employable young man should be available for temporary hire. Inquiry revealed that Benazouz had just been released from prison. He had been rounded up in Algiers, along with members of the two major underground nationalist movements, following a disturbance and bloodshed in a distant hill town. Nor was this his first arrest. During World War II he had dreamed that he was being arrested and his dream was soon fulfilled on the suspicion that he was involved in black-market activities. Despite the likely psychological interpretation of his dream, he professes innocence and did, in fact, escape sentence.

Benazouz is not, however, the colorful figure these incidents might lead one to expect. As seen in 1950, he is a young man in his twenties who affects a Western appearance and expresses progressive, modern ideas. His European clothes are very neat and his total appearance is more French than Arab. Although he has had only four years of French schooling and considers himself essentially uneducated, his French is exceedingly good.

This young man is one of the two Arabs in the sample who were not born in Sidi Khaled. Both his parents were born in the oasis and were postadolescent when their families moved to Algiers. Related through their fathers, their marriage was a traditional, lasting, and monogamous union. Benazouz is the second of three children. The father works as a laborer in a French winery—acceptable employment, despite the Moslem antipathy to alcohol. While Benazouz gives the appearance of a clerical worker, he has, in fact, had a succession of unskilled jobs.

His life goals are clear in his mind. Although he believes that ideally a man should be married at twenty-two, he has not yet married because it is important for him to have a good job first. "If you are married, you have children in spite of yourself," he says. He wants a secure position, a comfortable apartment, and four children including two girls "for their mother." Illustrative of the same goals, Benazouz has beaten his younger brother for keeping bad company and refusing to go to school.

His cultural values are a mixture of Western scepticism and deprecation, of the backwardness of many of his fellow Arabs on the one hand, and unquestioning adherence to Koranic teaching on the other. His attitudes toward the seclusion of women are liberal. Indicating that these customs are not required by the Koran, he asserts they would not be necessary at all, if adequate education were "permitted" (by the French, is implied). Polygyny, he thinks, is declining in direct proportion to the increasing respect for women, who formerly had no rights. Now their protests against this custom, which produces so many quarrels among co-wives, are being listened to. His response, however, to the question of what he would do if he ever found a strange man in his house is the usual Arab one, "I would kill him." He erroneously considers this response unique.

He holds only those supernatural beliefs, such as in the evil eye and genii, which he can trace to the Prophet and the Koran. Since Benazouz has the Westerner's faith in doctors and their medicines, he calls the *talebs*, who make charms, "not men of science but charlatans." Nor does he believe in fortune tellers "who talk about everything and hit some things right." He does maintain, however, that he can foresee his own future in his dreams and cites the instance of his arrest, which he had already dreamed about. His only other supernatural belief is in *sahharas* who have the magic power of making a girl love a man. He denies that they have any power to impair a man's virility.

Throughout his contact with Benazouz, the anthropologist found him a reliable, relatively flexible person with whom to work. He showed a minimum of personal defensiveness, not finding it necessary to enhance himself at others' expense. He never made any reference to his nationalist activities.

The psychological integration suggested throughout the Rorschach protocol is somewhat more mature, with much less pervasive internal pressure over sexual conflict than in the case of Mohammed (Case No. 50). He shows strong obsessive-compulsive propensities (Dd% = 17, 5 S), obsessive and arbitrary thinking in the form of several instances of precision alternatives, exactness limitations, and arbitrary responses.

Benazouz' record suggests a person with much potential anxiety (anxiety affective index = 30; total shading: 12 with 3 YF, 1Y); sensitivity (5 FT); and responsiveness to environmental stimuli (1FC', 2FC, 3CF). His sensitivity and responsiveness are well controlled (F + % = 86) but pervasive. He maintains an attitude of guardedness and evasion, having a number of evasive responses such as maps. Even though Benazouz has strong labile propensities (3CF, including a volcano), he attempts to remain objective and realistic. In spite of repression of inner resources (1M), he is a relatively flexible person (rigidity score = 33). He scores eighth lowest among the Arabs in this regard and is well within the range of the Normal American sample. Certain deep-set feelings of inferiority (7 FV) are resolved by compensatory emphasis on self-assertion and aggressiveness. Many of his animals are fierce, aggressive creatures such as lions, crocodiles, bison, and eagles. Although there is an obvious concern with achievement of an assertive self-identity, at the same time there are suggestions of unresolved relationships with a strong authority figure. He wants to be a bigger and stronger person than he already is.

His assertiveness can be oppositional and negativistic in nature (5S). This oppositional feeling is likely to be turned outward, since his responsiveness to his environment is strong and there are repressive forces at work preventing introversion (M: Σ C = 1:4). His problem of self-assertion is probably related to the social realm as he is strongly status conscious, looking down on groups he considers primitive or simple. In his human responses he sees a pair of men on Card III (nonelaborated), but he also sees Negro heads which he describes as "not as good-looking as whites." In identifying idols as belonging to primitive Negro tribes, he remarks that they are similar to those of the American Indians. Such responses indirectly express both his derogatory attitude towards anything primitive and respect for the power and prestige of Americans. That he looks both ways in his acculturation is suggested by his relatively large number of popular responses, both in terms of American norms (Total Beck P = 6) and in terms of responses popular only in the Arab sample (Arab P = 7). These results signify a combined awareness of Western percepts and a manifest sharing of modes of perception basically Arab in nature.

Benazouz respects horizons other than his own. He sees an American bison, a map of France, Swiss mountains, the mountains of California. This may be partially due to his interest in American films. One would guess that his anti-French attitudes do not extend to a general anti-Western feeling. In spite of maintaining his identity as a progressive Arab, his psychological propensity toward feelings of inferiority probably makes his social identity an ambivalent one. Most likely, doubts concerning his self-identity are repressed or denied by compensatory but realistic political and social activities which continually affirm his allegiance to Arab culture, at the same time expressing a belligerent attitude toward the hated, alien French.

Case No. 45: A Convert to Islam

One record of interest not in the Arab sample is that of Pierre, the teen-age son of French parents. He has asked for, and is receiving, Moslem religious instruction preparatory to marrying an Arab girl who lives in the same tenement building. He has also applied for official papers making him a Moslem French citizen with the name of Mohammed. The administration does not, however, approve the change and Pierre contends that they are putting difficulties in his way.

Pierre's father, recently deceased, was an irreligious roughneck who worked as a laborer and lived in the Casbah, fraternizing with its lower-class inhabitants to such a degree that he spoke both Arabic and Kabyle with ease. He was almost the stereotype of a "tough." Pierre recalls being beaten with a whip and, on one occasion, being chained to his bed for two days. His father never permitted him to go out at night or to smoke. He said that he would allow such liberties after Pierre had served his military term and was twenty-one. It is noteworthy that, immediately after describing his father's brutal strictness, Pierre comments, "If I were not afraid of God, I would not follow a religion."

Pierre's mother is sufficiently Catholic to have had her five sons baptized and sufficiently French to have insisted that he have five years' schooling. Aside from this the mother, who also was beaten by the father, seems to be a passive figure in her boys' lives. Two older brothers have migrated to France, but Pierre's younger brother, like himself, is considering conversion to Islam. Having grown up in a peer group of Arab children, the boys reached adolescence in intimate proximity to a family of six Arab girls. The necessity for conversion in order to marry these girls is the factor forcing formal recognition of their Arab identification. The cultural groundwork is already there. "To be French is death"; says Pierre, "to be Arab brings joy and marriage. What is misfortune for the French is joy to us." This pronominal identification with the Arabs typifies his utterances. His fez symbolically expresses the same identification.

Like most converts, Pierre is more Arab than the Arabs. In contrast to many urban Arabs, Pierre's supernatural beliefs are all characteristically like those of the oasis people, whom he has never seen but whose culture comes to the Casbah with the southern migrants. Expressing very restrictive views concerning the seclusion of women, he shows some interesting non-Arab divergences. These, significantly, manifest a lack of the ego threat to an Arab man which is involved in the idea of a wife's adultery. Pierre would prefer that his wife go out of the house with her mother, rather than with his, for then, "if she were unfaithful, the fault would lie with her family and the marriage price would be returned upon divorce." He gives an even more aberrant response to the hypothetical situation of finding a man with his wife. He contends that he would have intercourse with the man's wife in front of the erring couple and then divorce his wife. Another unique feature is his belief in love as a basis of marriage, an idea completely foreign to the Arabs.

The Rorschach record shows certain features similar to the Arab records. It is quite high in over-all rigidity (rigidity score = 54), demonstrating obsessive-compulsive thought patterns (maladjustment score = 74). A very limited range of interests is apparent and Pierre is most concerned with physical wants. He is very concrete in approach, constrictive and limiting elaboration characterizing a number of the responses. Obviously functioning at a normal intellectual level, he is highly stereotyped in his thinking. Sixteen of his 20 responses are animals; the remainder are botanical. There is a selectivity, however, that suggests a basic feeling of inner inadequacy and an oral-dependent orientation. His animals are, characteristically, butterflies, beetles, cockroaches, and a tortoise. The only exceptions are two sea rays. In the majority of the responses he is concerned with pointing out the mouths. His three botanical responses are edible plants, a lettuce, and cabbages. One can surmise that this person has relinquished all inner assertiveness and striving.

Of interest in ascertaining whether his percepts are Arab or Western are the five Western populars and the total lack of the Arab vista responses. He does give a sea creature (a ray) on Card IV, which is a popular among the Arabs, but such a response is not rare in Western records. The psychological motives for this person becoming an Arab are doubtless complex. The rigidity and constriction of his personality structure are not contrary, however, to that found in certain Arabs. He identifies himself with a harsh parental role, saying, for example, he would beat his children and chain them if necessary. The record suggests that he does not consider himself strong or adequate. The Arab identity may be a way for him to achieve adult male status reinforced by the rigid support of such status which Arab society affords. As a Frenchman, he may not feel as readily self-assertive. He is, in some respects, the parallel of the Arab adolescent (Case No. 1) who shifts toward French identity as a means of resolving certain inner conflicts.

B. SOME DEVIANT PATTERNS

Case No. 26: A Retired Soldier

A noncommissioned officer during the latter part of his career, Abderrahman had many years service with French native troops in Algeria. Now past middle-age, he has employment in a responsible but unskilled position in Algiers. Clean, dressed in European clothes aside from his fez, Abderrahman speaks good French, which he says he learned to read and write on his own. His only formal schooling consists of three years of Koranic training.

His father, a farmer in Sidi Khaled, married Abderrahman's mother after the death of his first wife. Abderrahman is their only son. The mother died when Abderrahman was a small child. After his father's death, when the boy was eleven, he lived for three years with an uncle. At fourteen he came to Algiers, where the number of jobs had increased during World War I. His army service fell between the two wars. Retiring from the *Spahis* with a modest pension, Abderrahman married and divorced one wife before seeking his present mate from a nomad group. Her two children by a previous marriage are being reared as his own, a very unusual situation in this strongly patrilineal society. Of the six children he has had by this wife, only two are still living.

Abderrahman has a wealth of opinion concerning supernatural beliefs. His respect for modern medical techniques explains his contempt of traditional Arab practices, such as the use of charms. Insisting that a person's welfare depends upon one's own character, he claims that few *talebs* are possessed of real supernatural power enabling them to help others. Although he is not afraid of the evil eye, he believes that some aggressive people do have supernatural power *(baraka)* and that the evil eye is the natural result of this power and aggressiveness. As for afreet, "Solomon purified the world of them. Hitler and Stalin are human afreet and Stalin is the biggest afreet alive."

When questioned about *sahharas*, Abderrahman admits that they can make love potions, which he considers harmful as the materials now used have been introduced by the French in order to weaken the people. These substances attack the stomach and lungs, whereas the ingredients used in the old days were harmless. "A *sahhara* takes a person's nail clippings or hair and puts them in a potion which makes the victim sick. Fingernails are dirty. Even if you touch your eyes with dirty hands, you get eye diseases." He knows from old Arab books that the Arab drugs reinforced sexual powers, whereas the present ones just weaken a man. The authorities, however, close their eyes to this, as they do to the drug traffic. Jewish women have acted as the intermediaries in the introduction of the new drugs because they can speak Arabic. He reiterates that through these practices European control is continued. His first wife tried to use this kind of magic on him, debilitating him so that he was powerless to sleep with other women. It was then that he studied the subject. He learned of two old Arab practices: A woman will love a man a great deal if he massages his penis with honey before intercourse; if a man washes his hands well and then gives a drink to a woman, it will make her love him. When questioned as to whether he follows these customs, Abderrahman says, "No. If a woman doesn't like me, I don't bother with her." Finally he took his wife home to her parents, intending to teach her a lesson and then to take her back in three or four months. She took his marriage papers with her, as well as other papers in his name, so he divorced her.

SOME INDIVIDUAL PATTERNS OF ADJUSTMENT 167

His bitterness towards the French appears frequently. For instance, he blames them for the decline of Arab astrology. They have limited the study of this science, although they use it themselves, as witnessed by the observatories they have built. His hostility is again evident when he discusses tattooing. He is careful to hide a tattoo of Western design on his hand, saying that he detests tattooing, introduced by early Catholics in North Africa prior to the Arab invasion. As a matter of fact, many of the indigenous Berbers, who did tattoo, were Catholic, but the emphasis on the religion of the French is significant. Abderrahman says that the French are responsible for the present lack of respect for women. Since the French occupation, if women are molested in the streets, the authorities will do nothing. If a woman is picked up as a prostitute, the police just let her go. He maintains that the Arabs do not want to keep their women shut up in the house but are forced to do so in order to protect them. Actually, he has permitted his daughters to attend school, accompanied to and from class by their mother. When an older daughter was returning from school one day with her mother, she was accosted by some men, one of whom threatened the women with a knife. Only the screaming of the women frightened the men away as the police did not even appear.

Abderrahman is distrustful of the purpose of the Rorschach testing as described, seeing the anthropologist's work as some sort of political inquiry. He believes the ink blots are deliberately constructed drawings. While in itself this suspicion is not diagnostic of paranoid pathology, it fits in with the nature of the record. He indicates, at the end, that he had a definite approach in mind in giving the responses; namely, to present the "real spirit of Arab mentality." In one sense he does this by presenting, in extreme form, certain types of thought found scattered with less intensity throughout many of the records. The responses of this anti-French soldier, if given in a psychiatric setting, could only be described as diagnostic of paranoid ideation, with grandiose overtones, in an extremely intelligent individual.

Here are briefly some of the types of illogical and projective-type thinking found in Abderrahman's record:

1) Throughout the cards there is the use of grandiose, fabulized symbolism of world forces in conflict or great evils, threatening to overpower and destroy. The red and the black of the cards are used to represent various abstractions of such things as "greed and evil."

2) The affect attributed to the cards is overvalenced and extreme in nature. Attention is focused on the "feeling" in the cards. Form is not used much as a determinant except to start a chain of fabulized associative elaborations.

3) The language is "queer" and body parts are "vitalized" in an unusual way. For example, on Card IV: "It's a person—completely savage— *all that comes out of him* is savage. It's a devil." "The arms *go out from the body but come back to it.* They are not free. The top part is a covering of some kind. Black legs come out below. The covering represents the normal, but the thing isn't normal. It is set on a pillar instead of on its legs—savage—bad."

4) Continual attention to coverings, invisibility, hiding, and guarded passages such as the fortified Suez Canal on Card VII is found mostly in individuals of an extremely suspicious, paranoid nature.

5) The fear of penetration, which appears in milder form in many of the other Arab records, takes on a more malignant tone here. The feeling is represented almost independent of concrete content. For example, on Card VI; "It is something which opens a breach in all the rest and remains superior to all the rest.... It splits open all that was in the previous cards. This black represents the arrow which made the breach and turned part of the black into white. The black is evil that has become somewhat white and conserved its strength. It is strong because it is on top and has more arrows." (Here one can note the indirect sexual symbolism.)

6) Card VIII brings out an extreme form of illogical juxtaposition of elements technically described as a "fabulized combination" or as "confabulation." The language too has a queer flavor. "*Now you show me* green flags (indicating the deliberate purpose of the examiner). Above them is a headdress of green. The red is the liver. The red animals put their feet on the headdress, the flag, and the liver. The liver is just for them to put their feet on. The paw on the headdress is black, *You aren't doing this for a book.*" (This implication that the anthropologist's work is political is a clear projection from his own percept to the intentions of the tester.) "The flag, headdress, and liver are all symbols of one people." On the actual percept the subject comments, "It looks like a lung," but he continues to use the word "liver." "Liver" is similar to our "heart" in symbolic content. By symbolizing his response, the subject rationalizes and thereby shows a need to maintain a surface logic. Such capacity helps explain how he can continue to function without some breakdown that would make the manifest nature of his paranoia more overtly nonadaptive.

The above is sufficient to indicate to the clinically experienced person the unequivocally paranoid ideation of this record. The question may occur, Is it fair to consider this record paranoid in the context of Arab culture, especially since the behavioral material presents an individual who seems to have made an acceptable adjustment to French military service and who now holds a position which demands at least moderate responsibility? It is the considered opinion of the psychological collaborator that the ideation presented on this Rorschach means the same as it would if it had been obtained from an American. What is not as easily determined from such a record (as is equally true for American records) is the nature of the positive ego forces which maintain this person in spite of paranoid structuring. The definition and diagnosis of paranoid pathology is difficult to define in psychiatric interviews. If the paranoid delusion coincides with sufficient outer reality to make it plausible to others, the person can maintain himself very well without drawing any undue attention to himself. It is only when the stresses of life exacerbate a situation that a latent paranoid structure reveals itself by the increasing implausibility of a persecutory system or a compensatory grandiosity.

There is nothing at present to indicate that Abderrahman is under any undue strain which would cause him to manifest such implausible ideation. Yet if we examine the report of his divorce from his first wife for weakening his sexual power through magic, we find a story with definite paranoid elements. It is noteworthy that it is the weakening of his sexual ability that is projected to outside malevolent forces. His culture helps disguise the pathology of his story because the belief system of the relatively uneducated Arabs supports such ideation. In his case he gives a somewhat naturalistic explanation in terms of "drugs." Likewise, his hatred of the French and Jews and his blaming them for many of the evils of his own society is not uncommon for the Arabs. We must, however, point out that structurally Abderrahman's ego is nevertheless using mechanisms of projection whatever the license he receives from his culture.

Case No. 36 B: A Man Possessed by Genii

Thin to the point of emaciation, filthy, and ragged, Khaled is thirty-two years old. Living in very squalid circumstances with his mother and an abnormal brother, he has been periodically possessed by genii for eleven years and worries about the increasing frequency of such occurrences. His manner is nervous and distrait, but he converses coherently and can answer questions, even though he tends to equivocate in his responses.

Khaled's father is a *taleb* and at one time had a small store in the oasis. He had four wives and now lives with the last one. His first wife was his father's brother's daughter. He soon took a second spouse and, by subsequent marriages after the death of his second and third wives, maintained a polygynous household of two wives until he divorced the first, eighteen years ago. This woman was Khaled's mother, who bore half of the husband's twelve living offspring. Severe in his relation to the boy, Khaled's father beat him frequently, once slapping him so hard that he was knocked unconscious. The father would not let him play but kept him occupied either in the store, working in the gardens, or going to school. In addition to the Koranic training which Khaled received from his father, he studied five years with other Arab teachers and also attended the French school four years.

Khaled was fourteen when his mother was divorced. He continued to work in the store until it failed and also to work as a gardener. Making use of his Koranic training as a *taleb*, he taught children for a while. If we can trust his chronology, his first seizures by genii occurred before his first marriage. He was twenty-four when he married his father's brother's daughter, but the marriage did not last. Then he married one of his mother's relatives, who bore him two children. One of these, a boy of four, is still alive. His wife's father has taken home Khaled's wife and child but he permits the lad to eat his noon meal with Khaled. This arrangement is highly anomalous, although understandable, since Khaled has been so debilitated the past four months by his nightly seizures that he has not been able to work, thus existing only on the charity of relatives. It is not clear whether the withdrawal of his wife followed or preceded the increase in his seizures. One of Khaled's dreams, before the beginning of his present crisis, reflects his fear of aggression from his mother's relatives when he is not under his father's protection.

Even more anomalous is the fact that he and his brother live alone with their mother, although she has relatives in the oasis. Clearly this woman and her two abnormal sons have been rejected by their kin, at least so far as living arrangements and marriages are concerned.

Khaled's epileptoid seizures are like those characteristically attributed to attacks by genii. His mother follows local tradition in blaming the seizures on sexual congress with a genie, although Khaled alludes to them only as attacks by genii. His brother is not bothered by genii and people simply think he is crazy (*mahboul*). Now adult, he has always been abnormal. Half-naked and covered only by a torn, filthy robe, he squats silently in the courtyard, moving only to get food or to run to the wall to relieve himself.

It is interesting that this same family has other members who illustrate the third culturally recognized form of deviation, saintliness. Some of Khaled's cousins were regarded as holy because of their peculiar behavior, which consisted of never washing and of sitting for hours in the market place, completely withdrawn and speaking to no one.

SOME INDIVIDUAL PATTERNS OF ADJUSTMENT 171

We get some picture of what it is like to be attacked by genii from Khaled's own account:

> I see things like smoke. My heart tightens and I can't move or talk. When I get better, I get normal again. Until four months ago, I could fight it off with words of God, but then they get into my head, and I can't get them out. I can hear them laugh. They are like the wind. They wrap around me and I begin to feel them going into my chest. I begin to have fear. When they leave, I can talk and move. They go out like a shadow from my chest.

Khaled has sought charms to exorcise his genii from all the *talebs* in the region. Recently he even consulted a *guezzana* in an attempt to foresee his fate. Both with regard to the use of this latter, religiously disapproved practice and his search for help in books on love magic, his interview responses are evasive and contradictory. He even used his contact with the anthropologist to seek some Western medicine which might cure his condition. The only real help he has ever had was after his initial seizure, when a "great" *taleb*, now dead, cured him for a year with a Koranic charm and potion.

He feels threatened by the evil eye and believes that this is the source of his genii attacks. Similar seizures, which he experienced a year ago, he believes were due to the envious remark of a man who, seeing him hard at work in a garden, commented, "You have a motor in your back."

Khaled's Rorschach, approached quantitatively, does not evidence any outstanding disturbance. While his record shows certain disorders in the area of thought, these are found sporadically throughout the other records. There is, however, a combination of qualitative indications of severe pathology which do not contribute to the score on the maladjustment scale but which, nevertheless, do attest to a malfunctioning ego structure. He was one of the few Arabs tested who "edged" the Rorschach cards. This turning of the surface of the card almost parallel to the line of vision has been clinically reported as quite a rare occurrence, found almost solely among psychotics. One conjecture as to the basis of edging behavior is that the person perceives something on the card as overly real and turns the card sideways to see if the object is actually three-dimensional. Some approximation of this visual phenomenon may be found in a perfectly normal reaction to viewing bright red colors on color film transparencies under certain conditions. The red colored images sometimes appear to stand out from the film. With debilitation of the ego, a similar effect may occur when the individual looks at the Rorschach cards.

Khaled also shows "confusion" and "fluidity" in certain responses. One could not determine whether this confusion was due to a lack of desire to commit himself or whether he had forgotten, in the inquiry, what he had said earlier in the free association. He describes some of his percepts in very vital terms: "Trees throw all their force into the end." He also makes such remarks as, "This is a picture that drives me crazy." On the other hand, the content of his responses is not bizarre or weird, nor is the use of determinants or location areas in any way aberrant. It is almost as though there were a healthy part of himself which fights off some debilitation that he feels as alien and "outside" himself. He has somehow objectified his illness as an extraneous force but not necessarily a supernatural one. In attempting to obtain from the anthropologist American medicine to control his illness, he indicates that he does not attribute his sickness to supernatural forces alone.

Case No. 9: A Taleb Who Hennas His Beard

His relatives and neighbors thoroughly dislike sixty-two-year-old Saïd. They accuse him of having the evil eye and maliciously gossip about him for staining his chin whiskers with henna so that he will not be a "grey-beard." He indirectly supports this interpretation by contending that Mohammed recommended henna, but not black dye, for beards. Henna, for Arabs, is associated with holiness. Saïd's vanity does not stimulate him to care for his person or clothes, both of which are dirty and unkempt. He spits on the walls of his room or under the carpet and wipes his nose on the sleeves of his robe.

A Koranic teacher, he rants at his half-dozen pupils, often beating them, and is generally violent in his emotional expression. All his shouting and aggressiveness cannot cover his cowardice. Once he brutally struck a boy with a stick when he caught the lad pushing his six-year-old daughter about in the street. When the boy's angry father came to Saïd's house, the *taleb* fled.

He has no obvious political convictions, nor any other kind, for that matter. He seeks to please rather than to inform. His manner toward the anthropologist was unctuous and he tried in every way to ingratiate himself. There is nothing unusual in his religious beliefs. Although he occasionally writes charms for nomads and knows how to exorcise genii, he is defensive about the lack of demand for his services.

Saïd's mother was his father's third wife, taken in polygynous marriage. She was divorced while Saïd was a young boy and for eight years he was sent to live in a *zaouia* in the neighboring oasis of Ouled Djellal. There he studied under the marabout and other teachers of the religious fraternity. At thirteen, his father gave him a bride of eighteen, his father's brother's daughter. The surviving children of this marriage are four daughters, a very inadequate progeny for masculine-oriented Arabs. When his wife reached the climacteric, he married the daughter of another of this father's brothers, a woman more than ten years his junior. The fact that the co-wives were first cousins did not stop them from quarreling or even actively fighting.

The younger wife bore one son and three daughters. The mothers' rivalry extended to bickering among their children but now the elder wife is dead and her daughters are married. When asked if he wanted another wife, Saïd answered that he had "a young wife who pleased him greatly." Even this indirect reference to the sexual adequacy of his wife is very anomalous for an Arab and may also reflect his desire to appear young and virile.

How much his son means to Saïd was obvious when the boy fell seriously ill. The anthropologist brought in a doctor who was able to save the boy. Saïd was pitifully grateful. His strong attachment to his son is even more apparent when he literally fights the lad's battles for him, beating other boys who have hurt his son. As in the case of aggression against his daughter, his punitive violence toward other men's children goes beyond local norms for rough coercion. He is equally undisciplined in his relation to his spoiled youngest daughter, whom he indulges in every way, giving her privileges usually reserved only for sons.

Saïd's Rorschach is not very revealing. A generally constrictive, stereotyped protocol of fifteen responses, the record does not suggest more than average intellectual functioning. The rigidity score of 71 is extremely high. He hedges cautiously on many of his responses. In his reactions to the last three cards, he finds an easy solution to the necessity of producing responses by giving practically the same content of "an animal in a tree" to all three. Subsequently, in the inquiry, he tries to rationalize the response by giving some details to make it acceptable. His thinking, in general, tends to be more concerned with self-justification than with being logical or coherent in organization. Of his fifteen responses, ten are animals and three are trees. Nothing very personal is revealed. In spite of his hedging and a tendency to withdraw earlier responses during the inquiry, he does not reject any card. He voices difficulty throughout the test, stating that he "cannot understand" and, at one point, that he is perspiring because of the strain which makes him "suffer." There is no doubt that he finds the test an ordeal.

Of note is his total of eight Arab populars, a very high total when compared with the mean number of three populars for the group as a whole. Such emphasis on P responses usually suggests a need to conform to commonly held thought patterns. The populars in Saïd's record raise the question as to what this means in terms of his aberrant, disturbed behavior. His level of form adequacy is within the normal range and, with all its constriction, the record suggests no pathology. Whatever his difficulties, they do not seem to be due to lack of reality orientation. Rather, one might infer that he is sensitive to general opinion and would like to be highly regarded. He probably knows himself to be something of a bluffer, attempting to hide from others any revelation of his basic inadequacies, although not very successfully. He maintains a very superficial, stereotypic perception of human relationships and, coupled with a basically undisciplined, primitive, emotional structure, he is almost pathetically transparent as a sycophant. His undisciplined, even unprincipled behavior leads him to be despised by others, in spite of his constant attempts to cover up and be accepted in his role as *taleb*.

Blind Rorschach analysis did not, in itself, suggest this sort of integrated picture. Although many of the elements were separately predicted, there was not accurate prediction of this man's primitive affectivity. As in a number of other cases, Saïd's color responses, despite their extratensive balance, do not reflect the propensity for uncontrolled emotional display which distinguishes him.

Case No. 8: A Hawker of Charms and Nostrums

By dint of eight years' Koranic schooling, Hocine presents himself as a *taleb-toubib*, a "teacher-doctor," adept at using magic for diagnosis and making charms for curing various ills. He is a specialist, self-styled, in venereal disease. Having no office, he carries the instruments and materials of his practice in his pockets and in a sack, setting up shop in cafes or wherever his clients may be. The sophisticated urban Arabs are contemptuous of him and laugh when Hocine denounces his more successful rivals as charlatans. A marginal person in a highly competitive profession, his dirty, slovenly appearance loses him possible wealthier patients.

Now middle-aged, he has been in Algiers intermittently for eighteen years. He is the next to the youngest of the nine children in his father's household of four polygynous wives. The father was a gardener but is now deceased, as are his three elder wives. Hocine's mother, wife, and children live in the oasis while he comes alone to the Casbah for half of each year. His grandmother was a *guezzana* who, with a mirror immersed in a platter of water, could see past and future. She also dealt with genii. Others of his paternal family have *baraka* and specialize in making cuts on the foreheads of sick children to let out fever.

Hocine has seen genii and, as a *tour de force,* can make children or adults who are in a state of purity also see them. He claims belief in, and is well informed about, all Arab supernatural forces. Showing marked interest in any kind of magical power, he would like to have "Solomon's ring," for then he could control genii and be all-powerful. Hocine is sure that Aladdin's lamp, guarded by all the afreet, is somewhere in Algeria. In common with many other Arabs, he has "Satan's dreams." He says that a dream of intercourse with mother or sister is significant of good luck and success in business. A dream of fighting with one's father in which the son wins indicates that the son will be devoted to his father. If the father wins, the son will be dissatisfied and eventually quarrel with the father.

Hocine's protocol presents a picture of severe internal disturbance (maladjustment score, 86, the seventh highest score in the group). His low rigidity score of 29 indicates a failure to use ego constrictive defenses to bind up his internal difficulties. Sadomasochistic content and proof of disturbed sexual adjustment pervade the record. Such responses are found on six of the nine cards (Card V was rejected). The partial record follows:

Card II: The lower part of a woman, opened up. It's divided along here. The sexual part is also cut in two. This side is the part in which the baby is formed. The other side is the anus and rectum. You can't see the external sex parts.

Card III: A person cut in half, with two lungs. It's all part of one person when folded together.

Card IV: This way—a person cut open. The thigh. There is the backbone, split open. Even the backbone is opened up.

Card VI: The body of a person opened up. Just a body cut open. Those are the sexual parts below. It looks like a man. They are interior parts on the front of a man.

Similar responses were given to Card VIII, identified as a female vagina, cut open, and to Card X, described as throat, kidneys, and sexual parts of a human.

Hocine's protocol indicates a strong desire for contact with others. He is probably painfully aware of the feeling of others toward him. One surmises that he is superficially compliant and passive (4 texture responses, 3 of them TF; 3 passive movement responses) and that he cannot readily show direct aggression or anger. Covertly he is hostile and aggressive (hostility content, 18 per cent of all responses; bodily preoccupation content, 19 per cent), but he cannot assertively express these emotions. Counterpart to his inability to overcome his helpless submission and attachment to power, which he expresses symbolically in the content of certain Rorschach responses, is his conscious preoccupation with the magical means of obtaining power. For example, on Card I there is a borderline movement response, "two genii attached together"; and similarly, on Card IX, "Siamese twins attached at the legs, hands resting on something." The figures are tied to each other, symbolizing some ambivalence about deep dependency. A praying figure on Card III again suggests a dependent relationship on outside power.

While the anthropologist provides no supportive evidence, Hocine apparently tries to accomplish through slyness, deceit, and submission itself what he cannot achieve by direct assertion. He feels pathetically vulnerable to attack at all times. His pervasive preoccupation with men's and women's bodies, split open and exposing their internal sexual organs, is evidence of the severity of his sexual disturbance. Such a record suggests that this man would engage in homosexual activities which, for him, would be an unconsciously directed means of wresting masculine power from other men.

This protocol, interpreted according to certain psychoanalytic surmises concerning homosexuality, is typical of those formed among men not able to master the difficulties arising from a dominant, overpowering father image. Hocine's resort to magic and, inferentially, to chicanery are the means of finding a formula to supply himself with what he did not obtain in his own distorted maturation. Through his manipulation of charms and nostrums he can gain at least some sense of power in reference to the weakness of others.

Case No. 25: A Happy Man

In contrast to the foregoing personalities, Amar is an unusually cheerful, outgoing individual, so well liked that he is often chosen as a semiofficial greeter for the village council or the cafd. Living in the oasis community, he is a well-to-do landowner, forty-eight years old. He has remained totally Arab in habits and dress but this does not imply that he is anti-French. He says that politically he stays to the middle of the road but some of his compatriots accuse him of being too subservient to the French. He freely admits that he consulted the French administrator before agreeing to work with the anthropologist and that he was impressed by the latter's rapport with the administration. He has long represented his sib on the *djema'a*.

His strong sense of responsibility explains Amar's kindness and helpfulness. He likes to joke and to tease, but never maliciously. In most situations he appears self-assured but not aggressive. The only indication of inner tension is his habit, like Ahmed's, of cracking his knuckles.

We can infer a strong paternal identification as Amar's relationship with his father was very good. He describes the old man as generous and kindly. The father died at the age of one hundred and three, having had four wives and thirteen children. It is interesting to note, with regard to identification, that Amar's marriage pattern is identical with that of his father: two monogamous marriages, each followed by divorce; then a subsequent polygamous marriage to two women. Now a patriarch in his own right, Amar has twenty-three individuals in his household, including two married brothers and their families.

Some people say that Amar occasionally flies into terrible rages at home, when he scolds and yells at his sons. He created a similar scene in the market place, screaming at a craftsman who had tried to cheat him. Religious but sceptical about peripheral supernatural beliefs, he has no faith in genii and tells a humorous anecdote about one of his sisters. She wanted a divorce from her husband, who refused to let her go. Then she said she was being attacked by a genie, to which the husband replied that he would chase out the genie and he beat her with a stick. "The genie left and never returned!"

Amar's Rorschach record confirms the behavioral pattern. He ranks next to the lowest of the total group on the rigidity scale and ninth lowest on the maladjustment scale, while demonstrating in his affective symbolism a generally positive affective cathexis. A relatively open record when compared with Arab averages for the production of movement, color, and texture, it demonstrates a generally happy emotional adjustment. The color-dominated color responses, as well as the movement responses, are mild and pleasurable. The nature of his movement responses suggests a basically positive attitudinal stance toward others, with mature attitudes and expectations definitely predominating. One-fourth of the responses are positive in tone, the amount of unpleasantly toned material being relatively low, not more than 9 per cent of the responses. (A critical level for disturbance is above 40 per cent.) Some sexual preoccupation appears in his response to Card I: "A woman with a vulva." Since such content, however, is not repeated and since the tone of the record becomes increasingly positive, this response does not weigh heavily in the balance.

Looking at the protocol in terms of cognative processes, it is strikingly Arab in character. Amar's responses contain many unrealistic relationships, with no attempt made to be methodical. Beginning with small details, he may shift to a whole response; or he may respond with a series of details on one card, giving a whole response on the next. His reasoning throughout may be characterized as naïve and egocentric. The Rorschach record includes six of the twelve specific responses found most popular for the entire Arab group.

Amar's record is singularly devoid of any hostile content. Instead, various positive features of nature (garden vegetables, fruit trees) or recreation (costumed Negro dancers, a moving picture) are paramount in his associations. His thinking processes coincide with the Bleulers' characterization of the Moroccans as self-centered, undisciplined, and illogical. But, in general, Amar shows a fairly rare personality pattern for an Arab. The record is significant in that his good adjustment in Rorschach terms corresponds with his good social adjustment.

CHAPTER X

THE CULTURAL CONTEXT OF PERSONALITY

The fact that cultural norms could not be predicted from personality data does not, of course, imply that there are no meaningful relationships between the two sorts of phenomena. We turn, therefore, to the task of discovering some of the ways in which specific Rorschach measures of Arab personality are related to Arab culture traits. The procedure is exploratory and, while we can suggest theoretical explanations for the relationships which emerge, this does not constitute a test of the theory involved.

One of the facts which became apparent in the tests of Professor Hutt's hypotheses was that culture traits which would seem to have similar personality implications were not always found to be related to personality traits in the same way. We shall now be concerned with expanding our knowledge of these culture and personality linkages and be discovering how they are related to the changes attendant upon urban contact. It is well to recall that our analysis of the personal backgrounds of the oasis and urban groups demonstrates that the cultural and personality differences found between the groups can be interpreted with assurance as being due to acculturative change.

Method of Analysis

The personality measures to be discussed are the Rorschach rigidity and maladjustment scores and three indices of affective content in the Rorschach. The latter include positive content, anxious content, and combined indications of hostility and body preoccupation.[1] The proportion of these last, combined types of content increases significantly in the city. The other four scores remain relatively constant except for some tendency for positive content to decline in the city.[2]

---

[1] Anxious content is separated from the other two types of unpleasant content because, if not separated, the high proportion of anxious material and its lack of association with the culture traits mask the significant relationship of some culture traits to Rorschach implications of hostility and body preoccupation.

[2] See Appendix M for distributions of data and levels of significance not presented in the text and footnotes of this chapter.

Scores on each of the five personality measures were divided into "high" and "low" categories, the dividing point being one standard deviation away from the mean score of the Normal American sample. For all of the measures, except positive content, the division is above the mean, thus making it possible to compare those cases which are extremely high in the trait with all others. For the indices of positive content, the extremely low scores are compared with the remainder.

The cultural characteristics analyzed were personal cleanliness and traits which were discussed earlier under the headings of seclusion of women, punishment of children, and supernatural beliefs. The variation within each trait was divided so as to produce as near a dichotomy of cases as possible. Comparison was then made between each of the cultural distributions and each of the personality measures for the total sample of Arabs and for the oasis and urban groups separately.[3] As anxiety showed no significant relationship to any culture traits, it will be omitted from further consideration. The results of the other analyses of the total sample are presented in Table XV with indications of the levels of statistical significance of the relationships discovered.

Cleanliness

Previous analysis of this trait has shown it to be marked in the cultural ideals but often not fulfilled in practice. Its fulfillment is related to urban contact only in the upper economic group. We also found in the analysis of Professor Hutt's hypotheses that adherence to cleanliness norms has the same sort of link to the personality trait of anality as occurs among Western individuals. The further analysis of personality concomitants of cleanliness produced no statistically significant relationships.

There are, however, trends in the data which strongly suggest that high rigidity and maladjustment are associated with lack of cleanliness. In the oasis group, alone, the relationship to rigidity is significant at the .06 level. The probable anality component in rigidity and the significant relationship of the former to cleanliness lends further significance to the trends. The type of personality associated with lack of cleanliness also suggests an individual so rigid and maladjusted as to make economic success unlikely.[4]

---

3. The separate oasis and urban analyses were used to ascertain if there were significant urban changes in the personality implications of the traits. Only one was discovered, which will be discussed in appropriate context.

4. For evidence of the tendency for rigidity and maladjustment to be related to economic position, see Appendix M, Part II.

Table XV

LEVELS OF SIGNIFICANCE OF RELATIONSHIPS BETWEEN
RORSCHACH AND CULTURAL VARIABLES*

	High Rigidity	High Maladjustment	Medium or High in Positive Content	High in Hostility and Body Preoccupation
Cleanliness				
Meticulous or clean	-.10	-.10		
Seclusion				
Requires veiling of one or both eyes	.10	.01		-.10
Forbids wife to go out with her mother				
Wife's seclusion ends at 56 years or older	.001	.01		-.15
Punishment				
Beats severely or prefers beating	.05			-.15
Uses isolation				
Uses food deprivation	-.05	-.10	.05	
Supernatural				
Uses charms			.05	-.01
Believes in genii				-.15
Believes in power of *sahhara*				-.05
Protects against or has been affected by evil eye			.05	-.01
Interprets his dreams				
Believes in power of *guezzana*				

*Total sample analyzed with two-tailed tests of significance. Minus signs indicate an inverse relationship between the variables. See Appendix M for data.

Seclusion Practices

The relationship of three seclusion customs to the personality variables will be seen from the accompanying table. The degree of veiling required and the terminal age for the seclusion of women both showed a statistically verified and consistent relationship to rigidity and maladjustment. The more restrictive customs were preferred by Arabs who were very high in these qualities and, interestingly enough, somewhat low in symbolic indications of hostility and bodily preoccupation in the content of Rorschach responses. Concerning the acceptability of a wife's mother as her chaperone, however, there is a striking lack of relationship to the psychological variables, despite the seeming similarity of the personality implications of the three seclusion customs.

If we place the evidence in the general context of what was learned about Arab personality, we conclude that the relatively maladjusted Arab, whose psychic problems are inferentially markedly sexual in origin, rigidly imposes strict controls on his women.[5] In the tendency for an inverse relationship to exist between severity of restriction and hostility or bodily preoccupation symbolism, we see evidence that the rigid, maladjusted Arab who follows such restrictive practices does not tend to develop more internalized and intrapsychic conflicts over the handling of his aggressions. In a sense, they are "taken out on the women" in acceptable cultural ways which produce no overt or even covert hostile tensions.

The above cultural expression of personality characteristics is based on analysis of the total Arab sample. Comparison of the oasis and urban groups reveals how these apparently functional links between culture and personality operate under acculturative influences.

Considering veiling norms first, we note that the shift to the more liberal requirement of allowing the exposure of both eyes is so general in the city that only four of the urban Arabs continued to insist on more complete covering. The demonstrated personality implications of differences in veiling practice are, therefore, essentially an expression of the oasis situation. The relationship of maladjustment to veiling is significant in the oasis group, in which it is still possible to measure differences in veiling practice (P = .03). It is revealing, however, to examine the urban "traditionalists" despite their small number. Of these four more restrictive Arabs, all are high in rigidity, three are high in maladjustment, and three are low in both hostility and bodily preoccupation, paralleling the oasis findings.

5. In this connection, the test of Professor Hutt's hypothesis X showed both maturity and cathexis to be significantly related to less rigid seclusion practice.

It is meaningful to ask if the change in cultural norms occurred despite the apparent psychic "utility" of the oasis norms in personality integration, or whether the changes in cultural attitudes are paralleled by personality shifts attendant upon urban residence. We have already seen that overall indices of rigidity and maladjustment do not change in the city, but Rorschach content symbolizing hostility or bodily preoccupation increases. The total evidence indicates, therefore, that change in veiling practice goes on despite its significant relationship in the oasis to personality traits which do not change with movement to the city. The urban increase in hostility symbolism or anatomical responses is consistent with the decline in severity in attitudes toward veiling. As will be further discussed below in relation to supernatural belief, it would not be unreasonable to assume that the external social pressures of the Casbah affect cultural beliefs. As the customs change, alterations in psychological integration occur, since the individual loses beliefs and practices around which he has made psychological adjustments which circumvent intrapsychic conflict. The person who finds himself bereft of reassuring supernatural beliefs and cultural practices is also more exposed to the French world and what is perceived as its threatening domination.

There is much less difference between the oasis and urban groups in the age at which a woman may come out of seclusion. The relationship of these customs to Rorschach scores on rigidity and maladjustment[6] is, nevertheless, similar to the results with veiling. Those who are the most rigid and maladjusted are more severe, whereas those who give more hostile or bodily preoccupation content are prone to be less severe.

Punishment of Children

The psychological implications of the methods employed in punishing children are markedly varied. The use of isolation as a punishment shows no relation to the personality measures employed. The use of severe physical punishment is characteristic of the most rigid Arabs and of those who do not tend to show marked hostility or bodily preoccupation.[7] But, unlike seclusion customs, such beating of children shows no relationship to

---

6. In the oasis, age out of seclusion is significantly related to rigidity at the .02 level and in the city at .08. In the oasis, the relationship to maladjustment does not reach significance, but in the city it is significant at the .05 level.

7. The tendency for an inverse relationship to hostility was also found in testing Professor Hutt's hypothesis VI.

maladjustment. Beating does not become less severe in the city[8] nor does rigidity decrease, but the expression of preference for such beating as the best form of punishment does decline.[9] The Arab seems to beat his sons through rigid adherence to the pattern learned on the receiving end in childhood. The father's domination of his children is not altered by contact with the French, but he is probably not so likely to express, at least to a non-Arab, what he knows will be taken as an unduly punitive position.

The most rigid Arabs, however, are significantly less likely to punish children by depriving them of a meal, limiting their food, or even delaying their meals. The explanation here seems to be that beating is the usual form of punishment and only the less rigid Arabs are likely to depart from the pattern and employ other means. Interestingly, it is also those who tend to be better adjusted and who give more positively toned affectual material in the Rorschach who punish by food deprivation. Such Arabs show no less tendency to use physical punishment. It is as though those who use deprivation to punish their children do so with the feeling that "it is for their own good." Despite the association of the stable personality factors with food deprivation, this kind of punishment increases in the city (P = .06).

Supernatural Beliefs

Rigidity and maladjustment, which showed such striking relationships to the preceding culture traits, are not related to any of the six supernatural traits analyzed. One interesting thing, however, was found with regard to maladjustment. Its relationship to belief or disbelief in fortunetelling *guezzanas* was significantly different in the city and in the oasis (P = .02). In the desert, eleven of the twelve disbelievers are very high in maladjustment. It is possible that the religious interdiction of fortunetelling is responsible for the tensions associated with this custom, but the direction of the relationship would have been hard to predict.

The most marked personality concomitant of the supernatural beliefs which were rated is the inverse relationship which exists between the intensity of four of the beliefs and indications of hostility or bodily preoccupation. Rorschach content symbolism indicates that, as with seclusion customs, approved belief in supernatural forces seems to function to obviate the formation of

---

8. See Appendix M, Part II.
9. As was seen in Chapter V, P = .02. The number of Arabs who preferred such punishment was too small to analyze with the psychological variables.

aggressive sets, either turned outward toward others or directed inward against the self. Customs concerning charms, the evil eye, and love magic of the *sahhara* show this pattern at statistically significant levels, while beliefs in genii show a trend of a similar nature. The only beliefs which diverge from this pattern are the two involving prognostication.[10] As a concomitant of the inverse relationship of four of the traits to types of unpleasant Rorschach content, two supernatural beliefs show significant direct relationships to positive content in the test.

One may provisionally conclude, on the basis of these results, that the personality implications of the supernatural traits hold without regard for acculturative changes. Customs concerning charms, genii, and *sahharas* wane significantly in the city, where there is a concomitant increase in evidence of hostility or bodily preoccupation symbolism. But concern over the evil eye, which has similar personality implications, is not altered by urban contact. In fact, all of the evidence we have presented indicates that culture change goes on in response to social pressures, without much regard for the previous personality implications of the traits involved. It would certainly have been impossible to have predicted which culture traits would change on the basis of our knowledge of their psychological significance for the individual in the oasis and our knowledge of the personality shifts attendant upon urban contact. There is probably some sort of threshold beyond which given personality types cannot adjust to certain cultural behaviors. Our investigation, however, seems to indicate a marked tendency for personality predispositions and cultural configurations to develop new kinds of equilibria during acculturation.

It is important to point out also that half of the urban group came to the city when they were fourteen years of age or older and three-fourths were over nine years old. The changes which they underwent, both culturally and psychologically, demonstrate that the effect of early training and experience is not conclusive in personality formation. It is the continuity of influences through life, and not just the impact of early influences alone, which makes men as they are.

In summary then, the evidence shows a consistent pattern. The attenuation of traditional beliefs among the urbanized Arabs is related to increasing intrapsychic tensions that are expressed

---

10. We have seen that fortunetelling is significantly and differently related to maladjustment in the oasis and city. Similarly, the use of dream interpretation is directly related to low anxiety in the city ($P = .05$) and the city differs from the oasis in this regard ($P = .11$). The only other significant finding with respect to supernatural traits in the subsamples was the inverse relation of use of charms to hostility or bodily preoccupation in the urban group taken alone.

in symbolic form in Rorschach content. The minority position of the more acculturated urbanized Arab is reflected in his perception of the social environment as hostile and threatening. He must cope intrapsychically with the implications of this psychological set. Direct expression of reactive hostility is not possible short of the open rebellion which has since occurred. Feelings are focused on being oppressed by the dominant French. Those who adhere more tenaciously to traditional beliefs sometimes show greater rigidity and score higher on maladjustment. In adhering to the old social and religious beliefs, however, such Arabs are not forced into patterns of adaptation that cause them to experience a great degree of personal threat coming from their own projected hostility.[11]

The Cultural Setting of Personality Formation

French and urban influences, however, seem to have had various effects upon the Arabs, depending upon initial differences in their personalities. In a minority of cases, the personality pattern developed by those in the city approximates the norms of the Normal American sample. On the other hand, the urban situation produced increased intrapsychic stress, so that another minority of individuals evidences a more adverse intrapsychic adjustment than that found in the oasis. We note that rigidity and maladjustment are correlated in the city but not in the oasis. This suggests that migrants who arrive in the city with highly rigid personalities experience such great difficulty in relating to the new situation that they become markedly maladjusted. Less rigid migrants, on the other hand, appear to react favorably to their new setting and work out their problems of psychic adjustment in the process of making the social adjustment.

Despite such oasis-urban differences, the personality type which marks the Arabs as a group rests on the common developmental experience which the culture dictates. The Algerians show no particular evidence of fixation at, or regression to, the earliest stage of ego development in which personal relationships are concerned with nurturance. Their Rorschach records are characterized far more as showing ego defenses related to the level of development which is most concerned with the

---

11. Analysis of Rorschachs of urban American Negroes shows them to have similar patterns of personality integration. This is highly suggestive for understanding the effects of minority group status on individual integration where pronounced rejection by the dominant group makes actual assimilation impossible. See Goldfarb's analysis of Negro records in A. Kardiner and L. Oversey, *The Mark of Oppression*. (New York: W.W. Norton and Co., 1951).

internalization of disciplinary controls and a conscious relationship to authority figures. It seems clear that the feared authority figure tends to be a threatening father, given to uncontrolled rage and physical abuse.

There are no real sanctions in the culture against the display of violent affectivity toward women and children. Fear of retribution can keep such behavior toward peers or superiors in check, but children are a man's possessions and cannot be alienated by aggressive behavior. Genuine affection is no doubt felt toward children but, when the father is angered, he has no compunction about beating them. A child learns not to be directly assertive in any way which will provoke anger. There is little room for logical discussion, and recourse to objective fact is not often used as a way of settling issues. Their handling within the family does not tend to develop objectivity or logical thinking.

One method of relating to others, which is modally adopted, is that of passive submission. This passive submission has certain sexual components. Early experience associates mother and siblings with sexual stimulation. Later, very strong sanctions are imposed against continued orientation toward these sex objects and no legitimate substitute is provided until later in life. Psychosexually there is a retreat from Oedipal stimulation and rivalry, under a severely developed sense of threat. There is a culturally prevalent pattern of homosexual submission of younger preadolescent males to older ones. Homosexual submission as a means of placating authority can be considered a culturally modal defense maneuver, but the assumption of a passive, submissive attitude is culturally interpreted as a female role and hence raises subconscious questions of masculine identity.

The authority figure is not only perceived as threatening but often as suspicious and distrustful as well. In fact the father, instead of assuming the loyalty and integrity of his wife and children, distrusts them and is often actually deceived by their ruses. Family members can intrigue against one another for the father's favor or they can combine in deceiving him. Deviousness becomes another mode of relating to authority. One learns not to trust most people, and relationships of trust are reserved for intimate, strong, personal ties which usually have an underlying homosexual flavor.

Psychological difficulties are particularly apparent in men's relationship to women. With great importance placed on virility, concern over impotence is common. The intense distrust and suspicion of women is related to basic feelings of inner inadequacy about being active, authoritative men. Shaky about their virility, men are apt to blame women for sexual inadequacy, as in the case of those who accuse their wives of using *sahharas* to make them impotent. Potential rage toward possible initiators of adultery with one's wife goes hand in hand with fantasies of adultery with the wives of others.

It is not difficult to relate these patterns to unresolved childhood rages toward an aggressive, dominant, and fearsome father. Since one usually retreats from actual conscious rivalry or rebellion, the conscious feelings expressed toward the father emphasize respect rather than hostility. The better adjusted men resolve possible difficulties by making an active identification with their fathers.

The removal of the preadolescent boy from the group of women and younger children is an abrupt one. Before he becomes capable of active assertion as a young man, he resides for a few years in a limbo of observing the activities of the older males. This is also the period in which homosexual relationships are most common. Adolescent growth toward maturity is filled with attempts to attain an active masculine role. One must defend himself against his former passive proclivities. Paranoid-like projection and obsessive-compulsive character defenses are in common use to prevent a return to passive submission. Relatively few attain the dominant, active role without a struggle.

When personal economic independence is achieved the Arabs tend toward asocial seclusiveness, each within his own domain. A man makes of his own home a fortress against outside attack, yet memories of his own deviousness make him mistrust even those within the house. Not all men become dominant. Some enter into passive economic relationships with brothers or other near kin and live as dependents. Such a relationship can be mutually satisfactory. The support of one's kin attests to the prowess of the family head. As for the dependent, he can settle into passive, devious submissiveness and cease to struggle against it.

In the process of personality formation, supernatural beliefs are used to bolster inner defenses. There is definite evidence that those individuals who actively employ supernatural forces have less internal tension. Some of these supernatural powers have peculiarities attesting to underlying intrapsychic concerns. It is not difficult to equate the concern with love magic and the relative prevalence of fear of impotence. Concern over being attacked by genii seems to reflect fear of being penetrated by a threatening force. The emphasis on the sexual nature of a genie's attack and the belief that the body of either a man or woman is entered by the genie evidences the concern with penetration.

From a psychological standpoint, belief in the evil eye and the use of protective charms against it can also be considered indicative of fear of attack from outside. The evil eye, with its emphasis on the eye of an envious person destroying a desired object possessed by another, suggests the voyeurism of some children. Psychoanalytic therapy reveals that the unconscious associations of such children treat the eye as though it were a weapon of attack. In such an equation, one destroys what one desires, incorporating it through the eyes.

In the oasis, where the social order is more stable and beliefs more firm, the Arabs develop a more secure, though highly constricted, personality. Those who move to the Casbah live in more stressful surroundings. Some Arabs internalize these stresses; others achieve a more adequate adaptation to their new, half-Western world; but the lack of development of more objective controls is still quite apparent. The decline of supernatural beliefs decreases the protection from stress which they provide in the oasis. In many instances psychic stress becomes focused on political and economic problems. While the problems themselves are quite real, they are approached with more affectivity than objectivity. The Algerians know how to hate and whom to hate, but they are not always capable of using less emotional and more pragmatic means of achieving their goals.

APPENDIX A

DEMOGRAPHIC DATA

Population

The census of 1948[1] gives 5,612 as the population of Sidi Khaled. In addition to residents, this figure includes all men who had left the oasis to work in France and those who had been working in Algerian cities for less than one year. On the basis of the previously described random sample drawn from the civil register, it was found that over 5 per cent of the population, or some three hundred men, were in France. The sample likewise indicates that a similar number were working in Algerian cities, although the length of such urban residence is indeterminate. It is, therefore, impossible to know exactly how many of the latter were excluded from the census.

Natality and Mortality

The civil register is maintained by the Administration of the Commune Mixte des Ouled Djellal, in which Sidi Khaled is included. This is simply a register of births and deaths and does not indicate migration. The data for Sidi Khaled are indicated below.

The natural increase between 1932 and the end of 1948 amounted to slightly over 30 per cent, or 1,315 persons. This figure, added to that of the corrected 1932 population registration, is 5,631. The census of October 31, 1948, counted 5,612 persons in the population of Sidi Khaled, indicating that emigration to the Algerian cities is balanced by sedentarization of nomads and other new settlement.

The high number of births in 1943 and 1944 is paralleled in the oasis of Ouled Djellal and is probably a war phenomenon. The high death rate in 1942 is associated with famine.

---

1. Service Statistique Générale, Gouvernement Générale de l'Algérie, *Résultats Statistiques de Dénombrement de la Population Effectué le 31 Octobre 1948* (Algiers: Service de Statistique Générale, 1950), p. 122.

Years	Births	Deaths
1933	67	51
1934	168	110
1935	125	45
1936	157	52
1937	143	87
1938	96	58
1939	129	49
1940	152	45
1941	182	79
1942	170	117
1943	250	45
1944	194	61
1945	150	84
1946	201	105
1947	149	87
1948	152	95
1949	98	99
Total	2,485	1,170

Age Distribution

In connection with the drawing of a random sample, an analysis was made of the age distribution of the first three hundred individuals in the alphabetically arranged population registration of 1932. The demographic picture, therefore, is as of that date. Jobs were few in the cities in that depression year, but the list includes men who had left the oasis to work in the city and who were believed, by their families, to have gone only temporarily. The original registration, which was not complete, included 3,931 names. There were subsequent additions of 385 individuals, largely births during 1932, but also including many women who were omitted in the original count. The following data include the additions. The ages are the individuals' own estimates and, from forty years upward, they tended to be given in multiples of five.

Age	Male	Female
0-4	22	19
5-9	21	18
10-14	21	22
15-19	13	14
20-24	9	13
25-29	16	8
30-34	9	12
35-39	7	12
40-44	6	5
45-49	5	5
50-54	5	6
55-59	6	3
60-64	4	4
65-69	2	1
70-74	4	3
75+	5	0
Total	155	145

APPENDIX B

ANALYSES OF EDUCATION, MARRIAGE, AND ECONOMIC STATUS

	Father's Marriage		French Education (Total Sample)	
	Polygynous	Monogamous	None	Some
Koranic education				
+5 years	7	8	9	8
0-5 years	7	24	38	9
	P = .15		P = .05	

	Father's Economic Status			
	Oasis		Urban	
	High	Low	High	Low
Informant's economic status				
High	13	0	6	2
Low	1	5	5	7
	P = .001		P = .03	

	Father's Marriage		Koranic Education	
	Polygynous	Monogamous	+5 years	Less
Father's economic status				
High	7	18	10	15
Low	2	10	3	11
Father's origins				
Nomadic	5	7		
Sedentary	9	15		

	Economic Status	
	High	Low
Cleanliness		
Meticulous to clean	17	4
Dirty to filthy	10	24
	P = .01	

APPENDIX C

ANALYSES OF THE EFFECT OF INFORMANTS' BACKGROUND ON OASIS-URBAN DIFFERENCES IN PSYCHOLOGICAL AND CULTURAL TRAITS*

Part I
BACKGROUND FACTORS AND PSYCHOLOGICAL TRAITS

	N	Background Factors (Oasis and Urban Samples Combined)			
		Father's Marriage		Koranic Education	
		Polygynous	Monogamous	+5 years	Less
		14	32	15	33
Anxiety rating					
High: 18+		6	17	8	16
Low: 0-17		8	15	7	17
Hostility rating					
High: 7+		6	17	5	19
Low: 0-6		8	15	10	14
Body preoccupation					
High: 1+		6	14	4	16
Low: 0		8	18	11	17
Unpleasant content					
High: 28+		7	17	8	17
Low: 0-27		7	15	7	16
Positive content					
High: 9+		7	16	9	16
Low: 0-8		7	16	6	17
Oral content					
High: 1+		8	16	8	18
Low: 0		6	16	7	15

*Two-tailed tests of significance were used with the psychological variables; one-tailed tests with the remainder. Variations in total N result from incomplete data.

APPENDIX C

Part II
BACKGROUND FACTORS AND CULTURE TRAITS

		Background Factors (Oasis and Urban Samples Combined)			
		Father's Marriage		Koranic Education	
	N	Polygynous 14	Monogamous 32	+5 years 15	Less 33
Actual age at first marriage—women					
12-15 years		3	7	6	5
Older		3	7	5	6
Ideal age at first marriage—women					
12-15 years		9	14	9	14
Older		5	18	6	19
Confidence					
In some women		0	14	3	11
In none		12	17	12	17
		P = .005			
Wife may be accompanied by her mother		5	24	5	24
Wife may not be accompanied by her mother		9	8	10	9
		P = .01		P = .02	
Wife may go out					
Day or night		2	22	4	20
At night only		12	10	11	13
		P = .0005		P = .03	
Veiling					
Both eyes exposed		9	25	12	22
One or both covered		5	7	3	9
Begin toilet training					
At 1 year or earlier		1	8	2	7
Later		4	6	3	9
Importance of children					
Most important of choices		3	4	3	6
Not most important		9	23	11	21

APPENDIX C

Part II *(con't)*

	N	Background Factors (Oasis and Urban Samples Combined)			
		Father's Marriage		Koranic Education	
		Polygynous 14	Monogamous 32	+5 years 15	Less 33
Beating of children					
Preferred punishment		4	2	4	3
Not preferred		10	30	11	30
Isolation of children					
Used as punishment		7	20	8	19
Never used		7	12	7	14
Knowledge of French					
Some		6	23	9	20
None		8	9	6	13
		$P = .05$			
Clothes					
European		4	12	1	15
Arab or mixed		10	20	14	18
				$P = .01$	
Cigarette smoking					
Yes		11	19	11	20
No		3	13	4	13
Charms					
Not used		7	22	7	22
Used		6	10	8	10
Genii					
Disbelief		5	6	2	9
Belief		9	26	13	24
Sahhara					
Disbelief		3	12	6	9
Belief		7	15	6	18

APPENDIX C

Part III
OASIS-URBAN COMPARISONS, CONTROLLING FOR BACKGROUND FACTORS*

	Only Those with Five Years or Less of Koranic Education		Only Those with Monogamous Fathers	
	Oasis	Urban	Oasis	Urban
Confidence				
In some women			2	12
In none			7	10
			P = .11	
Wife may be accompanied by her mother	5	19	4	20
Wife may not be accompanied by her mother	5	4	5	3
	P = .07		P = .03	
Wife may go out				
Day or night	1	19	1	21
At night only	9	4	8	2
	P = .0002		P = .0001	
Knowledge of French				
Some			2	21
None			7	2
			P = .01	
Clothes				
European	0	15		
Arab or mixed	10	8		
	P = .0005			

*Only those culture traits and background factors found to be significantly related in Appendix C, Part II.

APPENDIX C

Part IV
RELATION OF BACKGROUND FACTORS TO
CULTURE TRAITS, WITH URBAN CONTACT CONTROLLED*

	OASIS		URBAN	
	Father's Marriage		Father's Marriage	
	Polygynous	Monogamous	Polygynous	Monogamous
Confidence				
In some women	0	2	0	12
In none	8	7	4	10
	Koranic Education		Koranic Education	
	+5 years	Less	+5 years	Less
Wife may be accompanied by her mother	3	5	2	19
Wife may not be accompanied by her mother	7	5	3	4

*Only those culture traits which did not show a significant oasis-urban difference in Appendix C, Part III.

APPENDIX D

DISTRIBUTIONS OF CASES IN TESTS OF HUTT HYPOTHESES*

I	Anxiety Rating				IV (Con't.)		
	1-2.5	3-4.5				Oasis	Urban
(a) Supernatural experience	5	6			Some disbelief	4	17
No such experience	23	23			Belief in all	15	11
						P = .01	
(b) Uses charms, protects vs. evil eye	15	20				Anxiety Rating	
						1-2 2.5-3.5 4-4.5	
Does not do so	14	8			Oasis	8 6 3	
					Urban	8 9 10	
II	Anxious Immature	Mixed	Non-anxious Mature		V	Hysterics	Others
					(a) Oasis		
Disbelief, non-use, most supernatural powers	10	19	7		Interprets dreams	0	11
Others	5	10	5		Does not do so	5	1
						P = .002 Reversal	
III	Anxious Constricted		Others		(b) Urban		
Uses charms, protects vs. evil eye	11		15		Interprets dreams	6	19
Does not do so	12		18		Does not do so	3	4
IV	Anxiety Rating				Total sample Interprets dreams	7	32
	1-2.5	3-4.5					
2-3 disbeliefs	7	3			Does not do so	9	8
1 disbelief	8	9				P = .03 Reversal	
Belief in all	12	17					

*For all psychological ratings, a high numerical index indicates that the quality being rated is more marked. The number of cases varies slightly as some data were not available for all subjects.

APPENDIX D (*Con't.*)

	Hysterics	Others
V (*Con't.*)		
(c) Oasis		
Belief in fortunetelling	2	4
Disbelief	3	8
(d) Urban		
Belief in fortunetelling	1	6
Disbelief	8	15

VI	Latent Hostility 1-2 Anality 1-2	Latent Hostility 3-5 Anality 3-5
Prefers severe punishment	27	9
Others	13	7

	Overt Hostility 1-1.5 Anality 1-2	Overt Hostility 2-5 Anality 3-5
Prefers severe punishment	23	13
Others	14	7

(Alternate)	Combined Hostility Scores	
	1-5	6-10
Prefers severe punishment	22	12
Others	14	9

VII

Urban contact	Assimilation Index				
	1 (low)	2	3	4	5 (high)
None	8	1	0	0	0
Up to 4 months	1	3	5	2	0
4 months to 5 years	2	1	4	2	0
5 to 20 years	1	3	4	6	6
20 years or more	1	0	2	3	9

$P = .001$
(16 cells at extremes collapsed into 2x2 table)

APPENDIX D (Con't.)

VII (Con't.)	Assimilation Index	
	1-3	4-5
Rorschach "urbanization" rating		
1-2 (low)	18	14
3-4	12	12

	Urban Contact	
	Up to 5 years	5 years or more
Rorschach "urbanization" rating		
1-2 (low)	15	17
3-4	9	15

VIII

	Supernatural Belief Index	
	Low	High
Rorschach "supernatural" rating		
1-2 (low)	15	13
3-4	12	17

	Power of Charms	
	Believes in	Does not believe
Rorschach "supernatural" rating		
1-2 (low)	13	14
3-4	22	7

$P = .05$

IX

	Anality Rating	
	1-2	3-4
(a) Food deprivation		
Uses	17	12
Does not use	15	13
(b) Evaluation of money		
Important	10	13
Not important	22	12
(c) Cleanliness		
Meticulous or clean	7	13
Dirty or filthy	19	10

$P = .05$

APPENDIX D *(Con't.)*

	Anality Rating	
	1	2-5
IX *(Con't.)*		
(d) Begins toilet training		
Before 1 year	6	4
1 year or after	4	8

	Maturity Rating	
	1-2	2.5-4
X		
Beginning of seclusion		
11 years or less	13	14
12 years or more	15	15
End of seclusion		
55 years or less	10	17
56 years or more	19	10
	P = .01	

	Extreme Cathexis Ratings	
	1-1.5	2.5-4.5
Beginning of seclusion		
11 years or less	8	15
12 years or more	14	6
	P = .05	
	Reversal	
End of seclusion		
55 years or less	8	18
56 years or more	14	15

Appendix E

COMPARISON OF RORSCHACH SCORING CONDUCTED BY De VOS AND HUTT

Both Dr. De Vos and Professor Hutt used graduate assistants in scoring the Rorschach protocols but closely supervised the process and personally checked the results. Hutt's median scores are available for only a limited number of determinants. De Vos's analysis includes seven additional cases to that of Hutt and the statistical forms of the two sets of data are different.

	De Vos Means	Hutt Medians
R	18.5	18
W%	41.7	35
D%	51.3	51
Dd%	9.2	14
F%	68.1	66
A%	46.3	46.4
P	2.7	1+

APPENDIX F

Part I

RORSCHACH MEASURES OF QUALITATIVE ASPECTS OF MENTAL FUNCTIONING

	ARAB						AMERICAN					
	Oasis		Urban		Total sample		Normal		Neurotic		Schizophrenic	
N	20		28		64		60		30		30	
	Mean	S.D.	Mean	S.D.	Mean	S.D.	Mean	S.D.	Mean	S.D.	Mean	S.D.
Approach												
W	5.4	3.2	6.1	2.1	6.0	3.0	5.0	3.5	5.3	3.2	3.6[b]	2.3
W%	39.7	20.2	44.2	23.5	41.7[a]	21.3	18.6	13.6	19.3	10.7	16.5	20.3
D%	53.1	20.7	50.7	19.5	51.3	19.2	73.5	11.4	72.1	10.7	72.0	18.4
Dd%	6.9	10.7	6.5	13.4	9.2	12.6	8.7	7.1	9.2	7.2	12.3[b]	12.1
Organization												
Z Score	19.5	11.9	24.7	9.5	22.3	11.6	22.4	15.2	24.0	20.5	20.8	20.9
Communality												
American P	2.6		3.2		2.7		6.8	2.4	5.8	2.0	4.7	2.6
Arab P	4.3		3.8		3.9							
Form Accuracy												
F+%	65.2	18.2	64.5	27.7	66.6[a]	23.8	80.7	9.8	70.4	16.1	60.7	22.4
Extended F+%	66.1	19.9	67.2	25.5	67.3	22.5						
Blocking, Stereotypy, Constriction												
Time, Init. Resp.												
R	49.9	33.7	44.1	28.0	45.8[b]	28.9	32.4	15.2	35.7	17.5	38.3	32.6
F% (Beck)	17.1	8.7	17.8	10.6	18.5[a]	11.5	30.9	12.8	32.7	29.8	31.2	19.0
F% (Klopfer)	70.0	13.7	62.1[b]	18.4	68.1	16.4	71.3	14.3	74.7	13.1	72.3	14.9
A%	60.4	20.0	54.9	20.4	59.6	19.0						
A%	50.6	10.4	40.7	20.5	46.3	20.5	48.7	13.4	51.3	14.3	39.7	20.6
Lds%	6.6	10.4	16.8	20.7	10.9[a]	16.1	3.2	6.5	1.5	4.0	0.8	3.9
Bot%	17.5	9.6	9.2	14.0	12.7[a]	12.3	1.3	4.3	1.9	6.7	0.0	0.0

Key to significance of differences (calculated for means only):
a. Compared with Normal American P = .001
b. Compared with Normal American P = .01

APPENDIX F
Part II
NUMBER OF CASES SHOWING VARIOUS RORSCHACH RESPONSES INDICATIVE OF THINKING DISORDERS*

	ARAB				AMERICAN	
	Oasis	Urban	Total Sample	Normal	Neurotic	Schizophrenic
N	20	28	64	40	25	25
Associative Constriction						
Rej	4	6	11	4	7	6
Delay	11	15	34	17	12[b]	11
Descrip	0	2	3[df]	5	11[b]	5
Demur, Deny	9	10	24[b]	2	10	9
Olig	6	3	12	3	1	2
Unclear	2	5	9	4	13	5
Affective Associative Elaboration						
Af Pos, Af Ng	6	3	10	4	5	3
Pers	9	6	19[c]	5	4	5
Symb	0	4	4	2	1	4
Fab El	5	13	23[e]	11	15[b]	9
Obsessive and Arbitrary Thinking						
Preoc (2 or more responses)	1	7	9	7	7	5
Wdr, Cmpl (2 or more responses)	4	7	15[c]	3	3	1
Pr Alt, Exact, Arb Ds	11	11	30[e]	11	19[b]	16
Cor Rig, Arb R	9	14	30[bf]	4	8[c]	5
Arb Cb	8	13	31[b]	5	10[c]	7
Ratn	8[g]	4[g]	20[b]	0	6	3

*See Appendix F, Part III, for meaning of abbreviations and method of scoring.

Key to significance of differences:
a. Compared with Normal American P = .001
b. Compared with Normal American P = .01
c. Compared with Normal American P = .05
d. Compared with Neurotic American P = .001
e. Compared with Neurotic American P = .05
f. Compared with Schizophrenic American P = .05
g. Comparison between Oasis and Urban Arabs P = .05

APPENDIX F

Part II (Con't.)

		ARAB				AMERICAN	
	Oasis	Urban	Total Sample	Normal	Neurotic	Schizophrenic
N	20	28	64	40	25	25
Associative Debilitation						
Irrel	2	0	3	0	0	3
Prsvr (2 or more responses)	1	3	4	0	0	0
A Phr	0	0	0	0	0	1
Prpl, Impot	1	2	5	3	4	3
Conf, Vague, Fluid	5	4	11	2	2	11
Autistic Disturbance, Impaired						
Logic						
Det C	0	0	0	0	1	3
Aut Ob	0	1	1	0	0	1
Verb	0	0	0	0	2	6
Absrd	0	1	1	0	0	2
Fab Pa, Fab Cb	1	7	13	5	6	6
Conf	0	2	4	0	5	4
Cntam	0	1	3	0	0	1
Aut Lg, Posit	1	1	4	0	1	4
Self R	0	1	1	0	4	4
Cn	0	1	1	0	0	1
Blot Dynamism	1	2	3	0	1	1

APPENDIX F

Part III
BRIEF DESCRIPTION OF THE SCORING OF
THINKING DISORDERS[1]

A. *Associative constriction* is a constriction of thought or a blocking of perception as part of a defensive reaction of the ego. These constrictive reactions are of several types: total rejection, excessive time delay, the use of various kinds of description rather than giving a response, inability to give final response, denial of previous responses, or excessive constriction of a response by using only part of the area perceived in a normal response.

Abbreviation	Category	Criteria
Rej	Rejection	Phillips, p. 165f.
Delay	Delay	Footnote 2
Cddes	Card Description	
Cdes	Color Description	Klopfer, p. 153, 284.
Symet	Symmetry Verbalization	Phillips, p. 172; Rapaport, p. 355
Demur	Demur	Phillips, p. 169

1. The system of scoring signs of thought disorder which was used by De Vos employed criteria adopted from several authors, as well as defining some original categories. Citations in this discussion refer to the following:
Bruno Klopfer and D.M. Kelley, *The Rorschach Technique: A Manual for a Projective Method of Personality Diagnosis* (Yonkers-on-Hudson: World Book Co., 1942).
Leslie Phillips, *Rorschach Interpretation: Advanced Technique* (New York: Grune & Stratton, 1953).
Jean Piaget, *The Child's Conception of Physical Causality* (New York: Harcourt, Brace & Co., 1930).
David Rapaport, *Diagnostic Psychological Testing* (Chicago: Year Book Publishers, Inc., 1946), Vol. II.
Roy Schafer, *Psychoanalytic Interpretation in Rorschach Testing: Theory and Application* (New York: Grune & Stratton, 1954).

2. Three arbitrary criteria were set up: (1) initial time of first response is over 1'30"; (2) there is a difference of 45" between the initial reaction time to one card and the initial reaction time to the following card (cf. analysis of *time of first response* in Phillips, p. 199); (3) the total time spent on one card with two or less responses is more than five minutes. But, if responses are discussed at great length or there is a disgression, delay is not scored.

APPENDIX F

Abbreviation	Category	Criteria
Deny	Denial of Previous Responses	Footnote 3
Olig	Oligophrenic Constriction	Rapaport, pp. 158-60
Unclear	Unclear	Footnote 4

B. *Affective Associative Elaboration* involves what Rapaport calls an "increase in distance" from the Rorschach blots as a stimulus for percepts (p. 529). Also included are responses showing *affective* loss of distance.

Abbreviation	Category	Criteria
Af Pos	Positive Direct Affective Reaction	Rapaport, p. 364; Phillips, p. 172;
Af Neg	Negative Direct Affective Reaction	Phillips, p. 172; Rapaport, p. 364
Pers	Personal Association	Phillips, p. 171
Symb	Symbolized Response	Rapaport, p. 354; Klopfer, p. 153
Fab El	Fabulized Elaboration	Phillips, pp. 153-61; Rapaport, p. 332

C. *Obsessive and Arbitrary Thinking.* This general category is characterized by various approaches to the Rorschach test which reveal rigidities in thinking which are found in either obsessive compulsive individuals or individuals with paranoid propensities. These approaches have a forced, arbitrary flavor. In extreme form, concepts are arbitrarily forced to fit the blot material or there is a manipulation of the blot areas in an arbitrary way to suit the concept. Another type of response in this category is that in which poor fit is rationalized so as to justify the response and make it more acceptable. All of these responses are characterized by a tendency to arbitrariness in logic and rigidity in thought.

Abbreviation	Category	Criteria
Preoc	Preoccupation	Rapaport, p. 299
Wdr	Whole Compulsion	Klopfer, p. 245
Cmpl	Completeness Compulsion	Klopfer, p. 241
Pr Alt	Precision Alternative	Phillips, p. 169
Exact	Exactness Limitation	Klopfer, p. 216; Phillips, p. 14
Arb Ds	Arbitrary Discrimination	Footnote 5

3. This is scored when, in the inquiry, the subject denies a previous response and even when urged refuses to reproduce it.

4. Responses which lack precision or cannot be defined specifically and remain "unclear" to the subject. Such responses are sometimes accompanied by statements of lack of understanding.

5. Scored when a subject seeks to find a difference between the two sides of the symmetrical blots.

Abbreviation	Category	Criteria
Cor Rig	Correctness Rigidity	Footnote 6
Arb R	Arbitrary Response	Footnote 7
Arb Cb	Arbitrary Combination	Footnote 8
Ratn	Rationalization	Phillips, p. 33

D. *Associative Debilitation.* As the name implies, responses under this category are characterized by difficulties in marshalling mental energy in defining a percept, bringing it into clear focus, maintaining it, or, conversely, by shifting from a percept once obtained. Most of these signs are associated with the debilitation accompanying certain organic, neurological conditions. They are also sometimes noted in connection with schizophrenic, psychotic disturbance. The debilitation can either be related to difficulty in wresting from the blot a clearly perceived percept or related to an inability to convey an inchoate association to the examiner, the subject being unable to develop it or to maintain it at the level of a clearly communicable response.

Abbreviation	Category	Criteria
Irrel	Irrelevant Remarks	Phillips, p. 177
Prsvr	Perseveration	Rapaport, p. 299; Klopfer, p. 360; Phillips, pp. 160, 299, 344
A Phr	Automatic Phrases	Klopfer, p. 334
Prpl	Perplexity	Klopfer, p. 334; Phillips, p. 168
Impot	Impotence	Klopfer, p. 333; Phillips, p. 168; Rapaport, p. 353
Conf	Confusion	Phillips, p. 168; Rapaport, p. 353
Vague	Vagueness	Rapaport, p. 350
Fluid	Fluid	Schafer, p. 309; Phillips, p. 177, under "Fading"; Rapaport, p. 351

6. Scored when the subject gives a definite impression that he considers that there is only one correct percept for areas of a blot or the entire blot.

7. Arbitrary responses are those in which an individual, in an arbitrary manner, carves a response out of a blot area not forming a readily recognizable Gestalt. This is sometimes accompanied by "cutting off" parts of the blot, even going so far as to cover excluded areas with the hand to make the percept stand out more clearly.

8. This category includes responses combining or explaining characteristics of a percept which are highly improbable. They are usually forced rationalizations but often demonstrate an ability to be convincing, even though somewhat absurd.

APPENDIX F

E. *Autistic Associative Disturbance.* Responses in this category show a severe breakdown of ego functioning, evidenced in: an extreme increase in conceptual distance from the cards; a loss of ego control over the associative processes, so that primary processes interfere in associations; and a loss of ability for coherent communication.

Abbreviation	Category	Criteria
Det C	Deterioration Color	Rapaport, p. 361
Aut Ob	Autistic Obsession	Klopfer, p. 160
Verb	Strange Verbalization	Rapaport, p. 344
Incoh	Associative Incoherence	Rapaport, p. 352; Phillips, p. 170, "associative gaps"
Flgt	Flight of Ideas	Footnote 9
Absrd	Absurd Responses	Rapaport, p. 330

F. *Impaired Logic.* The following categories all contain responses manifesting some serious breakdown or lack of development of the logical, discriminating power of the ego. The breakdown in thinking is either implied from the nature of the concept or manifest in the explanation of the response. In the inquiry following these responses, there is sometimes an attempt to justify them from the nature of the blot evidence, but the evidence of the reasoning is clearly inadequate and of a primitive form dominated by the primary processes of thought. In the main, as discussed in reference to the various subcategories, they manifest several variations of what Rapaport terms "loss of distance." Various forms of primitive thought described by Piaget (p. 237ff.) and others are in evidence, such as syncretism, transduction, participation, and realism. The cards become overly "real" to subjects given to producing the type of responses described in the following categories.

Abbreviation	Category	Criteria
Fab Pa	Fabulized Particularization	Rapaport, p. 331
Fab Cb	Fabulized Combination	Rapaport, p. 332
Blt Rl	Blot Relationship	Rapaport, pp. 356-58
Conf Tr	Confabulation Transductive	Rapaport, p. 333; Phillips, p. 20

9. Associational flight from the percept or the blot is related, in most respects, to Associative Incoherence and involves unregulated free-association and the loss of connection with the original percept or idea. These responses are usually characteristic of manic conditions per se.

Abbreviation	Category	Criteria
Conf Pa	Confabulation Participation	Footnote 10
Cnt Td	Contaminative Tendency	Footnote 11
Cntam	Contamination	Rapaport, p. 338
Aut Lg	Autistic Logic	Rapaport, p. 341
Posit	Position	Footnote 12
Self R	Self-Reference	Phillips, p. 171
Cn	Color Naming	Klopfer, p. 331

10. Responses in this category show a type of primitive thinking which is related to what Rapaport describes as "participation." Things that share a single common quality are equated or considered related. In certain Rorschach percepts, arbitrary relations are made between blot areas per se or between objects on a primitive "participation" basis. In some cases the equation is made from a common quality.

11. This category contains responses in which the type of impaired thinking found in full-blown contaminations is incipient and not fully demonstrated.

12. Position responses were scored separately, although they may be legitimately subsumed under "autistic logic," following Rapaport. The use of position as a determinant, rather than form, etc., has traditionally been considered separately in Rorschach scoring. Position as a determinant is also often used in extremely autistic "symbolic" responses. This secondary use of position is somewhat more common than its use as a sole determinant.

APPENDIX G

COMPARISON OF DIFFERENT CRITERIA FOR CERTAIN AMERICAN POPULAR RESPONSES AND THEIR CONTRAST WITH ARAB P

Card	Location	American P, Revised Criteria	Beck's Criteria	Herz's Criteria	Klopfer's Criteria	Arab
II	D_1, D_6	animal	only bear and dog	only bear and dog	include rabbit, bull, hippo	include elephant, jackal, pigs, etc.
II	D_3	butterfly etc. eliminated	butterfly or moth	not P	not P	butterfly and moth did not appear
III	W, D_1, D_9	human figure	human figure	human figure	human figure	W, D_1, D_9 human figure; D_{11} d_6 human head
V	W	bat, butterfly, and bird	only bat, butterfly, and moth (no bird)	include bird	any winged creature	bat, butterfly, and bird
VIII	D_1	animal	four legged animal; no cat, lion, tiger	four legged animal	only acting animal; no bird and fish	four legged animal, incl. lion, chameleon, cat, and tiger
X	D_{12}	sheep eliminated	sheep	not P	not P	sheep did not appear
X	D_4	vermiform animal	not P*	worm, caterpillar, sea-snake, serpent	caterpillar, garden snake, worm	vermiform animals did not appear

*Worms and snakes are considered different; hence not combined into single P, although frequency of caterpillars, worms, and snakes together is greater than certain other percepts considered as P. See S. J. Beck, *Rorschach's Test*, Vol. I, p. 199.

APPENDIX H

NUMBER OF CASES SHOWING VARIOUS TYPES OF AFFECTIVE SYMBOLISM IN RORSCHACH PERCEPTS

	ARAB			AMERICAN		
	Oasis	Urban	Total Sample	Normal	Neurotic	Schizophrenic
N	20	28	64	60	30	30
Hostility						
Deprecatory	1	5	7[a]	22	12	5
Hostile-anxious	3	6	10[a]	26	18	12
Hostile-anxious tension	1[e]	9[e]	11	11	7	7
Distorted	4	9	19[a]	5	5	3
Sadomasochistic	4	7	17[c]	6	5	5
Anxiety						
Rejection	4	6	13[c]	4	7	7
Dysphoric-depressive	4	7	13[c]	3	2	2
Body-Preoccupation						
Bone anatomy	0[e]	7[e]	10[a]	27	20	14
Flesh and viscera	2	11	16	13	11	12
Dependency						
Childishly toned	1	3	4[a]	20	17[c]	10
Religious	7	7	23[c]	12	4	6
Positive Feeling						
Sensual body-contact	1	5	7[a]	50	19[cf]	11[af]
Recreation	6	4	13[b]	28	10	9
Positive toned nature	10	12	30	40	15	12[c]
Ornamental	2	5	12[a]	29	11	11

Key to significance of differences is given on next page.

APPENDIX H (Con't)

	ARAB			AMERICAN		
	Oasis	Urban	Total sample	Normal	Neurotic	Schizophrenic
N	20	28	64	60	30	30
Oral*						
Oral aggressive	7	3	13	13	10	7
Oral dependent	0	0	1	4	4	8
Positive oral	8e	2e	13	16	13	10
Miscellaneous oral	10c	6	22	11	3	2
One or more percepts	16d	10d	36	30	16	15
Anal and Sexual						
Anal anatomy	1	5	8	3	1	7
Miscellaneous anal	1	3	6			
Sex anxiety	1	1	3	2	2	2
Sex organs	2	3	5	1	2	8
Sex anatomy	0	0	1	2	1	4
Miscellaneous sexual	1	5	9			

*Category included in\the) overall indices of Hostility, Anxiety, etc., as well as being considered separately.

Key to significance of differences:
  a. Compared with Normal American P = .001
  b. Compared with Normal American P = .01
  c. Compared with Normal American P = .05
  d. Comparison between Oasis and Urban Arabs P = .01
  e. Comparison between Oasis and Urban Arabs P = .05
  f. Comparison between Neurotic and Schizophrenic Americans P = .05

APPENDIX J

FREQUENCY OF HUMAN AND MOVEMENT PERCEPTS IN ARAB RORSCHACH RESPONSES

	OASIS	URBAN	TOTAL SAMPLE
N	20	28	64
Total R	341	498	1186
Human percepts			
Number of H (including body)	16	50	82
Number of H/ & (H)	7	6	16
H%	6.7	11.4	8.3
Subtypes			
Persons (sex indeterminate)	0	11	13
Men	9	17	33
Women	3	6	12
Strange H or humanoid	7	6	16
Body	4	16	24
Human parts			
Number of Hd	7	19	39
Hd%	2.1	3.8	3.3
$\frac{H + H/ + (H)}{Hd}$	3.28	2.94	2.51
Head or face	4	17	28
Hand or thumb	1	0	5
Legs or feet	2	2	6
Anatomy	0	32	42
At%	0	6.4	3.5
Human movement			
M (including M in Hd)	11	30	55
M%	3.2	6.0	4.3
Quality of action			
Active percepts	5	11	19
Probably Arab	1	7	9
Foreign	3	2	6
Humanoid	1	2	4
Indefinite	0	3	4
Passive	6	16	32

APPENDIX K

Part I
MEANS AND PROPORTIONS OF RESPONSES AND M/C RELATIONSHIP

	ARAB				AMERICAN		
	Oasis	Urban	Total Sample	Normal	Neurotic	Schizophrenic	
N	20	28	64	60	30	30	
Total R	341	498	1186	1855	963	916	
Mean R	17.1	17.8	18.5[a]	30.9	32.7	31.2	
Mean M	.5	1.1	.8[a]	3.4	2.6	2.7	
Mean C	2.5	2.1	2.2[a]	3.3	2.8	3.2	
Mean V	.8[f]	1.5[f]	1.1	1.2	1.1	1.5	
Mean Y	1.6[f]	2.9[f]	2.4	2.3	3.0[g]	1.4[g]	
FC+%	30	22	25	32	29	14	
CF+%	42	32	38	28	28	19	
FC−, CF−%	28	22	25	21	29	34	
C, Cn%	0[d]	24[d]	12	19	14	33	
Total %	100	100	100	100	100	100	
FY, FC', FT%	77	66	65	68	59	63	
YF, C'F, TF, Y, C', T%	23	34	35	32	41	37	
F% (Beck)	70.0	62.1[b]	68.1	71.3	74.7	72.3	
F% (Klopfer)	(60.4)	(54.9)	(59.6)				
FM%	9.3	8.0	8.3				
m%	1.8[d]	8.6[d]	5.1				
M%	3.2	6.0	4.3[b]	10.9	9.0	9.8	
C%	14.7	11.8	11.8	10.3	8.4	10.6	
Y%	9.1[e]	16.3[e]	13.0[a]	7.2	8.2	5.4	
V%	4.7[f]	8.2[f]	6.9[b]	3.7	3.2	4.2	
Total %*	112.8	121.0	117.5	103.4	103.5	102.3	

*Totals over 100% due to double scoring of blends.

Key to significance of differences on next page.

APPENDIX K

Part I (*Con't*)

	ARAB			AMERICAN		
	Oasis	Urban	Total Sample	Normal	Neurotic	Schizophrenic
N	20	28	64	60	30	30
Total R	341	498	1186	1855	963	916
M > ΣC	4	7	15	30	10	12
M < ΣC	16	16	41[b]	22	15	15
M = ΣC	0	1	1	5	1	1
M = ΣC=0	0	4	7	3	4	2

Key to significance of differences:

a. Compared with Normal American P = .001
b. Compared with Normal American P = .01
c. Compared with Normal American P = .05
d. Comparison between Oasis and Urban Arabs P = .001
e. Comparison between Oasis and Urban Arabs P = .01
f. Comparison between Oasis and Urban Arabs P = .05
g. Comparison between Neurotic and Schizophrenic Americans P = .05

APPENDIX K

Part II
FREQUENCIES OF OCCURRANCE OF RORSCHACH DETERMINANTS

		ARAB			AMERICAN		
		Oasis	Urban	Total Sample	Normal	Neurotic	Schizophrenic
		20	28	64	60	30	30
M	0	12	15	37	9	12	12
	1	6	6	16 ⎫	7	5 ⎫	3 ⎫
	2-4	2	6	10 ⎬ a	27	8 ⎬ c	11 ⎬ c
	5+	0	1	1 ⎭	17	5 ⎭	4 ⎭
Total C	0	2	6	14 ⎫	7	7	4
	1	9	7	21 ⎬ b	12	4	8
	2+	9	15	29 ⎭	41	19	18
FC+	0	12	21	45 ⎫	21	15	21
	1	5	3	9 ⎬ c	23	8	7
	2+	3	4	10 ⎭	16	7	2
CF+	0	10	18	38	31	15	18
	1	7	7	16	15	9	5
	2+	3	3	10	14	6	7
FC−, CF−	0	9	18	36	34	14	8
	1	9	9	24	15	10	13
	2+	2	1	4	11	6	9

Key to significance of differences:
   a. Compared with Normal American   P = .001
   b. Compared with Normal American   P = .01
   c. Compared with Normal American   P = .05

APPENDIX K

Part II (Con't)

		ARAB			AMERICAN		
		Oasis	Urban	Total Sample	Normal	Neurotic	Schizophrenic
		20	28	64	60	30	30
C, Cn	0	20	22	57	42	19	15
	1	0	2	3	7	8	8
	2+	0	4	4	11	3	7
Y	0	4	6	15	18	6	16
	1	9	6	17	13	8	6
	2–4	6	10	22	20	10	5
	5+	1	6	10	9	6	3
V	0	10	12	30	25	19	16
	1	6	5	17	15	4	4
	2	1	6	8	10	1	5
	3+	3	5	9	10	6	5

APPENDIX L

BRIEF SUMMARY OF THE RORSCHACH RECORDS OF THREE WOMEN

Case	No. 13	No. 27	No. 37
R	10	31	15
W	9	5	6
D	1	24	6
Dd	0	2	3
Total S	3(2Ws)	6(2Ws)	3(1Ws)
F%	70	74	
M	0	1	0
FM	0	1	2
FC	1	2	1
CF	2	2	3
C	0	0	0
Y	0	1	0
Rigidity score	67	31	69
Maladjustment score	70	54	51
Content			
H, Hd	0,0	1,0	1,2
A, Ad	1,0	5,4	4,0
Fd, Cg	5,0	0,6	0,0
Hh, Orn	0,0	2,2	0,1
Bot, Flo	6,2	3,3	4,2
Nat, Arch	0,1	0,5	1,3
Affective Symbolism			
Host %	0	0	0
Anxiety %	18	1	13.3
Body Preoc. %	0	0	0
Dependent %	0	12.3	16.6
Positive %	72	31.6	23.3
Neutral %	10	51.6	46

APPENDIX M

Part I

RELATIONSHIPS BETWEEN RORSCHACH AND CULTURAL VARIABLES*

	Rigidity Score		Maladjustment Score		Positive Content Score		Hostility and Body Preoccupation	
	-44	45+	-50	51+	-7	8+	Low†	High‡
Cleanliness								
Dirty to filthy	8	26	8	26	13	21	24	10
Meticulous to clean	10	11	10	11	7	14	17	4
	P = .10		P = .10					
Veiling								
Both eyes exposed	16	26	19	23	15	27	29	13
One or both covered	3	18	3	18	9	12	19	2
	P=.10		P=.01				P=.10	
Chaperonage								
Wife may be accompanied by mother	12	25	14	23	12	25	27	10
Wife may not be accompanied by her mother	7	19	8	18	12	14	21	5
End of seclusion								
55 years or younger	16	15	16	15	10	21	21	10
56 years or older	3	29	6	26	14	18	27	5
	P=.001		P=.01				P=.15	
Beating of children								
Never, mild, and not preferred punishment	11	12	7	16	9	14	15	8
Beats severely or prefers beating	9	32	16	25	15	26	34	7
	P=.05						P=.15	
Isolation of children								
Never	9	21	10	20	11	19	24	6
Uses as punishment	11	23	13	21	13	21	25	9
Food deprivation as punishment								
Never	6	26	8	24	16	16	24	8
Delays or limits meal	14	18	15	17	8	24	25	7
	P=.05		P=.10		P=.05			

APPENDIX M

Part I *(Con't)*

	Rigidity Score		Maladjustment Score		Positive Content Score		Hostility and Body Preoccupation	
	-44	45+	-50	51+	-7	8+	Low†	High‡
Charms								
Does not use	13	26	16	23	19	20	25	14
Uses	6	18	7	17	5	19	23	1
					P=.05		P=.01	
Genii								
Does not believe in	4	11	7	8	8	7	9	6
Believes in	15	33	16	32	15	33	39	9
							P=.15	
Sahhara								
Does not believe in	3	15	7	11	10	8	9	9
Believes in	11	18	7	22	12	17	23	6
							P=.05	
Evil eye								
Does not protect against and never affected by	8	20	9	19	15	13	17	11
Protects against or has been affected by	12	24	14	22	9	27	32	4
					P=.05		P=.01	
Dream interpretation								
Never uses	6	15	7	14	8	13	16	5
Uses	13	29	15	27	16	26	33	9
Guezzana.								
Does not believe in	12	27	14	25	14	25	32	7
Believes in	8	17	9	16	10	15	17	8

*For the total sample. Differences in totals are due to lack of data for some informants.

† Low = Hostility score 0-15 and Body Preoccupation score 0-9.

‡ High = Hostility score over 15, or Body Preoccupation score over 9, or both.

APPENDIX M
Part II
SPECIAL ANALYSES FOR CHAPTER X

	Maladjustment Score			Hostility and Body Preoccupation	
	-50	51+		Low†	High‡
Veiling in oasis			Charms in city		
Both eyes exposed	6	5	Does not use	9	12
One or both covered	0	9	Uses	7	0
	P=.03			P=.02	
End of seclusion—oasis				Oasis	City
55 years or younger	4	6	Beating of children		
56 years or older	2	8	Never, mild and not preferred punishment	7	11
End of seclusion—city					
55 years or younger	9	6			
56 years or older	2	10	Beats severely or prefers beating	13	17
	P=.05				
Those who do not believe in *Guezzana*					
Oasis	1	11			
City	11	8			
	P=.02				

	Maladjustment Score			Combined Maladjustment and Rigidity Scores	
	-58	59+		Lowest	Highest
Economic status			Economic status		
Upper	19	12	Upper	8	4
Lower	14	19	Lower	4	8
				P=.15	

	Rigidity Score			Anxiety Score	
	-44	45+		-25	26+
Cleanliness in oasis			Dream interpretation in city		
Dirty to filthy	1	10	Never uses	2	5
Meticulous to clean	4	3	Uses	16	4
	P=.06			P=.05	
Seclusion in oasis					
55 years or younger	6	4	Those who do not interpret dreams		
56 years or older	0	10	Oasis	6	1
	P=.02		City	2	5
Seclusion in city				P=.11	
55 years or younger	7	8			
56 years or older	1	11			
	P=.08				

† Low = Hostility score 0-15 and Body Preoccupation score 0-9.
‡ High = Hostility score over 15 or Body Preoccupation score over 9, or both.

BIBLIOGRAPHY

Alexander, L., and Ax, A. F. "Rorschach Studies in Combat Flying Personnel," in P. Hoch and J. Zubin (editors), *Relation of Psychological Tests to Psychiatry*. New York: Grune & Stratton, Inc., 1951, 219-44.

Beck, Samuel J. *Rorschach's Test*. New York: Grune & Stratton, Inc., revised, 1950.

_____, Rabin, A., et. al. "The Normal Personality as Projected in the Rorschach Test," *Journal of Psychology*, XXX, 1950, 141-98.

Bleuler, M., and Bleuler, R. "Rorschach Ink-Blot Test and Racial Psychology: Mental Peculiarities of Moroccans," *Character and Personality*, IV, 1935, 97-114.

Bousquet, G.-H. "L'Islam et la Limitation Volontaire des Naissances," *Annales de l'Institut d'Etudes Orientales*, VII, 1948, 95-104.

Cherbonneau, Auguste. *Dictionnaire Français-Arabe pour la Conversation en Algérie*. Paris: Librairie Hachette et Cie., 1884.

deBussy, Th. Roland. *Petit Dictionnaire Français-Arabe et Arabe-Français de la Langue Parlée en Algérie*. Algiers: A. Jourdan, 1874.

Desparmet, J. *Coutumes, Institutions, Croyances des Indigènes de l'Algérie*, Vol. I, *L'Enfance, le Mariage et la Famille*. Trans. by Henri Pérès and G.-H. Bousquet. Algiers: Imprimeries la Typo-Litho et J. Carbonel réunis, 2nd ed., 1948.

De Vos, George. "A Quantitative Approach to Affective Symbolism in Rorschach Responses," *Journal of Projective Techniques*, XVI, 1952, 134-50.

_____. "A Quantitative Rorschach Assessment of Maladjustment and Rigidity in Acculturating Japanese Americans," *Genetic Psychology Monographs*, LII, 1955, 51-87.

_____, and Miner, Horace. "Algerian Culture and Personality in Change," *Sociometry*, XXI, 1958, 255-68.

_____, and Miner, Horace. "Oasis and Casbah—a Study in Acculturative Stress," in M. K. Opler (ed.), *Culture and Mental Health*. New York: Macmillan Co., 1959. , pp. 333-50.

Doutté, Edmond. *Magie et Religion dans l'Afrique du Nord*. Algiers: Adolphe Jourdan, 1909.

DuBois, Cora. *The People of Alor. A Social-Psychological Study of an East Indian Island*. Minneapolis: University of Minnesota Press, 1944.

Eggan, Fred. "Social Anthropology and the Method of Controlled Comparison," *American Anthropologist,* LVI, 1954, 743-63.

Fisher, Seymour. "Pattern of Personality Rigidity and Some of Their Determinants," *Psychological Monographs: General and Applied,* LXIV, No. 1, 1950.

_____, and Cleveland, S. E. "Behavior and Unconscious Fantasies of Patients with Rheumatoid Arthritis," *Psychosomatic Medicine,* XVI, 1954, 327-33.

_____, and Cleveland, S. E. "Body-Image Boundaries and Styles of Life," *Journal of Abnormal and Social Psychology,* LII, 373-79.

Goldfarb, W. "The Rorschach Experiment," in A. Kardiner and L. Ovesey, *The Mark of Oppression.* New York: W. W. Norton and Co., 1951.

Hagood, M. J., and Price, D. O. *Statistics for Sociologists.* New York: Henry Holt & Co., revised, 1952.

Hallowell, Irving. "'Popular' Responses and Cultural Differences: An Analysis Based on Frequencies in a Group of American Indian Subjects," *Rorschach Research Exchange,* IX, 1945, 153-68.

_____, "The Rorschach Technique in the Study of Personality and Culture," *American Anthropologist,* XLVII, 1945, 195-210.

Hitti, Philip K. *History of the Arabs from the Earliest Times to the Present.* New York: Macmillan Co., 5th ed., revised, 1951.

Kane, Paul. "Availability of Hostile Fantasy Related to Overt Behavior," *Illinois Medical Journal,* III, No. 3, 1957.

Kardiner, Abram. *The Psychological Frontiers of Society.* New York: Columbia University Press, 1945.

_____, and Oversey, L. *The Mark of Oppression: A Psychological Study of the American Negro.* New York: W. W. Norton and Co., 1951.

Klopfer, Bruno, and Kelley, D. M. *The Rorschach Technique.* Yonkers-on-Hudson: World Book Co., 1942.

Levy, Ruben. *An Introduction to the Sociology of Islam.* London: Williams and Norgate, Ltd., 1930.

Linton, Ralph. *The Cultural Background of Personality.* New York: D. Appleton-Century Co., 1945.

Malinowski, Bronislaw. *Magic, Science and Religion.* Glencoe, Ill.: Free Press, 1948.

Mckeel, Scudder. Review of Abram Kardiner, "The Individual and His Society," *American Anthropologist,* XLII, 1940, 526-30.

McLellan, David S. "The North African in France, A French Racial Problem," *Yale Review,* XLIV, 1955, 421-38.

Miner, Horace. "Rorschachs of Arabs from Algiers and from an Oasis," in Bert Kaplan (ed.), *Primary Records in Culture and Personality,* Vol. III. Madison: Microcard Foundation, 1960.

Murdock, G. P. *Social Structure.* New York: Macmillan Co., 1949.

Phillips, Leslie. *Rorschach Interpretation: Advanced Technique.* New York: Grune & Stratton, Inc., 1953.

Piaget, Jean. *The Child's Conception of Physical Causality.* New York: Harcourt, Brace & Co., 1930.

Rapaport, David. *Diagnostic Psychological Testing.* Chicago: Yearbook Publishers, Inc., 1946.

Redfield, Robert. *The Folk Culture of Yucatan.* Chicago: University of Chicago Press, 1941.

Schaefer, Roy. *Psychoanalytic Interpretation in Rorschach Testing: Theory and Application.* New York: Grune & Stratton, Inc., 1954.

Service de Statistique Générale, Gouvernement Générale de l'Algérie. *Résultats Statistiques du Dénombrement de la Population Effectué le 31 Octobre 1948.* Algiers: Service de Statistique Générale, 1950.

Siegel, Sidney. *Nonparametric Statistics for the Behavioral Sciences.* New York: McGraw-Hill Book Co., 1956.

Spindler, George. *Sociocultural and Psychological Processes in Menomini Acculturation.* Berkeley: University of California Press, 1955.

─── , and Goldschmidt, Walter. "Experimental Design in the Study of Culture Change,"*Southwestern Journal of Anthropology*, VIII, 1952, 68-83.

Welch, Galbraith. *North African Prelude, The First Seven Thousand Years.* New York: William Morrow & Co., 1949.

INDEX

Abortion, 58
Acculturation, 16, 113, 122
  case studies of, 147-69
  and personality change, 179-89
  and Rorschach content, 114, 115, 128, 137
  see also Assimilation index; Culture change
Adultery, 56, 57, 81-83, 90, 100, 162, 164, 188
Affect, 133, 134
  dependent, 136
  expressed by women, 144, 145
  extreme, 167
  see also Emotions; Hostility; Rorschach test
Afreet, 97, 146, 166; *see also* Genii
Age
  distribution of oasis population, 191-92
  of informants, 8, 74, 75
  of marriage, 74, 76, 77, 195
  of personality formation, 6, 185
Aggression, 83, 157, 158, 160, 162, 170, 182, 187; *see also* Anger; Quarrels
Agriculture, 31-34
  crops, 33, 34, 36
  dates, 21, 31-34, 36, 52
  gardens, 22, 23, 25-28, 31-34, 36, 150, 152
  grain, 28, 34
  palms, 21, 23, 25, 26, 28, 31-33, 48
  water, 1, 22, 25-27, 29, 32, 49; pumps, 27, 28, 32, 36
Alexander, L., 139
Algiers
  case studies from, 154-69, 174-76
  history, 1, 23

informants from, 7, 8
population increase, 27
see also Casbah; Urban contact
Americans; *see* Sample American
Amusements, 46, 47
Anality, 114-16, 152, 180, 200-202, 213; *see also* Rorschach test
Anger, 45, 46; *see also* Quarrels
Animals
  domestic, 25, 34, 35
  treatment of, 47, 49
  see also Rorschach indices
Anthropologist, 3, 5, 6, 8, 9 (Miner) 10, 11, 15, 52, 54, 60, 144, 147-49, 151, 155, 158, 160-62, 167, 171-73, 176
Anxiety
  during Rorschach testing, 13
  evidence of in case studies, 150, 162
  interpreter influence on, 109, 110
  oasis-urban difference in, 143
  relation to cultural variation, 112, 113, 180, 199, 222
  Rorschach evidence of, 134, 135, 141, 212, 219
Assimilation index, 114, 115, 200, 201; *see also* Acculturation; Culture change
Authority figure, 187, 188
Ax, A. F., 139

Baraka, 21, 23, 50, 63, 95, 96, 166, 174
Beck, S. J., 123, 126, 129, 130, 203, 211, 215
Berbers, 18, 20, 21
Bestiality, 58
Birth, 42-44
  statistics, 190-92

227

Bleuler, M. and R., 121, 122, 125, 129, 178
Blocking
  in Rorschach test, 126, 203, 204, 206
Body preoccupation, 133-35, 138, 139, 144, 175, 194, 212, 219-22
  see also Hostility
Bousquet, G.-H., 43, 59

Cadi, 61, 74
Caid
  position of, 24, 25
Casbah
  Arab informants from, 11, 12
  charm seller from, 174-76
  Frenchman from, 8, 163-65
  interview conditions in, 14
  origin of, 1
  see also Urban contact; Urban group
Case studies, 147-78
Castration
  fear of, 138, 141
  see also Mutilation
Cathexis, 116, 118, 133, 137, 177, 182, 202
Catholic, 164, 167
Cemetery, 22, 42, 65, 93
Census
  of Sidi Khaled, 190-92; see also Population
Charms, 35, 174, 196, 201
  effect of urban contact on belief, 103-6, 185
  relation of beliefs to personality, 111-13, 115, 139, 140, 181, 199, 201, 221, 222
  use of, 43, 50, 59, 95-97, 101
Cherbonneau, A., 21
Childhood, 6, 44-50
Children
  desire for, 84-86, 195
  number of, 74, 75, 84
  see also Punishment
Circumcision, 45, 46

Cleanliness, 15
  lack of, 169, 170, 172, 174, 180
  relation to economic status and city life, 88, 90-92, 193
  relation to personality, 115, 116, 180, 181, 201, 220, 222
  in ritual and etiquette, 50, 51, 94, 102
Cleveland, S. E., 139
Climate, 30
Clothes, European, 15, 91, 92, 115, 145, 148, 158, 161, 165, 196, 197
Compulsivity, 149; see also Obsessive compulsive
Concubine, 63
Confabulation, 156, 157, 167, 168
Constriction, 112, 126, 130, 142, 149, 165, 173, 174, 175, 189, 199, 203, 204, 206
Contraception, 59, 155
Control group, 67, 70-75
Council; see Village council
Crafts, 35, 36; see also Economic status
Crime
  Murder, 23, 83
  Theft, 34, 38, 53
Crops; see Agriculture
Culture
  basis for selective description of, 16, 17
  change
    interpreted from oasis-urban comparison, 2, 16, 17, 73, 74
    relation to personality, 113-15, 179-89
    in specific traits, 74-106
  see also Acculturation; Assimilation index

Culture (con't.)
  contact
    of oasis and urban groups compared, 67, 68, 70, 71
    see also French contact; Urban contact
  relation to personality, 2-6, 17
    exploration of, 179-89, 220-22
    tests of predictions regarding, 107-20, 199-202
  traits, as distributions of behavior, 6, 7

Dates; see Agriculture
Death, 64, 65, 154
  from afreet, 97
  statistics, 190, 191
  as reason for visiting, 82
de Bussy, Th. Roland, 21
Deceit, 149, 150
Defecation, 51; see also Toilet training
Dependency, 136, 137, 160, 212, 219
Desert, 18, 30, 34, 77
  Sahara, 18, 19, 24, 30
  and vista responses, 128, 145
Deviance, 11, 122, 147, 165-78
De Vos, George, 117, 122, 123, 130, 132, 202, 206; see also Psychologist
Diet; see Food
Disease; see Health
Divorce, 42, 59, 77, 154, 164, 166, 170, 172
Djema'a, 10, 39, 61, 78, 151, 176
Dogma, Islamic, 93, 95, 99, 103, 105
Doutté, Edmond, 95
Dowry; see Marriage
Dreams
  Arabs' interpretation of, 101, 102, 104-6, 152, 162
  relation of personality to, 113, 114, 118, 181, 185, 199, 221, 222
  sexual, 58, 102, 175
DuBois, Cora, 4, 5

Eating, 46, 50, 52, 170; see also Feast; Food
Economic status, 72, 73, 75, 90-92, 193, 222
Economy; see Agriculture; Economy; see Agriculture; Crafts; Market
Edging of Rorschach card, 171
Education
  French, 24, 28, 29, 46
  of oasis and urban groups, 71
  in relation to Koranic education, 70, 193
  Koranic, 25, 49, 50
  of girls, 28, 94, 167
  of oasis and urban groups, 70-72, 193
  provided by zaouia, 22
  relation to cultural variation, 73, 94, 95, 102, 195-98
  relation to French education, 70, 193
  relation to psychological variables, 73, 194
  see also Taleb
  relation to Rorschach popular responses, 128
Eggan, Fred, 66
Ego
  controls, 150
  defenses, 121, 132, 133, 141-43
Emotions, 54-56, 125, 132, 134, 141-43; see also Affect
Epidemics; see Health
Evil eye, 35, 55
  beliefs about, 43, 100-2
  charms against, 96, 97
  effect of urban contact on belief in, 104-6

Evil eye (con't.)
  relation of beliefs to personality, 111-13, 118, 181, 185. 188. 199, 221
Experiment, natural, 1, 66; see also Research design
Experimental group, 67, 70-75

Family composition, 71, 72, 74, 75
Famine, 23, 28, 190
Feast, 45, 46, 61, 63
Felatio, 58, 59
Fisher, Seymour, 68, 123, 139, 156
Flatulence, 52, 53
Folklore, 2, 52
Food
  deprivation, 87-90, 115, 181, 184, 201, 220
  preferences, 158
  staple, 33
  supplementary, 88
  see also Eating; Feast
Fornication, 57, 58
Fortune tellers, 162, 185, 200; see also Guezzana
French
  administration, 10, 67, 78, 176
  administrator, 24-27
  attitude, 148, 154, 158, 162, 164, 167, 176, 186
  conquest, 1, 23
  contact, 148, 151, 154, 158, 166; see also Culture contact; Urban contact
  domination, 154, 183, 186
  education; see Education
  influence, 24, 28
  language, 11, 12, 15, 24, 29, 91, 92, 108, 115, 148, 154, 158, 161, 165, 196, 197

Gardens; see Agriculture
Genii, 14, 174, 196
  beliefs about, 42, 43, 97-99
  charms against, 96, 99
  effect of urban contact on beliefs, 103-6, 185
  possession by, 99, 169-71, 177
  relation of beliefs to personality, 111, 112, 140, 181, 185, 188, 221
  in Rorschach content, 137, 146
Genitals, 42, 136, 153; see also Castration; Circumcision; Mutilation; Penis; Vulva
Goldschmidt, Walter, 66, 67
Government; see French administration; Djema'a; Village
Guezzana, 103-6, 171, 174
  relation of beliefs to personality characteristics; 113, 114, 118, 181, 184, 200, 221, 222
  see also Fortune tellers
Gunplay, 40, 41, 61, 62

Hagood, M. J., 68
Hallowell, Irving, 5, 127
Headman, council, 10, 11
Health, 35
  Disease, venereal, 35, 174
  Doctor, 25, 35, 105
  Epidemics, 1, 23
  Medicine, 171, 172
Henna, 49, 61, 64, 172
Hilali, 20, 21
Hitti, Philip, 20
Hoch, p., 139
Homosexuality, 58, 138, 139, 141, 152, 158, 160, 187, 188; see also Felatio; Sodomy
Hostility, 114, 134, 135, 137-40, 143, 144, 150, 156, 157, 175, 177, 186, 188, 194, 212, 219-22
  and body preoccupation, 179, 181-85

INDEX 231

Hostility (con't.)
  latent, 114, 200
  overt, 109-11, 114, 200
Humor, 53, 54, 56, 61, 65
Hutt, Max, 13, 107, 119, 179, 180, 182, 183, 199, 202
Hypochondria, 138, 139
Hysteria, 112-14, 199, 200

Imam, 36, 41
Impotence, 104, 141, 154, 157, 187, 188; *see also* Sahhara; Virility
Informants
  age of, 8, 74, 75
  background characteristics of, 7, 8, 12, 70-73, 193-98
  interviews with, 8, 10, 11, 13-15, 74
  selection of, 8-12
Intercourse, 42, 57, 80, 83, 94, 159, 160, 164, 166
  dreams of 58, 102, 175
  with genii, 97, 99
  premarital, 58
  see also Sexual relations
Interpreter, 12-14, 143, 148, 161; *see also* Translator
Irrigation, 32-34
Islam, 84, 93-95
  convert to, 163, 164
Islamic law, 52, 83, 94

Japanese Americans, 123, 127
Jews, 80, 100, 166, 169

Kabyle, 43
Kane, Paul, 138
Kardiner, Abram, 2-4, 6, 119, 186
Kaplan, Bert, 8
Kebir, 38, 39, 41, 63
Kelley, D. M., 133, 206
Kindred, importance of, 85, 86
Kinship, 37, 43; *see also* Sibs
Kitab, 43, 45, 96; see also Charms

Klopfer, Bruno, 133, 142, 203, 206-11, 215
Koran, 25, 35, 49, 50, 96-101, 105, 151; *see also* Education
Levy, Ruben, 94
Linton, Ralph, 3, 46

McLellen, David S., 31
Magic, 100, 103, 105, 113
  as means to power, 175, 176
  and personality, 139, 185, 188
  see also Charms; Evil eye; Sahhara; Supernatural
Maladjustment, 123-26, 136-38, 150, 152, 165, 175, 177, 180-86, 219-22
Malikite law, 52, 94
Malinowski, B., 103
Marabout, 21, 23, 53, 93, 152, 172; *see also* Saint
Market, 33, 36, 54, 82, 101
Marriage, 37, 38, 43, 44, 55, 59-65, 94, 103
  age at, 74, 76, 77
  by cadi, 61, 74
  by *djema'a*, 61, 74
  dowry at, 60, 63
  frequency of types of, 71
Masturbation, 58
Maturity, 112, 116, 118, 199, 202
Medicine; *see* Health
Mekeel, Scudder, 3
Menomini, 66
Menstruation, 57, 77
Methodology, 147, 179, 180
Migration
  selective, 12, 70-75
  urban, 1, 7, 10-12, 16, 27, 29, 73, 186, 190
Miner, Agnes, 13, 143
Miner, Horace, 5, 8, 10-13, 119; *see also* Anthropologist
Modesty, 50, 51, 98

232 INDEX

Money
  desire for, 84-86
  importance of 115, 155, 201
Moors, 21
Moroccans, 121, 122, 126, 128, 129, 178
Morocco, 18, 19, 24
Mortality; see Death
Moslem, 8, 20, 21, 23, 31, 51, 93, 94, 163; see also Islam
Mosque, 24, 36, 49, 94, 129
  percept in Rorschach, 130, 152
  whitewashing of, 14, 39, 41, 46
Mountains
  Atlas, 19, 21, 130
  Aurès, 19-21
  in Rorschach content, 126, 127, 128, 130
Murder; see Crime
Murdock, G. P., 30, 35
Mutilation
  fear of 45, 149
  in Rorschach content, 136, 138, 152; see also Castration

Nail-biting, 45
Naming, 44, 56, 102
Names, taboo, 56
Narcissism, 133, 153, 159, 160
Nationalsism, 1, 161
Negroes, 21, 25, 63, 64, 100, 186
  in Rorschach content, 137, 155, 157, 163, 177
Neurasthenia, 112
Neurosis, 112
Neurotic Americans; see Sample, American
Nomads, 44, 61, 83
  conflict with, 20-24, 34, 38
  sedentarized, 1, 21, 24, 25, 28, 34, 37, 73, 103, 190, 193

Nursing (of baby), 42, 43, 62, 88, 89

Oasis
  case studies from, 148-53, 169-74, 176-78
  culture compared with urban culture, 2, 7, 16, 17, 73-106, 113-15, 178-89, 197
  culture described, 30-65
  group
    background compared with urban group, 70-75
    definition of, 67, 68
  personality compared with urban personality, 109, 111, 114, 123-43, 179-89, 203-5, 212-18
  see also Sidi Khaled
Oberholzer, Emil, 4, 5
Obsessive compulsion, 132, 149, 152, 159, 162, 164, 204, 207, 209
Occupation; see Crafts; Economic status
Oedipal conflict, 58, 157
Orality
  content in Rorschach, 133, 140, 153, 160, 194, 213
  dependency, 159, 165
  passivity, 157
Organization of village; see Village organization
Ouled Djellal, 10, 18, 19, 21-29, 33, 37, 38, 46, 55, 59, 67, 78, 99, 190
Ouled Naîl, 22, 37, 62
Ouled Zekri, 22-25, 37, 38, 61
Oversey, L., 186

Palms; see Agriculture
Paranoia, 132, 157, 167-69, 188, 207

INDEX

Patrilineage, 44, 57; *see also* Sibs
Penis, 45, 56, 64, 160, 166
Pères, Henri, 43
Perseveration, 153
Personality
  age of formation, 6, 185
  of Algerians, 121-46
  of Americans; *see* Sample, American
  case studies, 147-69
  change in relation to culture change, 113-15, 179-89
  cultural setting of, 186-89
  relation to culture, 2-6, 17
    tests of predicted relationships, 107-20, 199-202
    exploration of interrelationship, 179-89, 220-22
Phillips, Leslie, 206-10
Phobia, 112
Piaget, Jean, 206, 209
Pilgrimage, 22, 36
Polygyny, 57, 77
  of informants' fathers, 70-73, 148, 150, 154, 193-96
Popular responses; *see* Rorschach indices
Population, 25, 26, 31
  age distribution in oasis, 192
  natural increase, 26, 190
  of Algeria, 1
  of Sidi Khaled, 190-92
  urban, 1
Prayers, 21, 39, 49-51, 63, 65, 78, 94, 95, 102, 160
Praying figure in Rorschach, 176
Pregnancy, 42, 57-59
Prostitutes, 35, 59, 80, 167
Psychologist (De Vos), 144, 147, 157, 169
Psychosexual development, 133, 140
Psychotic, 52, 63, 98, 138, 147

170-72; *see also* Schizophrenia; Paranoia
Puberty, 94
Punishment
  of children, 7, 50, 149, 170, 172, 173, 196
  oasis-urban difference, 87-90, 184
  relation to personality of parent, 114, 181, 183-85, 188, 200, 220, 222

Quarrels, 39, 44, 77, 150

Rabin, A., 123
Rahmania, 23, 39
Ramadan, 49, 78, 151
Rapaport, David, 206-10
Recording machine, 14, 15, 108, 149
Redfield, Robert, 84, 103, 113
Religion, 2, 20, 39; *see also* Islam; Moslem; Prayer; Supernatural
Research design, 7, 8, 66-68; *see also* Statistical tests
Rigidity; *see* Rorschach test
Rorschach indices
  animal percepts (A), 127, 132, 136, 146, 149, 162, 165, 173, 202, 203, 219
  color responses (C), 132-34, 141-44, 146, 149, 152, 155, 159, 162, 163, 167, 177, 215-19
  detail, large (D), 155, 202, 203, 219
  detail, small (Dd), 126, 142, 155, 159, 162, 177, 202, 203, 219
  form (F), 129, 131-34, 141, 142, 152, 155, 159, 162, 173, 175, 202, 203, 215, 217, 219
  human percepts (H), 130, 132, 136, 137, 141, 144, 146,

Rorschach indices (con't.)
  152, 153, 155, 156, 214, 219
  movement percepts (M), 132, 136, 141, 142, 144, 149, 152, 155, 156, 159, 162, 163, 177, 214-17, 219
  number of responses (R), 109, 110, 142, 144, 152, 155, 159, 165, 173, 202, 203, 215, 219
  popular responses (P), 127-30, 150, 163, 165, 173, 177, 202, 203, 211
  shading (Y), 109-11, 132, 133, 141, 142, 146, 152, 155, 159, 162, 215, 218, 219
  vista percepts (V), 109-11, 133, 141, 142, 145, 155, 215, 218
  whole responses (W), 122, 125, 126, 132, 149, 152, 155, 177, 202, 203, 219
Rorschach test
  administration, 12-15
  affective content, 132-43, 146, 179, 204, 207, 212, 213
  anal content, 114-16, 133, 138, 140, 141, 153, 175
  blind analysis, 4, 5, 17, 107, 108, 117, 145-48
  blocking in, 126, 203, 204, 206
  cross-cultural use of, 4, 5, 144-48
  indices of rigidity and maladjustment, 123-25, 186, 219
    relation to culture traits, 179-84, 220-22
  influence of interpreter on results, 108-11
  oral content, 133, 140, 153, 194, 213
  popular responses, 127-31, 211
  positive content, 134-36, 143, 179-81, 184, 185, 194, 212, 219, 220
  scoring of De Vos and Hutt compared, 202
  sexual content, 99, 133, 140, 141, 168, 175, 213
  unpleasant content, 134, 135, 179, 194

Sadomasochism, 138, 139, 152, 159, 175
Sahhara, 99, 100, 103-6, 118, 162, 166
  relation of beliefs to personality, 111-13, 181, 185, 187, 188, 196, 221
Saint, 20, 21, 39, 98; *see also* Marabout
Saintliness, 170
Sample
  American
    neurotic, 125, 129, 132, 134, 136
    normal, 123-32, 134, 136, 138, 140-42, 162, 180, 186
    schizophrenic, 129, 132
    tabular comparisons, including above subtypes, 124, 135, 203, 204, 212, 213, 215-18
  bias, 12, 70
    control of, 70-75, 193-98
  characteristics of Arab, 67, 68, 71-75
  random, 9-11
Schafer, Roy, 206, 208
Schizophrenia, Rorschach indications of, 208; *see also* Sample, American
Sedentarization, 1, 21, 24, 25, 28, 34, 37, 73, 103, 190, 193
Sex
  content in Rorschach, 99, 133, 140, 141, 168, 175, 213

Sex (cont'd.)
  conversation about, 56, 149, 158
  disturbance, 175, 176, 182; see also Impotence
  knowledge, 56-59
  play, 58, 187
  relations, 44, 57-59, 160; see also Intercourse
Sexes, separation of, 30, 31, 52, 57, 58; see also women
Shaduf, 26
Shame, 50, 52, 53
Sheikh, 24, 25
Siblings, 43, 57, 58
  informants' position among, 71, 72
Sibs, 37-39
Sidi Khaled
  oasis
    census, 190-92
    culture described, 30-65
    history, 18, 22-29
    location, 18-20
    saint, 18, 20, 22, 23
Siegel, Sidney, 68
Sleeping arrangements, 30, 44, 56, 57, 149
Smoking, 15, 91, 92, 115, 155, 164, 196
Sodomy, 58, 59, 149, 160
Soothsayers, 113, 114; see also Guezzana
Sorcery, 7, 99, 100, 105, 154, 157; see also Sahhara
Spindler, George, 66, 67
Statistical tests, 68, 70, 73, 123, 125
Status, 53, 193, 222; see also Economic status
Stealing; see Crime
Stereotypy, 127
Supernatural belief, 93-106
  index of, 115, 201
  and personality, 112-15, 118, 139, 181, 184-86, 188, 189, 221, 222

Rorschach rating of, 115, 201; see also Charms; Dream interpretation; Evil eye; Genii; *Guezzana*; *Sahhara*
Supernatural figures in Rorschach content, 137, 146

Taleb, 25, 35, 38, 59, 89, 96, 102, 103
  case histories, 172-76; see also Education, Koranic
Tattooing, 148, 167
Thinking
  arbitrary, 162, 204, 207
  disorders, 131, 132, 204-10
  illogical, 121, 122, 126, 129, 167, 205, 209, 210
  logical, 187
  obsessive, 204, 207
  projective, 167
Thumbsucking, 45
Toilet training, 86-88, 115, 116, 195, 202
Translator, 10
  influence on Rorschach, 108-11; see also Interpreter
Tunisia, 18-20, 24

Unemployment, 36, 72, 75
Urban contact, 7, 8, 27, 67, 68, 71, 72, 93, 115, 200, 201; see also Culture contact; French contact
Urban group
  background compared with oasis group, 70-75
  definition of, 67, 68
Urban personality compared with oasis personality, 109, 111, 114, 123-43, 179-89, 203-5, 212-18
Urbanization rating, 115, 201

Veiling, 62, 77, 80, 81, 181-83, 195, 220, 222
Village
  council, 10, 11, 39, 158; see

Village (con't.)
    also Djema'a
    organization, 37-41
    quarters, 22, 38, 39, 41
Virginity, 57, 58, 116
Virility, 173, 187; see also Impotence; Sahhara
Voyeurism, 188
Vulva percept, 160, 177

Water
    use of during Ramadan, 151, 152; see also Agriculture; Irrigation
Weaning, 43, 59, 88, 89
Welch, Galbraith, 20
Widows, 57, 65
Wife, chaperonage of, 80, 81, 181, 182, 195, 197, 198, 220
Wives, number of, 71, 72, 75, 77, 84, 85

Women, 30, 31
    beating of, 177
    confidence in, 80-82, 115, 149, 150, 195, 197, 198
    in Rorschach percepts, 136, 156
    Rorschachs of, 13, 143, 144, 219
    seclusion of, 16, 77-82, 101, 154, 161, 164, 167
    in relation to personality of men, 116, 118-20, 181-83, 202, 220, 222

Yucatan, 103, 105, 113

Z score, 126, 203
Zaouia, 21-23, 53, 93, 172
Zibane, 18, 19, 21-23, 30
Zubin, J., 139

www.ingramcontent.com/pod-product-compliance
Lightning Source LLC
Jackson TN
JSHW070313120426
100741JS00007B/40